THE TECHNIQUE OF
EARLY GREEK
SCULPTURE

THE TECHNIQUE OF
EARLY GREEK
SCULPTURE

By

STANLEY CASSON

FELLOW OF NEW COLLEGE ; READER IN CLASSICAL
ARCHAEOLOGY IN THE UNIVERSITY OF OXFORD ;
MEMBER OF THE GERMAN ARCHAEO-
LOGICAL INSTITUTE

HACKER ART BOOKS

NEW YORK

1970

First Published by Oxford University Press, London, 1933
Reprinted by Hacker Art Books, New York, 1970

Library of Congress Catalog Card Number 72-116353
SBN: 0-87817-041-3

PREFACE

A STUDY of the technique of a particular period of art is not necessarily a dull cataloguing of methods and tricks and conventions. The way in which a statue is made may, indeed, afford no little insight into the mind of the maker. For technical methods are bound to affect the style and outlook of the artist and so lead to modifications in his aesthetic intention. If technique is limited and poverty-stricken, then style will be equally limited and perhaps equally poverty-stricken. Invention in technical methods, on the other hand, can encourage freedom of style, though if that invention become too fertile it may lead the artist to prefer technical perfection to everything else. And this has, in fact, happened in every important period of artistic activity.

The intention of this book is to examine in the fullest detail the various technical methods used by the Greeks in the making of stone and bronze statues in order that the reactions of style upon technique and of technique upon style may be established and analysed. In the process some important chronological results emerge. If the date of the introduction of certain tools into the full use of the sculptor can be established, it follows that valuable chronological data are at once available. I have attempted in the following pages to make it clear what research is possible on these lines.

It is obvious that a work of art cannot be taken as a *fait accompli* if any critical study of it is to be made. It must be looked at both from the point of view of its maker and of those who behold it. The tendency for many years past has been to look at Greek sculpture from the purely historical point of view and to disregard the methods employed in its construction by Greek sculptors. This leads to fruitful results and, coupled with a balanced judgement of style and a critical analysis of stylistic qualities, to a satisfactory consideration of the whole affair. But it still leaves the sculptors

themselves out in the cold; it still makes it difficult for the
observer to grasp the intentions of the maker. By a close
study of the methods used by the maker from start to finish
the observer can in the end learn to appreciate more deeply
the aims of the sculptor himself.

There is no work in English of any kind on the subject of
Greek technique and, apart from the excellent study by Carl
Blümel in German, no book in any other European language.
Much good work is being done on technical lines by many
learned students, but, as yet, their research has not resulted
in any comprehensive publication. It is with the intention of
suggesting the outlines of such a study that this book was
undertaken. I have limited the period to that covered by the
finest products of Greek sculpture in any age. I have
attempted to deal with the prehistoric periods and the
archaic Greek periods in full detail in order to show what
connexion there is between the prehistoric and the historic.
I have closed the period with which I have dealt at approximately 450 B.C., since that date marks a turning-point in
Greek methods that was more important than any which
preceded it or which came after. Naturally I have had to
discuss methods and instances of dates as late as the fourth
century, but substantially the middle of the fifth century is
the limit of my inquiries. Subsequent technical methods are
of great variety and interest and deserve a separate volume:
but they do not change so rapidly or lead to such drastic
modification of style as do the methods of the archaic period
and of the early fifth century.

The neglect of excavators, or museum authorities, in the
past to search for or to preserve the various tools and implements of metal or stone used by sculptors has not made it
easier to reconstruct the technical processes. But the number
of tools which might be expected to survive would not in any
case be large and, in fact, surviving examples are of extreme
rarity.[1] The only archaeologist who has recorded every

[1] Petrie remarks of saws and tubular drills in Egypt (*The Temples and*

example of a technical instrument found and every instance
of the traces of the work of specialized tools is Sir Flinders
Petrie, whose admirable work on these matters for Egyptian
archaeology is beyond praise. It is the more tragic that he
records in a recent work[1] that Greek iron tools of various
types, found at Naukratis in conditions in which they could
be dated to 600 B.C., were lost. The best, he says, were sent
to the British Museum at the time of the excavations, but
were thrown away by the authorities as valueless objects!
The preservation of these tools would, as those who read this
book may realize, have been of the utmost value to any subsequent study of the subject of technique. Petrie also is the
only excavator who has meticulously preserved all objects
and instruments of emery-stone. One is tempted to wonder
how many similar objects of emery have escaped the notice
of excavators in Greece, for I know of none recorded in
excavation reports.

Readers will notice that some of the photographs in this
book are made from casts of the original sculptures. In some
cases I have found that a really good cast, which has not been
tampered with after casting, shows up more clearly the
particular surfaces which it is desired to photograph than the
original, for in some cases the surfaces of the original are so
stained or water-marked that the detail would not come out
well in a photograph. It is also possible to get clearer
shadows on the dull surface of a cast than on the original.
But wherever possible I have used photographs of the
original and in no case have I resorted to a cast where a
photograph of the original marble would show what was
wanted more authentically or more clearly. I am much

Pyramids of Gizeh, p. 78): 'That no remains of these saws or tubular drills
have yet been found is to be expected, since we have not yet found even waste
specimens of work to the tenth of the amount that a single tool would
produce. . . . Again even of common masons' chisels there are probably not
a dozen known.'

   [1] *Seventy Years in Archaeology*, 1931, p. 56: 'On my enquiring to see them
some years later, I was told that Mr. Newton said they were ugly things and
he did not want them, so they were thrown away!'

indebted to many friends for advice and help. To Professor Rhys Carpenter for helping me to get certain photographs made and to Herr Wagner of the German Institute at Athens for having made them; to Professor Beazley for help and suggestions in the matter of certain vase-paintings; to Mr. Alec Millar of Chipping Campden for advice and help in certain questions of bronze technique and in problems concerned with the use of certain stone-carvers' tools, and for his own continuous interest in the subject as a whole, an interest which his own skill has made the more valuable to me; to the Director of the National Museum at Athens and to the Trustees of the British Museum for permission to take and use photographs; to the particular skill of Mr. Waterhouse of the British Museum for taking some of the more difficult and technical photographs; to Dr. Welter of the German Archaeological Institute for the use of several excellent photographs; to Sir Arthur Evans and to Mr. Pendlebury of Knossos for very great help in obtaining for me certain photographs from Candia, and to Sir Arthur for permission to reproduce two of his most important illustrations. I am particularly beholden to Mr. de Garis Davies for permission to reproduce two of his admirable drawings of the Rekhmere tomb, and to Dr. Buschor for permission to reproduce a figure from Samos; and to Mr. Chaundy of the Ashmolean Museum for numerous excellent plates.

I have also to express my thanks to Professor A. B. Cook for advice and help and for some most valuable references; and to the bronzeworkers and silversmiths of Chipping Campden for the loan of metal-workers' tools and for their considered opinions upon some of my problems. Mr. R. H. Dundas of Christ Church has, with kindness, read the proofs. The Derby Trustees, by giving me a generous grant, made it possible for the book to be illustrated with adequate photographs which the Clarendon Press has made into plates of exceptional clarity.

CONTENTS

LIST OF ILLUSTRATIONS

BIBLIOGRAPHY

ASHMOLE, B. 'An alleged archaic group.' *Journal of Hellenic Studies*, l, 1930, p. 99.

BLÜMEL, CARL. *Griechische Bildhauerarbeit*. Berlin and Leipzig, 1927. (Ergänzungsheft des Deutschen Archäologischen Instituts.)

BLÜMNER, HUGO. *Technologie und Terminologie der Gewerbe und Kunste bei Griechen und Römern*, vol. iii, Leipzig, 1884, pp. 187–226.

CASSON, S. 'Bronze work of the Geometric period and its relation to later art.' *Journal of Hellenic Studies*, xlii, 1922, pp. 207 ff.

—— 'Some Greek seals of the "Geometric" Period.' *Antiquaries Journal*, VII (1927), i, pp. 38 ff.

—— 'Some Technical Methods of Archaic Sculpture.' *Journal of Hellenic Studies*, l, 1930, pp. 313 ff.

CARPENTER, RHYS. *The Sculpture of the Nike Temple Parapet*. Harvard University Press, 1929.

KLUGE, K. *Die antiken Grossbronzen*. Berlin and Leipzig, 1927.

—— Die Gestaltung des Erzes in der archaisch-griechischen Kunst. *Jahrbuch*, 1929, p. 1.

—— *Die Gestaltung des Erzes und ihre technischen Grundlagen*. Berlin and Leipzig, 1928.

LEPSIUS, G. R. Griechische Marmorstudien. Berlin, 1890.

LUCAS, A. *Ancient Egyptian Materials*. London, 1926.

PETRIE, SIR F. *The Arts and Crafts of Ancient Egypt*. London, 1909.

—— *The Pyramids and Temples of Gizeh*, 1883, Chapter VIII.

—— *Tools and Weapons*. 1917.

—— *Anthropological Journal*, 1883. 'Mechanical Methods of the Egyptians.'

RICHTER, G. M. A. *The Sculpture and Sculptors of the Greeks*: Yale University Press, 1930 (2nd edition).

PART I

THE DEVELOPMENT OF TECHNIQUE
HISTORICALLY CONSIDERED

I

PREHISTORIC PERIODS

I. CRETE

i. *Hard Stones.* The Minoans were not sculptors in the full sense of the term. But they made occasionally small figures in hard stone which must serve as the basis of any consideration of their technique in the manipulation of stone. This discussion of Minoan technique must not be taken to presume the continuity of Minoan with Hellenic civilization. No technique can presume that. But there is such a thing as regional survival, that is to say the survival in a given cultural region which has a unity of its own of certain technical tricks, habits, and methods which outlast all cataclysms and are transmitted by the survivors of one régime to the artists of the next. I need only cite as an example, the survival into classical Greece of black-glaze for pottery from a remote prehistoric period.

Styles of art may well perish with political or social catastrophes, but methods of art often, though by no means always, survive immense changes of fortune, and adapt themselves, provided they are suitable, to new styles and to an innovating aesthetic.

How the Minoans cut their stone figures and statuettes may thus have a considerable bearing upon how Greeks cut theirs, for Crete and the Minoan world is, in the main, commensurate with Greece and the early Hellenic.

But where artists and sculptors are incapable of working on a large scale in stone their work will in all probability bear some affinity with the work of lapidaries and gem-cutters of the period. It is thus impossible to distinguish with absolute precision the small sculptures from the gems of Minoan times from the purely technical point of view. On examination it will be seen that, in effect, there is no method of carving used in Minoan stone figures which is not also used by the gem-cutters. At the same time that does not mean that *all* the tools used for gem-cutting are used in Minoan stonework, but rather that *some* only are used and none that are not the tools of gem-cutters.

There are only two representations in stone of the human figure that have been found in Crete in reliable circumstances in the course of scientific excavation. The better of the two comes from Tylissos[1] and is of a hard green stone. It is the figure of a worshipper exactly in the manner of the bronzes of that type.[2] His right hand is held over his right eye, the stomach is protruded, as always in the bronzes. The left arm is down vertically by his side, and the whole figure stands on a small pedestal. It is, in fact, a copy in stone of a conventional type of bronze figure and, as such, of the greatest interest. The figure measures 8 cm. in height and has been made by a process of careful and painstaking rubbing with an abrasive. The lines of rubbing along the left arm and legs are very clear. No chisel or cutting instrument has been used. The line of contact of the rubbing instrument with the stone was always at right angles so that the rubber corresponds in action to the gem-cutter's wheel, with the difference that the wheel would have effected in a few minutes what the hand-worked rubber removed in the space of some hours. The principles of action of the two instruments are essentially the same.

The other figure[3] is altogether cruder. It comes from Porti and is the figure of a man in grey stone, complete

---

[1] No. 219 in the Museum at Candia. It has not been published. It has been suggested that this figure is a forgery, but I see no reason to accept this suggestion.

[2] W. Lamb, *Greek and Roman Bronzes*, pl. v, *a–d*.

[3] Xanthoudides, *Vaulted Tombs of Mesara*, pl. XXXIX, No. 171.

except for the left leg. The little figure stands 5·5 cm. high and shows a rigid human figure with the hands clasped on the breast. It has no obvious connexion with known types in bronze. In fact it appears rather to have been derived from the rigidly conventional 'Cycladic Idols' of the islands which were widely imported into Crete and seem to have become objects of considerable demand. Like the Tylissos figure this is made by rubbing.

From Kalathiana comes a small figure of a lion in hard grey stone about 4 cm. in length and pierced at the shoulders for suspension. This may be compared with the superb axe of schist from Mallia[1] which ends in a leopard *protome*. Neither of the two has ever been touched with a chisel or gouge; they are the product of a careful process of steady and intricate rubbing.[2]

The only other example of hard stone sculpture of the human figure attributed to Cretan workmanship is the statuette of a lady now in the Fitzwilliam Museum at Cambridge.[3] Since it does not come under the head of works whose pedigree is unimpeachable it will be dealt with separately after the authentic works have been discussed.

The most noteworthy examples of sculpture in hard stone (or relatively hard stone) other than of human figures are the two fine heads of a lion and lioness from Knossos.[4] With them must be associated the part of a muzzle of a precisely similar head found underneath the Temple of Apollo at Delphi.

The head of the lioness from Knossos is executed in a marble-like limestone, that of the lion in alabaster. The Delphian fragment is of the same marble-limestone as that of which the head of the lioness is made.

All three appear to be of Late Minoan date, probably

---

[1] Mallia, *premier rapport* (1922–4), pl. XXIII.
[2] Aided in the case of the Mallia axe by a burin for incising detail and a tubular reed drill for rendering the facial markings.
[3] A. J. B. Wace, *A Cretan Statuette in the Fitzwilliam Museum*, 1927.
[4] Evans, *Palace of Minos*, II. ii, pp. 827 ff.

L.M. I, the Delphian example being certainly a Cretan import to the Greek mainland; Sir Arthur Evans, indeed, thinks that it comes from the same Knossian workshop as the others, and the fact that the Delphian example has been mended shows that it was not possible for it to be replaced by mainland artists.

The primary stages of the working of these three heads cannot be established. We can only infer the final methods. Those methods seem to have involved, in the main, a process of laborious abrasion, since the shapes precluded all turning on a lathe. In the case of the head of the lioness the hollows of the ears, particularly the depression in front of each ear, and above all the smooth furrows between the eye and the brow can only have been achieved by continuous rubbing. The eyes and the groove of the mouth, on the other hand, indicate the use of a cutting instrument, while the fringe of hair round the jowls was incised with a pointed burin. A drill was probably used for the two small holes above the eyes at the end of each brow as well as for the structural holes round the neck and through the muzzle.

The lion-head of alabaster (now in the Ashmolean) is fragmentary, but enough survives to show that exactly the same processes were followed. The abrasive process is, however, more manifest in the case of the finely rendered facets to the cheeks, which can be restored reliably from the surviving fragments, which show their starting-point. The same type of depression between the eyes and the brows, the same drill-holes over the eyes and in the muzzle, and the same clearly cut eyes and mouth testify to exactly the same mode of sculpture.

The Delphian fragment is too small to permit of any inferences, but there is nothing in it to contradict the conclusions here made.

In general it can be said that these heads in their final states were achieved entirely without the aid of the chisel or gouge and, for the main surfaces, by means of continuous rubbing with abrasive stone. There is no instrument of metal which could have rendered the fine furrows of the brows or the facets of the jowl of the lion. They are in the tradition of a Stone Age and not due to the sophistries of a new age of metal. The use of abrasive and of burin show the influence of the gem-cutter's art. In any case there is a direct contrast with the methods used in the carving of soft stone, such as steatite, where the use of the knife suggests comparison rather with the technique of wood-carving.

The stone statuette of a goddess in the Fitzwilliam Museum at Cambridge is in a class by itself. It is the only elaborate representation of a human (or divine) figure in hard stone which has ever been attributed with some show of evidence to the Minoan period. A not dissimilar figure in soft steatite comes from Tylissos (see below, p. 11), but its detailed appearance and technique are quite different: its technique in particular is thoroughly characteristic of soft stone, that is to say it is carved mainly by means of a simple blade, as if it were wood.

The Cambridge figure is made of hard reddish breccia, a favourite material of Cretan lapidaries and a stone of local origin. Being of a very hard and intractable material, a simple knife-blade, even of very hard copper or bronze, would be almost useless for its manufacture. In fact its final surface was worked in the following way.[1]

(a) The lines round the lowest zone of the skirt. These are carefully filed and kept roughly parallel. They could have been made with a fine-edged tool of abrasive stone. It is improbable that a metal file of copper or bronze would have been used in Minoan times, since such a tool would be worn out with great rapidity. A modern steel file, on the other hand, of the most common style, could make these lines. As they are to-day, however, there is nothing

[1] This description is based on a close examination which I was allowed, by the kindness of the Director of the Fitzwilliam Museum, to make in August 1931 and 1932.

about them to suggest the modern forger rather than the ancient craftsman.

(b) The vertical grooves of the four zones of skirt above this lowest zone. These are uniform all round the skirt and are cut from above or from below with a narrow gouge, each cut being made with one or more sharp strokes. The grooves so made are independent in each zone, that is to say, they do not join up with the grooves of the other zones or lie in relation to them.

(c) The pattern of the apron. The hem-pattern of the apron consists of small circular depressions within a border. These holes or depressions are almost exactly similar to those of the apron of the Tylissos goddess. In the case of the Cambridge figure they are certainly made with a blunt-headed drill. The hem lines, however, and the crossing lines of the body of the apron are carefully incised with a graving tool or burin.

(d) Fingers and hair. The fingers are divided by a burin or chisel and the lines of the hair are cut with a similar instrument.

(e) The hole by which the two parts of the figure fit at the waist is a rectangular one and seems to have been made with a blade, perhaps a flat chisel. It has certainly not been made with a drill. The hole on the base which attached the figure to its pedestal is round and was made in the same way, not with a drill.

There is no direct evidence of surface to show how the face was cut or how the triangular depressions in the bend of each arm were cleared. I am inclined to think that a flat chisel was used both for the face and for these depressions. I cannot, however, detect any precise traces of the flat chisel which are beyond dispute.

From this detailed examination it will be clear at once that the main tools used are, with one exception, tools that were known in the Minoan periods as far as our present knowledge goes. The abrasive file, the burin, and the drill are all alike exactly the tools which we should expect to find in hard-stone sculpture of the Minoan age. But the one exception is an important one. The gouge is not an instrument which, as far as we know, was known either to the wood-carver or to the hard-stone carver and lapidary of Minoan times. There is, as will be shown below, ample evidence for the use of the flat chisel, at any rate, in woodwork, and its use on hard stone, while extremely improbable, must not be wholly ruled out. But the use of the gouge is quite unusual, in fact unique. This is the only Minoan work in hard stone in which its use is known. That the grooves of the skirt are cut by a gouge is certain. They are not the kind of grooves which an abrasive can make, for their surfaces are striated by the gouge-blade in many instances and their outlines have the characteristic unsteadiness of outlines defined by the gouge. Lines made by the flat chisel have the same unsteadiness (see below, p. 140 and Fig. 66). These vertical grooves show the starting-point and the end of each stroke. They are not steady and even but shaky and narrow at top and bottom. Such would be true of any gouge mark of an inch in length made by the gouge on hard stone with swift strokes.

The fact that these grooves are so made seems to me to make acceptance of this statuette as genuine impossible. As we have seen, the technique of Minoan work in hard stone followed rigidly the technique of the gem-cutter and the lapidary. But here we find a tool in use which was not known in Minoan times[1] and which first came into use in Greek lands in the sixth century B.C. It may, of course, be argued that its use here is the only evidence for its existence as a Minoan tool, and this is a possible line of defence. But against this it must be urged that this hypo-thetical Minoan gouge would, of necessity, have been

[1] Petrie in *Tools and Weapons* (1917), p. 22, states: 'It (the gouge) is almost entirely a northern tool, there being only three (Bologna, Vetulonia, Athens) from all the Mediterranean area. . . . There are hardly enough examples to trace the course of varieties.'

made of bronze or copper, and it is hardly credible that such a tool could cut into the surface of hard breccia of this type without being immediately blunted or broken after a few strokes. The evidence, indeed, from these gouge marks seems to me to be decisive (see Appendix, p. 236). They can only have been made with a steel or iron gouge.

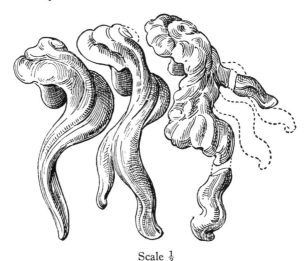

Scale ⅓

FIG. I.   Curls cast in solid bronze (from Knossos).

It may be added that the pedigree of the figure is unknown and the doubts cast upon its authenticity on grounds of style and general character are serious.[1] Leaving these on one side we can at least say that on purely technical grounds the statuette does not conform to the known practices of Minoan times and that one tool, hitherto unknown to the Minoan repertoire, but a favourite stone-worker's tool to-day, is extensively used on the surface. The fact that that tool must have been of steel or iron makes the attribution of the statuette to the Bronze Age untenable.

ii. *Wood.* The only material in which it seems certain that large statues were made in Minoan times in Crete was wood. This knowledge we owe to the brilliant inference drawn by

---

[1] *Journal of Hellenic Studies*, xlvii (1927), p. 299.

Sir Arthur Evans[1] from the association near the East Hall of the Palace of four massive bronze locks of hair embedded in a heavy deposit of carbonized wood. The bronze locks for long had remained in the Candia Museum unidentified. But comparison with smaller figures, such as a miniature ivory head with bronze-wire tresses attached[2] and a similar head without the tresses but with the attachment holes clearly seen,[3] showed the purpose of these larger bronzes. The charcoal deposit indicated the material to which they were attached. From the scale of the tresses Sir Arthur computes, on the principle of *ex pede Herculem*, a colossal wooden statue of a female some 9 feet in height. He proposes a most interesting parallel with the statue of Apollo Aleus found at Ciro[4] in Calabria, which had a marble head with a wig of bronze hair, marble hands and feet, and a presumed wooden body, long perished.[5]

Scale $\frac{1}{10}$

FIG. 2. Suggested restoration of head of statue, with bronze curls on a wooden figure.

This evidence for the existence of large wooden statues at Knossos at once throws back the history of the Hellenic xoanon, at any rate from the point of view of technical processes, to a very remote pre-Hellenic age. Of the actual technique of this Cretan statue we know nothing, but must draw the inevitable inference that it was fashioned according to the manner of woodcarving and achieved with knife and chisel and perhaps plane, though the use of the latter tool is

---

[1] *Palace of Minos*, iii, p. 522; E. J. Forsdyke, *Minoan Art* (British Academy), 1929, p. 20.   [2] Ibid., p. 432, fig. 298.   [3] Ibid., p. 433, figs. 299 and 300.

[4] For this work see the references in Evans, op. cit., p. 523, and MacIver, *Greek Cities in Italy and Sicily* (1931), p. 68.

[5] Pindar, *Pyth.* v. 40, speaks of a statue of a single cypress block dedicated at Delphi by Cretans.

not necessarily to be included.[1] The remarkable painted head made of stucco or plaster which was found by Tsountas at Mycenae on the west side of the acropolis may be itself a cult figure. The care with which the head is painted and the fact that the painting and moulding are done with equal care all round (Fig. 16) preclude us from attributing it to a mural decoration in relief. It is certainly the head of a figure intended to stand by itself. Its date is problematical, but there are grounds for attributing it to the close of the last Mycenaean period.[2]

iii. *Soft Stones*. Various forms of steatite were at all periods extremely popular among Minoan artists. The knowledge of the material and possibly the methods of working it probably came to Crete from Sumeria, where it was popular at all periods.

Steatite, when used for plain vases and cups, is usually turned on a lathe. But, when used for figures or for elaborately ornamented vessels like the Chieftain Vase or the Harvester Vase, the vessel itself is turned but the decoration is done, perhaps before the turning, almost exclusively by means of a knife, as if it were woodwork. Proof of this is difficult, but the traces of a knife-point are visible in several instances. Moreover, by a process of elimination we are driven to assume some tool of the knife type. For there are neither chisel-marks nor file-marks, nor would it have been possible for the intricate designs of steatite reliefs to be cut by an abrasive process. The softness of steatite, together with the compact nature of the stone and its absence of cleavage or lamination makes it an ideal material for hand-carving. It is certainly more tractable than ebony but harder

---

[1] Evans, op. cit., iii, p. 522; and Ridgeway, *Early Age*, ii, p. 490 and n. 6. The ears, hair-band, lips, and tatoo markings are dull red. The hair and eyes are deep black. Both colours are painted over a chalk-white slip. The nostrils are bored and uncoloured. Bosanquet thought that it was the head of a sphinx, the head free and the body in relief. But the head in such a case would certainly show an attachment at the back. No such attachment is visible.

[2] Ridgeway, loc. cit.

than box-wood. Its compact nature makes it possible for detail to be rendered upon its surfaces with high success, and the fact that it takes a polish gives it some of the virtue of marble without the defects of that material. For steatite does not chip or flake.

Nevertheless it seems unlikely that any actual carving or relief in steatite was allowed to remain with its natural surface visible. The famous cups decorated in relief certainly were encased in a thin covering of gold-leaf. The only statuette we have in this material[1] was covered with a thin coating of stucco and then painted. The authenticity of this statuette is, however, not assured.

Conceivably the soft stone known as *Lapis Siphnius*, not yet accurately identified, is a steatite. Certainly the habit of turning it on a lathe and so fashioning it into vessels survived into classical times, for we are told by Theophrastus[2] that it can be worked into any form by virtue of its softness and that after the vessels are made they are oiled and so achieve a black colour. That the habit of turning vessels in soft stone should have survived so late in one of the Cyclades, suggests the continuity of a prehistoric island technique. No surviving instances, however, of this Siphnian ware are known.

Gypsum is rarely used for sculpture, but there are two important instances in the shape of the two bull-reliefs brought by Lord Elgin from his brief excavations in the dromos of the so-called 'Treasury of Atreus' at Mycenae. These reliefs have been shown decisively by Sir Arthur Evans to be Cretan work on imported Cretan stone from Knossian quarries.[3] The one relief shows a charging and

---

[1] Evans, *Palace of Minos*, iii. 427.

[2] Theophrastus, Περὶ τῶν λίθων, lxxiv: ἐν Σίφνῳ τοιοῦτός τις ἐστὶν ὀρυκτός, ὃς τρία στάδια ἀπὸ θαλάσσης, στρογγύλος καὶ βωλώδης, καὶ τορνεύεται καὶ γλύφεται διὰ τὸ μαλακόν . . . ποιοῦσι δ' ἐξ αὐτοῦ σκεύη τὰ ἐπιτράπεζα; and Pliny, *N.H.*: 'In Siphno lapis est qui cavatur, tornaturque in vasa coquendis cibis utilia vel ad esculentorum usus.' Pliny has translated the substance of Theophrastus.

[3] *Palace of Minos*, iii, pp. 192 ff.; *Brit. Mus. Cat. of Sculpture*, I. i, Nos. A. 56 and 57.

the other a stationary bull. Only in the case of the former can any attempt be made to examine the technical methods, for the latter is too much weathered. The 'Charging Bull Relief' seems to have been cut with a chisel and a knife, while the carefully cut striations on the bull's neck were engraved with an abrasive point of metal or stone, used in the manner of a burin.

In essence, then, these gypsum reliefs seem to have followed the fashions of steatite carving where the detail, as we have seen, was rendered with a knife, the blade of which was used for paring off the inset surfaces and the point for engraving the detailed lines and features. There is one particularly interesting example of stone-carving in red gypsum which can, not unreasonably, be classed as sculpture.[1] It comes from the palace at Knossos and is probably of the third Middle Minoan period. It was apparently part of a revetment in stone from a wall decoration. It represents the characteristic Middle Minoan marine rocks from a sea scene. Its importance in this context is that it is, in a sense, a kind of fretwork cut from a flat slab of gypsum. The indentations on the edges which show the characteristic rocky outlines have clearly been filed away carefully with files of varying sizes. Different pieces of abrasive stone would clearly have effected the various curves and cuts in the outline far more easily than a metal file, if indeed metal files existed in Minoan times.

Although gypsum is here classified as a soft stone, this particular kind of red gypsum, resembling porphyry in some respects, may, perhaps, rank rather as a hard stone.

iv. *Ivory*. None of the surviving ivory Minoan figures permit us to draw certain conclusions as to the methods by which they were cut, since their surfaces in every case have been damaged by the passage of time. But there seems little doubt that they were principally cut with the knife, and that the drill was occasionally used for boring holes, as, for instance,

[1] Evans, *Palace of Minos*, iii, p. 366, fig. 243.

for the insertion of wire tresses on the heads or of other detailed ornament. Similar drills are, on occasions, used for boring holes in steatite or in hard-stone vessels. The drill was certainly part of the equipment of the lapidary as well as of the sculptor of small works in hard or soft stone.

v. *Bronzes.* Human and animal figures in bronze of Minoan workmanship are by no means common. In all there are hardly more than a score of well-executed and artistic figures. These are limited severely to types, with one notable exception (see below, p. 15), and strictly follow the same technique in every case. The main types are two, male worshippers and female worshippers, always in the characteristic Cretan attitudes of adoration. The one exception is the splendid group of a Bull and Acrobat, now in the collection of Captain Spencer Churchill.

But all alike have exactly the same technique. They are cast solid and hardly ever worked after casting.[1] There seems to have been in the Minoan artistic character some hint of impressionism, for it is difficult to understand why these statuettes were left uniformly as they came, rough and untouched, from the mould.

One thing is certain—that the Minoans had no knowledge at all of hollow casting by the *cire-perdue* process. Curiously enough, the Minoans took no hint from contemporary Egyptian bronze or copper work in which metal was saved by employing beaten sheets and filling them with bitumen[2] in the case of large statues, while in the case of small statuettes the surface of solid figures was often meticulously finished. The Minoans quite definitely followed a technique and a tradition entirely their own. But it was a short-lived tradition, for the earliest datable bronze statuette belongs to the

[1] The best account of these statuettes as a whole is to be found in Miss W. Lamb's *Greek and Roman Bronzes* (1929), pp. 19 ff.

[2] The famous copper statue of Montesupis, son of Pepi I (c. 2700 B.C.), was made of sheets of copper beaten over a wooden core or block. This technique was never transmitted to Crete from Egypt although elaborated at so early a period.

period 1700–1580 (M.M. III), while the latest, still of the same general style, hardly post-date 1470. The subsequent bronzes show a rapid deterioration both of style and of technique and soon assimilate themselves to a crude general style common to most shores of the eastern Mediterranean.

In the case of the main series of Minoan statuettes of the best type there seems to have been a uniform method followed in the casting. What is now seen as the pedestal upon which the figure stands, which itself is part and parcel of the flat footplate holding the feet, is technically formed from the crude bronze which was left in the orifice down which it was, when liquid, poured by the caster. This is most clearly seen in the case of an interesting statuette found in the Harbour Town of Knossos.[1] Here the pedestal consists of a solid button-shaped mass of bronze formed by the last drops that were poured into the mouth of the mould: it is joined to the feet by two separate pipes of bronze which were formed by the two separate holes that led the liquid metal down the cast into each leg. In the case of the usual male 'worshipper' the junction between the footplate and the mouth of the mould is effected by a single simple tube which, in the casting, filled up with bronze and so made a rod of metal, joining to a flat plate.[2]

In the case of the female 'worshippers' the ample skirts provided their own basis of support, and there are no additional pedestals.

The lack of finish, even where it involved the smallest conceivable after-treatment, is seen in the case of the statuette of a male from the Harbour Town of Cnossos. The casting, as in most of these figures, was a rough one, probably from a sand-mould, and small lumps of metal, caused by defective casting, are still adhering to the surface. The simplest process of final surface polishing would have removed them.

---

[1] Evans, *Palace of Minos*, II. i, p. 234 and fig. 132. Also Lamb, op. cit., pl. VIII *b*.   [2] Lamb, op. cit., pl. V and VIII, *a, b*.

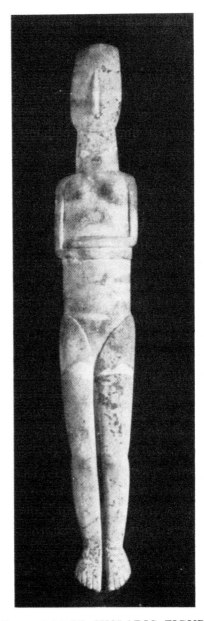

FIG. 3. LARGE CYCLADIC FIGURE,
No. 3978, in the National Museum, Athens.
Height 149 cm. Breadth 21·5 cm. Depth 6 cm.

The bronze of the bull and the acrobat, unique in our knowledge of Minoan bronzework, is a small masterpiece of ingenuity. Its casting must have been extremely difficult. Its preservation is not complete enough to show what sort of pedestal it had, but the forelegs of the bull have a protuberant boss of bronze. Yet we cannot guess how it stood or upon what kind of basis.

Here, too, there is a surprising lack of final finish. Nothing at all seems to have been done to it after the casting.

2. CYCLADES

i. *Hard Stones.* The diminished force of artistic invention seen in the products of the Cycladic islands makes the study of the technical methods employed there a matter of less difficulty. Where artists are less artistically inventive they tend to be more conventional in the technical methods they employ. For a long period there were produced in the islands small idols in hard white marble which differed as little in style as they did in the methods of their manufacture. Here and there a sculptor was tempted to some unusual feat of artistry, but tended rather to exhibit his originality by means of size than by any lapse into naturalism or experiment in complexity.

Cycladic artists invented a simple and convenient form of idol which, for some reason which we do not know, had an immense vogue over a wide area. Even the more sophisticated Cretans imported Cycladic idols in large numbers[1] while at the same time producing in other branches of art

[1] *Palace of Minos*, i. 115 and n. 1. These imported idols were apparently considered as objects of value since in almost all cases they show traces of having been mended. Six were found in graves at Koumasa (see Xanthoudides, *Vaulted Tombs of Mesara*, trans. P. Droop, 1924, p. 21). Although only three of these are of island marble it is unlikely that the other three were made in Crete. One comes from Platanos (ibid., p. 121) and another from Pyrgos (*Arch. Delt.* 4. 163), one large and eight small from Haghios Onuphrios (Xanthoudides, p. 21), four from Tylissos and a head from Trypete near Candia (ibid.), and some others the provenance of which is not known.

objects far more artistic than those usually produced in the islands.

The Cycladic idol as we know it seems to have evolved from the very simple type found in the earlier settlements of Troy. In origin it is probably Anatolian. Certainly what seem to be the most primitive types, shaped like fiddles, are found at Troy. These are made of marble as a general rule, though sometimes of slate[1] or other hard materials.

The same fiddle-types are found in the Cyclades. They seem to have been made by taking a simple rectangular slab of marble, removing two rectangular pieces from the corners so as to leave a protruding neck, and then cutting a simple indentation on each vertical side to make a waist.

But the ingenuity of these island artists was considerable. The same general process was applied with greater imagination and observation, and slowly a less geometric and schematic representation of the human figure emerged (Fig. 3). But, once the fuller type was fixed, variation was rare. As a rule the only element that varied was the size. Thus we have typical island female idols that vary from 3 inches in height to nearly 5 feet[2] with little or no variation in appearance or method of manufacture.

With so large a number of a fixed type available for study and with every size to examine it is not difficult to see how they were made. The marble was first selected as a rectangular slab. It was then trimmed to the outline of a human figure with arms folded, legs together, and feet slightly apart. The head was erect and given, as a rule, a slight tilt backwards. The division between the legs gives the clue to the process of manufacture of the whole. It is effected by abrasion with a wedge-shaped tool which cuts a simple groove into the marble surface. Sometimes the pressure of the tool

---

[1] Schliemann, *Troy* (1875), p. 36, No. 17.

[2] See Tsountas and Manatt, *The Mycenaean Age*, p. 257, fig. 132. The head of one still larger has been found in Amorgos (P. Wolters, *Ath. Mitth.* xvi, p. 46). No. 6195 in the National Museum (see Stais, *Guide*, p. 211) measures 0·59 m. in height, and was found at Spedos.

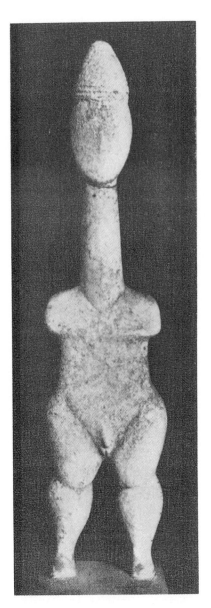 

FIG. 4. CYCLADIC FIGURE, No. 3911,
in the National Museum, Athens.

Height 25·2 cm. Breadth 6·1 cm.
Depth 2·5 cm.

FIG. 5. CYCLADIC FIGURE, No. 3919,
in the National Museum, Athens.

Height 30·5 cm. Breadth 7·2 cm.
Depth 3·3 cm.

FIG. 6. CYCLADIC HARPIST, No. 3908. National Museum, Athens
Height 23 cm. Breadth 11 cm. Depth 16·5 cm.

is such as to cut right through the marble, perhaps in-advertently, so as to make a hole. With another tool of abrasive the rough outlines of the arms are cut, the fingers and the toes indicated by lightly grooved lines, and the only feature of the face which is ever rendered—the nose—is achieved by rubbing a flat surface on two sides of the face, so leaving an unrubbed boss projecting. Noses are thus rendered in every case where a nose is shown. The top of the head is thus thinned off into a ludicrous knife-edge, which gives an exaggerated dolichocephalic appearance to an already fantastic object.

It is in any case clear enough that the statuettes are finished by a process in which rubbing and rubbing only is the artist's mode of work.

The rarer male figures (Fig. 4 & 5) are more rounded and realistic, and in one instance the arms are separated from the body by bored holes. But these holes do not seem to have been made with a drill. They were rather cut by a process of steady pressure with a pointed awl, like a splinter, of abrasive, used and revolved by hand. In a sense such usage implies the existence of a primitive drill, but at a stage of development before it had become a drill revolved by a bow-string or brace-bit and when it was merely a borer.

The rare instances of more elaborate island sculpture are extremely instructive. The famous harpist from Spedos in the National Museum at Athens[1] and the equally original flute-player show how the process of abrasion could be used to produce real *chefs-d'œuvre*. The harpist, who is male (Fig. 6), is seated on a backed chair and holds the harp on his knees. Except for the forearms and part of the harp and left leg the figure is complete. It is the work of a real virtuoso who has set himself a diverting problem in open-work! The connexion with the typical island idols is at once evident in the head, which has the thin wedge-end and the same nose that are seen in the female figures. The genitals

---

[1] Nos. 3908 and 3910 in the National Museum. Stais, *Guide*, p. 203.

are shown clearly. The figure is conceived exactly in the manner of the female idols, but bent into a sitting posture. Clear traces of abrasive rubbing are seen on every surface. It is a small masterpiece of a laborious mode of art.

The flute-player, which was found at Keros (Fig. 7), is simpler and must have been less difficult to make. It shows a male figure standing with the usual tilted head and protruding nose. Both hands are raised to the flute, which is a double one. The body is rounder and more bossy, the legs divided not by the usual cleft but by a wide cutting so that each leg can be made rounded and circular in section. The feet, of necessity, are supported on a pedestal or footplate[1] which is structurally part of the whole. Clear traces of the rubbing that fashioned the footplate are seen on its upper surface. Little examination is needed to show that the method of manufacture is essentially that of the more conventional statuettes.

A third exceptional work is the pair of harpists from Thera.[2] Each is seated on a stool. They correspond in all essential details with the harpist from Spedos.

It remains to ask what possibility there was of metal tools being used in the construction of these figures. It must be remembered that at the time when the bulk of the Cycladic idols were made the islanders were in a not very mature bronze age. Bronze chisels are by no means uncommon on Minoan and island sites, but it may well be asked whether bronze chisels would have been at all adequate to cut the hard crystalline Naxian marble of which the bulk of the statuettes are carved. Nor would bronze files last long for such work. A saw of copper was found at Naxos[3] and is considered by some to be the oldest in Greece. Certainly it is contemporary with the idols. In the earlier stages of preparing the marble blanks from which these idols are made a saw would have been useful, but it is doubtful how long a

---

[1] It is conceivable that this type of footplate suggested that used in Minoan bronze figures.   [2] Bossert, *Altkreta*, fig. 120 *b*.   [3] Stais, *Guide*, p. 214.

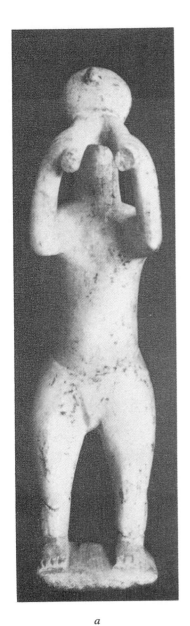 

a   *b*

FIG. 7, *a* and *b*. CYCLADIC FLUTE-PLAYER, National Museum,
Athens, No. 3910.

Height 20·5 cm. Breadth 5·3 cm. Depth of body 2·8 cm.

copper saw would have served its purpose in cutting so hard a material as island marble.

In dealing with these marble island idols, then, one is driven to assume the existence of abrasive tools of stone. It is no coincidence that precisely the kind of stone required is available in unlimited quantities in the very island from which the majority of the idols come and from which in antiquity it may be safely assumed that the fashion of making them originated. Although they have been found in Amorgos, Siphnos, Melos, Spedos, Thera, Syra, Paros, and Crete, Naxos has produced the largest number and the most varied types. It is in Naxos that are to be found also the famous mines of emery or corundum which is still used to-day by all modern sculptors as the most suitable medium for working the final mouldings and surfaces on a statue in marble. Emery from Naxos was famous in antiquity; it could have been used either as sand or as a tool, shaped according to the uses to which it was to be put. It was as accessible in the Early Minoan period to which these 'idols' belong as it is to-day when the annual output is some 20,000 tons.[1] There can be no reasonable doubt that the island statuettes were made with tools shaped from emery stone.

Corundum, or emery, is next to the diamond in hardness. It can be shaped only by grinding it with its own powder. But any natural pointed splinter would serve the purpose of engraving lines, as with a burin. The fingers and toes of the idols, or the fringe of hair on the lioness head above described (see p. 4) would easily have been rendered with such a tool. A wedge-shaped piece would equally well make the groove between the legs seen on the most common type of the idols. Pieces with flattened surfaces would do the simple rubbing such as is seen on the heads and faces of the idols and on their

[1] The emery mines were made a Government monopoly in the early days of Greek Independence in 1824. The deposits at Naxos have been estimated to contain five million tons and vary from 5 to 50 metres in thickness. See *Near East Year Book*, 1927, p. 705. Emery is also found in Asia Minor, but there is no evidence that it was ever worked there in antiquity.

smooth surfaces. It would in fact serve as a perfect tool for the speedy working of marble or of any hard stone. For soft stones, however, it would be more or less ineffective since its power of biting into the surface would make it too quick a tool for reliable use, and, as we have seen, there are no traces of steatite having ever been rubbed in such a way. For turning, on the other hand, an emery point fixed on to a lathe would be excellent, and we have certain information that it was so used by gem-cutters on their wheels.

The evidence from ancient sources as to its use shows that it was a famous export from Naxos in classical times. We hear a good deal of the 'stone of Naxos'. It is first mentioned in Pindar,[1] where a strong man is compared with a Naxian whetstone:

> Φαίης κέ νιν ἀνδράσιν ἀθληταῖσιν ἔμμεν
> Ναξίαν πέτραις ἐν ἄλλαις χαλκοδάμαντ' ἀκόναν.

That the material from which both whetstones and tools for artistic seal-engraving were made was roughly the same seems clear from Theophrastus,[2] who tells us that: ὁ λίθος ᾧ γλύφουσι τὰς σφραγίδας, ἐκ τούτου ἐστὶν ἐξ οὗπερ αἱ ἀκόναι, ἢ ἐξ ὁμοίου τούτῳ.

Both Suidas[3] and Stephanus of Byzantium[4] refer to Ναξία λίθος, but a curious confusion seems to have arisen in their sources between the emery of Naxos and a hard material for whetstone which seems to have been found at Oaxos in

---

[1] *Isth.* vi. 72.

[2] Περὶ τῶν λίθων, 77. The stone here referred to is not the Naxian but the Armenian, which, according to Pliny (*N.H.* 36. 22. 4), superseded the Naxian. Of the Armenian stone Stephanus of Byzantium (*s.v.* 'Αρμενία) says, παρέχονται δὲ λίθον τὴν γλύφουσαν καὶ τρυπῶσαν τὰς σφραγίδας.

[3] *S.v.* Νάξος· ἀφ' οὗ Ναξία λίθος, ἡ Κρητικὴ ἀκόνη . . . ἡ δὲ κριτικὴ ἀκόνη, ἐὰν διὰ τοῦ ι γράφεται ἡ διακρίνουσα καὶ φανεροῦσα σημαίνει. There is in addition some textual confusion in this passage, which has remained unsolved by the few editors of this author. The confusion of whetstone with touchstone may be due to the writer having drawn part of his information from Theophrastus, who discusses touchstones immediately after his account of whetstones.

[4] Νάξος πόλις, καὶ Ναξία λίθος, ἡ Κρητικὴ ἀκόνη. Νάξος γὰρ πόλις Κρήτης. Suidas more briefly cuts the Gordian knot!

Crete. Both these authors are our only record for the Oaxian stone, if indeed that can be taken as the explanation of their references to Crete. Whetstone of grit, not of emery, is to-day found at a place called Oxah,[1] but the modern Oxah is not the site of the ancient Oaxos, though it may well be the source of the whetstones exported by that city. Stephanus, not realizing that there were two possible sources for good abrasives, attempts without success to explain away his difficulty by the suggested reading of κριτική for κρητική. But in so doing he is adding the further confusion between a whetstone and a touchstone, for that is the only material to which the term κριτική could be applied.

That the Ναξία λίθος of these authors is from the island of Naxos and not from Crete seems certain, partly because of the existence of an enormous deposit of the stone on Naxos itself and partly because, if it came from Oaxos (or Ϝαξός, as it was called in earlier times),[2] it is hardly likely that it would have been known as early as the time of Pindar as Ναξία. If the stone known as Naxian came from Cretan Oaxos we should at least expect to find textual variants which might lead us to the Cretan name. But these, in fact, do not occur, and the mention of Crete is only found in the confused explanations of the two lexicographers.

Pliny, without any hint or suggestion of Crete, calls it, simply enough, 'Naxian', which his readers would without exception have taken to refer to the Cycladic island. And Pliny tells us more about it. In describing the process of cutting marble he tells us that a saw should be used with the aid of 'sand'.[3] The best sand was the Ethiopian, the next best the Indian and the Naxian. But the two latter have, he says, the same defect, which is shared by the Egyptian brand, of leaving an unequal surface on smooth faces. But we learn that the Naxian and Egyptian were in use in earlier times—

[1] Spratt, *Researches in Crete*, i. 127.

[2] Head, *Historia Numorum*, p. 459.

[3] *N.H.* xxxvi. 6, 9. Harena hoc fit et ferro videtur fieri, serra in praetenui linia prementi harenas versandoque tractu ipso secante, &c.

haec fuere antiqua genera marmoribus secandis. He adds that
Thebaic sand was used for *politura*, in stonework, and further
tells us that for long Naxian stone was preferred for the
polishing of marble statues and for the cutting of gems—
*signis e marmore poliendis gemmisque etiam scalpendis atque
limandis Naxium diu placuit ante alia.* Later,[1] he remarks
that among the abrasive stones which were used with water,
as contrasted with those which required the use of oil—
Naxiae laus maxuma fuit, mox Armeniacae.

From the silence of Theophrastus about Naxian stone
and his mention of the Armenian it may, perhaps, be inferred
that the Naxian had, by the fourth century B.C., gone entirely
out of fashion and been replaced by the Armenian. Certainly
Pliny's reference to the *antiqua genera* and his further
remarks, *Naxium diu placuit ante alia*, and *Naxiae laus
maxuma fuit, mox Armeniacae*, indicate something of the
kind.

But it is not quite clear in Pliny where the use of Naxian
sand can be distinguished from use of pieces of the actual
emery itself. Emery sand can be produced by crushing the
emery stone, or from sandy deposits in the proximity. Such
sand is referred to by Hesychius[2] and Dioscorides[3] as σμύρις
or σμίρις, and in the LXX Book of Job[4] as σμυρίτης λίθος.

The use of emery-stone as a cutting instrument must be
inferred both from the use of the term λίθος by Stephanus
and Suidas and the πέτρα implied in the passage of Pindar.
Pliny, on the other hand, refers to the sand when he calls it
Naxiae in one passage (*simile Naxiae vitium est et Coptitidi*),
but later, where he calls it *Naxium* and states how it was used
for statues and gem-cutting, he is thinking of it as the stone
itself, not of the shaped whetstone, the noun understood
being *saxum*. The final mention (*Naxiae laus maxuma fuit*,
&c.) takes *cos* as its noun from a preceding sentence.

[1] *N.H.* xxxvi. 22, 47.
[2] *S.v.* Σμίρις· ἄμμου εἶδος ᾗ σμήχονται οἱ σκληροὶ τῶν λίθων.
[3] v. 166: Σμύρις· λίθος ἐστὶν ᾗ τὰς ψήφους οἱ δακτυλιογλύφοι σμήχουσι.
[4] xli. 7: σύνδεσμος αὐτοῦ, ὥσπερ σμυρίτης λίθος.

In short, Naxian emery could clearly be used on statues in the two distinct ways.

It is not my intention to examine here the very rich evidence from Egypt as to the use by Egyptian artists of emery for the making of sculpture. But that it was so used, and extensively, is not even disputed by Egyptologists. Sir Flinders Petrie[1] explains how emery was used not only as sand for working saws, but also in fragments large and small as cutting-points and graving-tools. The hieroglyphs, for instance, on hard bowls of diorite are, he says, 'ploughed out with a single cut of a fixed point only one hundred and fiftieth of an inch wide'. Larger hieroglyphs on hard stones were 'cut by copper blades fed with emery and sawn along the outline by hand: the block between the cuts was broken out and the floor of the sign was hammer-dressed and finally ground down with emery'. The lapidary also used emery powder, and vases 'were ground out with stone grinders fed with emery'. One of the earliest instances of the use of emery is seen in a block of emery, now in the Ashmolean Museum (Fig. 15), which was used for smoothing and grinding hard stone beads. The block itself has been shaped.

In view of the various problems to be discussed below, these facts are of very great importance. For the same methods are found again both in the Minoan and Mycenaean periods and in Hellenic times.

3. MYCENAE.

i. *Hard Stones*. At Mycenae survives the one example of large-scale pre-Hellenic sculpture in hard stone. The Lion Gate is profoundly instructive both from an artistic point of

[1] *Arts and Crafts of Ancient Egypt*, 1909, pp. 73 ff. He also observes that as far back as prehistoric times blocks of emery were used for grinding beads, and even a plummet and a vase (now at University College) were cut out of emery rock. The knowledge of and import to Egypt of Aegean emery must thus in Egypt go back to a very remote period. See also *Tools and Weapons*, p. 45.

view, as showing the general aesthetic theories underlying its structure, and from a technical point of view as illustrating methods which appear to combine the outlook of the lapidary with those of the true hewer of sculptural form. It is the latter methods that I propose to examine now.

The heraldic lions and their central pillar, which constitute the 'Lion Gate' of Mycenae, are composed of a triangular block of hard grey limestone, probably of local origin. The heads of the lions were attached separately by dowels of which the dowel-holes are clearly visible.

The only technical consideration of the relief yet published[1] postulates the use of 'primitive and inefficient tools of bronze' and no other medium of working stone. The main lines of the relief are said to have been cut 'with the saw and the boring drill', both presumably of bronze. 'The straight lines of the capital and of the base and of the lions' legs and bodies', we are told, 'were cut out by the saw, whereas the curved lines between the lions' forelegs and round their paws were marked out by lines of drill-holes which, between the forelegs, are so close together that they have the appearance of a honeycomb.'

This account is partly accurate but insufficient as a technical description. It tacitly assumes the saw and the boring drill to be of bronze and fails to point out the most remarkable fact that the drill-holes are not mere holes, like the ordinary hole made by a solid drill, but are circles measuring 1·6 cm. in diameter, with protruding centres (Fig. 9). As such they were made by a tubular drill, which was revolved rapidly on a bow and used with the aid of emery sand. This type of drill goes back to Neolithic days and was used almost universally in Europe for the drilling of holes through axes or other hard-stone artefacts. It was used widely in Egypt for the purpose of boring large or small holes and for the main functional purpose of breaking down masses

---

[1] *B.S.A.* xxv, p. 16 and pl. 4. The plate, unfortunately, fails to illustrate the points made in the text.

FIG. 8. THE LION GATE RELIEF AT MYCENAE

Fig. 9. LION GATE RELIEF AT MYCENAE : lower part of the fore-feet of the lion on the right.

The deeper grooves have been cut out by a tubular drill. The marks of the drill are seen in the deepest part of the groove. The diameter of the drill was about 1·6 cm.

Scale 1/2. *From a cast.*

of stone.[1] Being hollow it started and ended on the surface of the stone by making a clear-cut ring, with a raised centre. As it bored into the stone it made a small pillar, or central core, which must have been broken off from time to time. When the required hole was ended the stump of this core remained.[2] It is these stumps that we see on the lion in the drill-holes of the Lion Gate Relief. In effect the tool used was identical both with the reed-drill which cut the holes of fine axes (of which the Trojan ceremonial axes are the most notable instance)[3] and with its modern equivalent the drill used for drilling artesian wells. It corresponds to some extent with the modern 'jumper-drill' of steel which is used by masons, particularly for the cutting of very hard stones like granite. The difference, however, is that the 'jumper-drill' is struck and turned slowly, and used with a mallet or hammer to strike it by hand, and not revolved by a bow-string or its equivalent. The holes made by the tubular drill of 1·6 cm. diameter are best seen on the Lion Gate Relief at the following places.

(*a*) Between the forelegs of the left lion: 5 clear drill holes with stumps preserved.

(*b*) Above the right paw of the forefoot of the left lion where there are 10 holes in a close-set row. Similar holes are above the left paw.

(*c*) Between the fore legs of the right lion. (See Fig. 9).

(*d*) Behind the right hind leg of the right lion—a series of 8 well-preserved holes.

(*e*) In the hollow oval beneath the column, 4 clearly marked holes at the back of this oval on the left prove conclusively that it was hollowed solely by drilling. (See Fig. 10).

That some form of saw was used on the Lion Gate relief

---

[1] Petrie, *Tools and Weapons*, p. 45.

[2] For examples of axes of the Bronze Age from Troy showing unfinished borings in various stages of incompletion of this type see Schmidt, *Schliemann's Sammlung*, Nos. 7182, 7201, 7219, 7227, 7233, and 7246.

[3] In these axes the surface decoration of knobs was done with the same type of drill.

seems certain. It was used on the basis of the column and on its capital but I can see no traces of it upon the bodies of the lions themselves. A saw is often presupposed for clear-cut lines, but its use is only possible in projecting parts, since the circular saw was unknown to antiquity and the straight saw, which was in early use, cannot cut into hollows. What look like the traces of a saw are often in reality the marks of abrasion[1] made by a stone tool.

But in the case of the marks on the column of the Lion Gate Relief the marks seem to me to presuppose the definite use of a sawing method. At the same time there is not the smallest necessity to presuppose a toothed saw of metal. Stone is even to-day best cut with a wire or blade used in conjunction either with emery powder and water or emery and oil,[2] and a thin wedge of wood used as a saw with emery powder can cut sometimes as effectively as a metal saw. It all depends upon the time spent and the pressure employed. The slower the method the better the results; nor have we any reason to think that the Mycenaeans were in a hurry! All saws used by stone-cutters to-day are toothless, consisting of simple blades. It is the sand which does the bulk of the cutting, not the blade.[3]

With these corrections in mind we can now see that the most ancient methods were employed to cut the Lion Gate Relief. How the final surface-mouldings were achieved must remain largely a matter of conjecture owing to the weathering of the surface, but I see no reason to doubt that the rubbing methods in use in the Cyclades for stone-carving were not also employed here, though with vastly more skill. Nor need this be mere assumption. For the central vertical

---

[1] Schrader, *Archaische Marmorskulpturen im Akropolis-Museum* (1909), p. 26, is possibly right in thinking that the deeper cuts are sawn in No. 1362. See fig. 80 below.   [2] Pliny, *N.H.*

[3] Vitruvius, ii. 7. 1, mentions a soft tufa stone which is so soft that 'it can be cut like wood with a toothed saw'. From this we are justified in inferring that only in remarkable cases like this could a toothed saw be used on even the softest stone.

FIG. 10. LOWER PART OF THE LION GATE RELIEF AT MYCENAE

Detail to show vertical cuts made by abrasive tools and horizontal saw-work. The vertical cuts could not have been made with a saw because at the top of the upper cutting is an overhanging moulding which would have prevented the use of the saw. The abrasive cuts correspond in shape with the cuts on Cycladic marble 'idols'. The oval hole was cut out by a tubular drill. Numerous holes made by the drill are seen on the original.

From a cast.

groove on the base of the column shows most distinctly a cutting which, from its position if not from its shape, could not possibly have been made with a saw. It is a groove of exactly the same type as the grooves between the legs of Cycladic idols (Fig. 3).

The surfaces of the lions have also been smoothed to some extent by a process of hammering or punching with a blunt punch. Similar surfaces are seen on the Atreus façade.

It is possible, therefore, to conclude that the main processes by which the Lion Gate Relief was made consisted of:

1. A preliminary blocking out of the design by means of a tubular drill which was used as a steel punch would be used to-day to remove superfluous stone.
2. The sawing of certain parts of the relief.
3. The abrasion of certain ornamental grooves.
4. The final smoothing by means of abrasion and hammering or punching.

We have thus been able to ascertain by analysis the tools used in this most important sculpture. To understand its methods of manufacture is to understand the ancestry of Hellenic methods in archaic times, since not only were the methods in this—the first full-size sculpture—known and inherited by successive generations of craftsmen, but also the sculpture has stood above ground since the day on which it was erected for every Mycenaean, Achaean, Dorian, and Hellene to see. If he wanted an example here it was to his hand. If art was in an eclipse owing to the catastrophes of those dark days of change between the Mycenaean hegemony and the slow gropings to sculpture of the 'Geometric' Greek, here at any rate was something which could afford a means of continuity of craftsmanship by serving as a model to examine and a masterpiece to imitate. Art, unlike politics, can live and grow by a contemplation of its own creations.

The fact that the heads of the lions on the Lion Gate were affixed separately is definite. From the nature of the dowel-holes it is as definite that the heads were in a heavy solid material and not in beaten bronze or wood. The dowels that held the head were thick and powerful. One must assume, then, that the heads were of stone or of solid metal. More than that cannot safely be inferred from the facts.

The use of a sawing process (which, as has been seen, does not necessarily imply the use of a toothed saw) is evident in Crete in the case of architectural features that go back to the beginning of the third Middle Minoan period,[1] and Sir Arthur Evans has already called attention[2] to the frequent discoveries of bronze saws among the domestic hoards of Knossos. It is also of some interest that Talos, the indigenous rival and pupil of Daedalus, was reputed to be the inventor of the saw.[3] At the same time I prefer to see in the surviving Minoan or Mycenaean saws tools of the carpenter's or butcher's trade rather than implements of the sculptor. For stone is never cut with such tools, unless it is so soft that it can rank for technical purposes with wood (see above, p. 26, n. 3). Campagna tufa, pumice, shale, and jet might all well be cut with a toothed saw. With harder stone it would be the saw that suffered!

A further method of sawing is illustrated by an interesting discovery from Tiryns recorded by Sir Flinders Petrie.[4] He states that he noticed at Tiryns a piece of hard limestone which had been sawn. 'I found', he says, 'a broken bit of the saw left in a cut. The copper blade had rusted away to green carbonate and with it were some little blocks of emery about a sixteenth of an inch long, rectangular and quite capable of being set, but far too large to act as a loose powder with a plain blade.' From this he infers the knowledge of a method in Mycenaean times for which we have no other certain evidence. The method presumed a copper saw of unhardened copper with small 'teeth' of emery inserted into the metal

[1] Evans, *Palace of Minos*, II. ii, p. 671.   [2] Ibid.
[3] *Diod. Sic.* iv. 76. 5; *Tsetzes*, i. 494 ff.; A. B. Cook, *Zeus*, i. 724 ff.; Frazer, note to Apollodorus, iii. 15. 8.
[4] *Arts and Crafts of Ancient Egypt*, p. 73. See also *Tools and Weapons*, p. 45.

cutting edge. This would give the saw enormous penetrative power.

At the same time, while evidence of sawn stone is clear enough from Mycenaean to early Middle Minoan times there are many cases of apparently sawn edges and surfaces which have in reality been achieved by a process of abrasion. The refined mouldings of the dado slabs[1] of close-grained hard greenstone from the North-west Corner Entrance of the Palace at Knossos are not the product of any sawing process but can only have been done by careful abrasion along ruled lines.[2] So too the upper and lower mouldings of the lime-stone friezes from the Palace show unevennesses and varia-tions from the horizontal and the parallel which would have been impossible had they been cut with a sawing process. The slight variations in question are due to the moulding having been done in stretches that were not long enough to run the whole length. Where each stretch of workmanship joined the next there were faint overlaps and adjustments. Abrasion is essentially a free-hand process, sawing is more mechanical. I can see no part of the Knossian friezes which could not have been done by abrasion pure and simple with variously shaped pieces of emery.

The similar frieze from the façade of the tomb of Atreus at Mycenae[3] shows the same technique (Fig. 11). The superb fragment (A. 53) in red porphyry of the type now worked at Tenos, is of particular and remarkable interest. The mouldings have exactly those unevennesses of line which are seen on the Knossian friezes. This presupposes quite definite rubbing in sections and not sawing. The triangular spaces between the spirals in all three rows of spirals have, on the other hand, been very carefully picked out with some form of punch, probably of hardened bronze. The process by which these cavities are made must have been extremely

---

[1] *Palace of Minos*, p. 598.

[2] They were, however, certainly sawn at the primary stage of workmanship Cf. Mr. Theodore Fyfe's note to Evans, *Palace of Minos*, ii. ii, p. 606.

[3] *Brit. Mus. Cat. of Sculpture*, i. i, A. 53–5, pp. 25 ff.

laborious and the amount of stone removed at each stroke very small. The wear and tear to the tools must equally have involved considerable wastage and replacement.

The central row of spirals differs from the others in having spirals which have not got returning centres. Here the centres of each spiral end in a complete circle which is disconnected from the main running lines. Each circle is very neatly cut with a thin line about 1 mm. wide. Each circle is exactly 1·6 cm. in diameter. All alike were cut with a revolving tubular drill, used with a bow-string at high speed. The base of the broken-off core is clearly visible in each case, and its very roughness makes the presumption certain that each hollow circle was intended to be filled, over the core, with glass or paste.[1]

The drill used for these central holes is identical in type with that used for the hollows of the Lion Gate Relief[2] already described (p. 25). It is even identical in size That both the Lion Gate Relief and the façade sculptures of the Treasury of Atreus were carved with the same tools, and that an identical type of drill was used in each, affords some reasonable if slight presumption for deciding that the two sculptures are contemporary.[3] It is of equal interest and importance to find that the centres of all the spirals on the faces of the two half-columns that flanked the gateway of the Treasury of Atreus[4] are done in exactly the same way with a slightly larger drill. For the rest of the decoration of these columns few conclusions can be drawn, since the

---

[1] This inference is, in fact, drawn by the author of the Brit. Mus. catalogue referred to, p. 25.

[2] The use of the tubular drill has been noted in the case of this façade slab by Wace (B.S.A. xxv, p. 344), but ignored in the case of the Lion Gate Relief.

[3] Naturally it concerns the dating of the relief only. No legitimate conclusion can be drawn as to the date of the gate itself, for the relief may have come from some other source and may not necessarily have been made originally for the gateway. It seems highly probable that it was originally designed for insertion above a tholos tomb which was never built.

[4] Brit. Mus. Cat., pl. III; and also on the fragments at Athens in the National Museum.

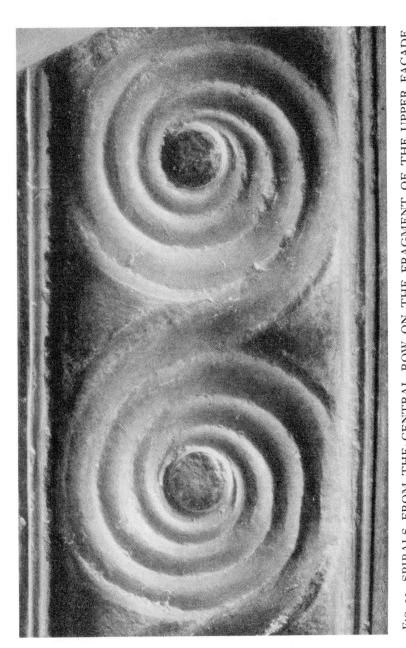

Fig. 11. SPIRALS FROM THE CENTRAL ROW ON THE FRAGMENT OF THE UPPER FAÇADE IN RED PORPHYRY OF THE TREASURY OF ATREUS, A 53 in the British Museum.

The central circles of the spirals were made with a tubular drill 1·6 cm. in diameter and the base of the core is visible inside the circle.

Scale 1/1.

Fig. 12. DETAIL OF THE RIGHT SHAFT OF THE
TREASURY OF ATREUS, in the British Museum
The centre of each spiral is a circle made with the tubular drill.

surfaces are far too weathered. But it is clear that the cross-hatching of the zigzags was done with a simple stone rubber.

Another fragment of façade from the Treasury gives information of a wholly different kind and equally instructive. This fragment (A. 54) shows one row of spirals with a moulding above and below, and below the lower moulding is a row of large disks of which four and a half survive. These disks are flat and resemble pole-ends; they are comparable to those over the capital of the Lion Gate Relief, and to similar terracotta pillars from Knossos,[1] as well as to a band surviving *in situ* in the 'Tomb of Clytemnestra'.

The method of their carving is remarkable. The flat surface of the stone was first divided into equal squares by the aid of a fine saw, perhaps semi-lunar in shape. The saw-marks on each side of each square can still be perfectly clearly seen. The circles were then marked out on the squares and the corners of each square carefully picked out with a pointed punch and the outlines of the circles finished freehand by rubbing on each side of each hollow so achieved. No compass was used at any stage in the construction of these disks. The following diagram gives some idea of the methods employed:

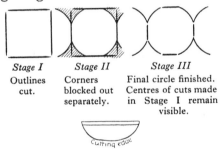

Stage I
Outlines cut.

Stage II
Corners blocked out separately.

Stage III
Final circle finished. Centres of cuts made in Stage I remain visible.

FIG. 13. Suggested shape of sawing instrument which cut the outlines of the circles.

It may be convenient at this point to collect the known instances where the use of a tubular drill is plainly demonstrable:

i. The pillars of the 'Treasury of Atreus' in the British

---

[1] *B.S.A.* viii, p. 29, fig. 14.

Museum. *Brit. Mus. Cat. of Sculpture*, vol. i. i, p. 18, A. 51 and A. 52; and the similar pillars in the National Museum at Athens. These pillars are of hard green limestone. (Fig. 12).

ii. The façade fragment of hard red porphyry A. 53 in the British Museum, derived from the same Treasury. *Brit. Mus. Cat. of Sculpture*, p. 25. (Fig. 11).

iii. The Lion Gate Relief. See above and *B.S.A.* xxv, p. 16. Hard grey limestone.

iv. Façade fragment in Nauplia Museum, from Mycenae, different from the British Museum fragment No. ii above. Evans, *Shaft-Graves and Beehive Tombs of Mycenae*, p. 75, fig. 53.

v. A small fragment of a spiral façade from the SW. Porch at Knossos. Evans, *Shaft-Graves and Beehive Tombs of Mycenae*, p. 75, fig. 54, and *Palace of Minos*, ii. i, p. 163, fig. 83 *g* and 84.

vi. A fragment of a façade decorated with rosettes. The centre of each of two surviving rosettes is done with a tubular drill. The fragment comes from the portal of the South Propylaeum at Knossos. Greenish-grey limestone. Evans, *Shaft-Graves and Beehive Tombs of Mycenae*, p. 72, fig. 48.

The following fragments of the Grave Stelai exhibit circular centres to spirals that measure 4·7 cm. in diameter and may also have been made by a tubular drill. But the condition of the surface makes certainty impossible.

i. Fragment of Stele from the Grave Circle at Mycenae. *B.S.A.* xxv, p. 139, fig. 32, xii b. Said to be of 'shelly limestone'. Tubular drill used as in i and ii above for the centres of spirals.

ii. Fragment of Stele VII a from the Grave Circle. *B.S.A.* xxv, pl. xxi.

iii. Fragment of Stele VII b from the Grave Circle. Ibid.

Painted versions of spirals from wall decorations in some cases reproduce the central drilled circle: the spiral frieze from the Bath Room at Knossos has the central circle filled by a rosette;[1] a stucco step of the Palace at Mycenae shows the central circles unadorned.[2]

Possibly the circles seen on some of the diadems of gold from the Shaft-Graves were first cut in moulds of stone. Into these moulds the sheets of gold were pressed or beaten, and the diameter of many of the gold circles corresponds roughly with the diameter of some of the circles on the stonework.

It is remarkable that the spiral-centres of the Orchomenos Treasury ceiling are not done with the tubular drill at all, but with a compass. The central point made by one compass-leg is clearly seen in nearly every spiral. The spirals, unlike those from Mycenae and Knossos, vary in diameter on account of the method by which they were made, whereas those made by the drill have a constant diameter. The Orchomenos circles measure from 1·5 cm. to 2·3 cm.—a large variation. Rosette-centres likewise are compass-made and not drilled on the Orchomenos ceiling. Clearly the sculptor-architects of Boeotia followed a totally different fashion from that in vogue in the south.

From the above list it will be seen at once that a coherent group of sculptures is emerging which we may reasonably consider as belonging to one period of art when the tubular drill was of no little popularity. The group can, therefore, be associated together in time, not, of course, with great precision. But when we find that on purely archaeological grounds the Knossos examples and those from the Treasury of Atreus are definitely associated and attributed to the close of the Middle Minoan period,[3] the technical characteristics which they have in common assume a greater importance. The Lion Gate Relief may seem to indicate that the tubular drill was also used two hundred and fifty years later, since on no grounds can the Lion Gate be dated before 1400. But

---

[1] Evans, *Palace of Minos*, iii, p. 383, fig. 254.　　[2] *B.S.A.* xxv, pl. xxv
[3] Evans, *Shaft-Graves and Beehive Tombs of Knossos*, pp. 71 ff.

it has long been thought that the relief on the Lion Gate is derivative from some other source; its style suggests an earlier period than 1400. The use in its construction of the tubular drill thus strengthens this view and justifies us in believing that the relief is earlier than the structure of the Gate itself. It may belong to an earlier planning of the Gate or even to a wholly different building.

There is indeed no evidence for the use of the tubular drill at the end of the last Late Minoan period. Its wide-spread use in Mycenae and popularity at Knossos point to a period of great artistic activity. Lapidaries seem at last to have turned into sculptors, though the tools they use are but enlarged versions of the tools of lapidaries. The period when the Treasury of Atreus was built and the Lion Gate Relief carved, was perhaps the first period in Greece when sculpture on the grand scale was conceived. A similar activity reigned at Knossos at the same time. Possibly one energetic mind was behind all the activity at Mycenae, for we find nothing at all in comparison at a later date, and after all these major works had been accomplished the tubular drill was forgotten. The vogue of the tubular drill did not extend to the northern half of the Mycenaean world, for, as we have seen, the spirals of the Orchomenos Treasury are done with a compass, not with a drill. But Mycenae and Knossos both favour the drill.

The fact that the tubular drill fell out of use after about 1600 or at latest 1550 B.C. explains why it was not one of the technical discoveries communicated across the cultural gap of 1200–1000 to the new masters of the mainland.

ii. *Soft Stones*. Steatite seems to have gone out of fashion by the third Late Minoan period. There are no Mycenaean figures of steatite in any way comparable to those done in Crete in Minoan times. Small ornaments and oddments only are made.

But the same stimulus that produced the large-scale

FIG. 14. LOW RELIEF, PERHAPS PART OF A
GRAVE STELE

From Mycenae. National Museum, Athens.

Scale 1/3.

FIG. 15. BASE OF A CUP OF EMERY STONE and a
SMOOTHED BLOCK OF EMERY STONE (half only):
(both in the Ashmolean Museum): both of the predynastic
period, from Egypt.

Each has been used as a bead-polisher and the polishing groove is
seen in each case. The cup shows on the other face the hollow made
by turning and the grooves of turning.

Scale 1/1.

sculpture of the Lion Gate led also to the production of large-scale reliefs mostly in hard stone in the shape of the grave-stelai from the Shaft-Graves.[1] The most complete and best known of these are unfortunately too weathered to allow any deductions to be made from a study of their detail. But there have survived some fragments in soft stone which are most instructive. These are classed by Mr. Heurtley as his Class I, which he thinks are the earliest.[2] Fragments X*a* and *b* and XI*b* show with perfect clarity that the reliefs which adorn them were cut quite simply with a knife. Moreover, the material of which they are made, described as poros (actually a soft grey limestone), was a stone which was much softer when fresh from the quarry than after a little exposure. The curiously barbaric figure on X*a* (Fig. 14), which Mr. Heurtley is tempted to identify as negroid in type and perhaps in action, looks to me as if it had come from a trial slab on which sculptors were experimenting. It can hardly have been part of an actual monument. An exact parallel for sculptors' trials of this type is seen in the case of the two heads found on the Acropolis of Athens, similar in material, in technique, and in their lack of serious intention.[3]

Whatever this peculiar monument was intended to be it must belong to the very close of Mycenaean culture. It may even be a work of primitive Geometric carving, made in an attempt to emulate the visible stelai of the Mycenaean princes.

But the main importance of these fragments is that they show that the tradition of soft-stone cutting, fixed long before in Middle Minoan times, still continued down to the twelfth century or even later. Soft stone was still cut with a plain knife-blade, as if it were wood.

[1] W. A. Heurtley in *B.S.A.* xxv, pp. 126 ff.

[2] It is much more likely that they are the very latest, contemporary with the decadent quasi-geometric art of the last phase at Mycenae. There is no reason at all to think that Mycenaean art in sculpture began crudely and emerged resplendent. The reverse was the case, for the Mycenaeans had learned their first lessons from Cretans when the latter were at the height of their artistic skill.

[3] Dickins, *Acropolis Museum Catalogue*, p. 72.

Summary.

A clear contrast has been observed in Cretan and Mycenaean times between the treatment of hard and soft stones. The hard stones are worked with abrasive rubbers for the general surfaces and outlines, with sharp pointed stone burins for detail, and here and there with the ordinary boring drill, which drills holes vertically to the surface. The Lion Gate and its associated group show the use of the tubular drill used for cutting hollows and depressions. The toothless saw or a sawing process was used for cutting projecting parts of stone masses.

All these tools except the tubular drill and possibly the saw, could have been of stone, almost certainly of emery, and the bronze saw in some cases had emery teeth in its blade. Since emery has a hardness infinitely greater than bronze or copper and was incomparably cheaper than either, it seems superfluous to assume that metal was used and is, in any case, contrary to the evidence. All these tools likewise correspond to tools used by gem-cutters. The variously shaped abrasive tools of emery are virtually the same as the knobbed and round-pointed tools which the gem-cutter of Minoan and Mycenaean times used, revolving at high speed, for achieving his hollows and rounded concave surfaces. The sculptor used similar tools slowly for producing convex surfaces. The pointed splinter or burin of emery corresponds to the burin used by the gem-cutter for incising detail freehand, in the same way as an engraver cuts the lines of a steel or copper plate. The manes of lions on Minoan gems are rendered in precisely the same way as is the jowl-fringe on the limestone head of a lioness from Knossos. The simple boring-drill is, of course, the most used in gem-cutting of all the gem-cutter's tools. The tubular or reed-drill, on the other hand, is more rarely used on gems of the Minoan and Mycenaean periods.

It is clear, then, that the sculptor's art in Crete and Mycenaean lands went hand in hand with the art of the gem-cutter. Whether it *developed from* the gem-cutter's art is a question for the answer to which there is insufficient evidence. Possibly both developed side by side.

The carving of soft stones, on the other hand, seems to have followed the methods of the wood-carver and the ivory-cutter. The well-known vessels of steatite that follow metallic or pottery shapes are turned on a lathe—itself a carpenter's tool—and the decorated surface is then cut with a knife-blade. The drill is used here and there, but rarely, and the incised outlines so frequently seen round the human and animal figures depicted on steatite vases are carefully cut with a knife-point.

The processes used for cutting hard stones seem to have been learned in part, at any rate, from the Cyclades, where the cutting of marble was an art that flourished before any hard-stone sculptural work of any consequence was cut in Crete. The antiquity of the famous idols of the Cycladic islands is considerable and the use of emery-stone as a medium must be dated back in the islands to the first cutting of marble. The use of emery for this purpose seems to have survived without interruption down to the present day.

That Crete learned many of her processes of working stone from Egypt is beyond dispute, but I am concerned here rather in showing what processes *were actually in use* in the Minoan-Mycenaean region than what was the exact origin of those processes. In fact some inventions, like the use of the saw, are actually attributed to Cretans, and the use of emery as an abrasive tool may have originated in Naxos, though it must be borne in mind that Egyptians and others must have imported emery from Naxos before the Naxians employed it themselves.

There is no evidence as yet that hard-stone sculptures were painted or adorned with other than incidental additions. The head of the lioness from Knossos had eyes that were made of jasper, inserted into the marble. The lion's head may have had similar eyes.

Figures in steatite, on the other hand, were apparently never left with their natural surface. Some were covered with gold-leaf, others painted with a thin coating of gesso.[1] The painted stucco head from Mycenae (see Fig. 16) may be a version in cheap material of a head that normally would have been rendered in steatite covered with gesso. It may also, as Sir Arthur Evans suggests, reflect the influence of contemporary wooden statues of large size.

Figures in bronze were invariably cast solid and the Cretans had no knowledge at all of the *cire-perdue* process, nor, as far as we know, of the technique of beaten bronze. Nor did they finish their cast figures with the chisel or burin. Cretan bronzework, in fact, lags far behind Cretan stone-work in technique. While the casting was, as in the case of the bull-jumper, elaborate and difficult, the process began and ended with the casting.

That Cretan statues of great size in wood, with bronze additions, were made for ritual use is now clearly established. This conclusion is of the greatest importance as showing that still another mode of art survived from prehistoric to classical times.

The survival of tools used in stone-craft is dubious. Chisels, awls, and punches are common on Minoan sites, but all may have been for domestic use or solely for employment in carpentry. The chisels in particular are rarely strong enough in fabric to have been used for primary or major work on stone, and the punches would have bent under a few strokes, so slight are they in build. The few saws that have been found are almost certainly wood-saws or meat-saws. The only surviving instance of a mason's saw is that found by Petrie (p. 28). Copper and bronze was too valuable to waste on stone-cutting when similar tools of emery or similar processes in which emery powder or teeth of emery on a metal blade were used were possible and avail-

[1] Evans, *Palace of Minos*, iii. 427.

FIG. 16. PAINTED STUCCO HEAD FOUND AT MYCENAE
Perhaps the head of a cult statue (National Museum, Athens).
Scale 3/10.

able. No intelligent craftsman would have employed metal when he had emery accessible, except in cases where, as on the Atreus façade fragments, cutting too fine for stone tools was required. And the example of the Cycladic marble-cutters was always before the eyes of Minoans and Mycenae-ans, to reinforce the knowledge acquired from technicians of the Neolithic period in the Aegean.

Lapidaries' work.

The simple methods of the lapidary, by which I mean the cutter and carver of stone vessels and ornaments, fall into a class apart. For the lapidary makes objects of use rather than works of art, and minor ornaments rather than masterpieces.

The lathe used by lapidaries is, unlike the carpenter's lathe, worked on the principle of revolving the object to be turned and keeping static the instrument that does the turning. The Cornish peasant-lapidary who turns vessels of serpentine works always on this basis. The matrix of stone to be turned on the lathe is fixed in plaster held in a vice upon a circular board which can be rapidly revolved by a foot-pedal. The tool which does the turning is fixed and immovable, once in position against the stone. The matrix revolves *against* the tool.

The ancient Egyptian type of lathe, on the other hand, reverses this principle. The drawing of a lapidary turning a stone vessel on one of the paintings in the Rekhmere tomb shows the lapidary holding the vessel firmly with one hand and revolving inside it a lathe, weighted from above and turned by a handle that probably continued revolving by the momentum given by the weighting. It seems hard to believe that this portable type of lathe was used at the primary stages on the raw matrix. I cannot see how it could possibly be so used. But after the vase had been hollowed against the lathe-tool the smaller portable hollowing-lathe might well have been brought into action. The process involved two separate instruments.

These relatively primitive types of lathe seem to be the

types which were employed by the stone-turners of Mochlos and of the various sites in Crete where the output of stone vessels was considerable. A typical example of a bowl of hard stone which has been turned inside and out on a lathe is seen in the grey and white marble bowl of the second Middle Minoan period which is now preserved in the Ashmolean Museum.[1] The traces of the turning are visible clearly on both surfaces, while the lugs and the lip have clearly been made by independent abrasion, probably with a stone tool.

Traces of a lapidaries' quarter have been found at the Harbour Town of Knossos,[2] where part of a vase of *Lapis Lacedaemonius*—the vivid green Spartan marble—and an unfinished limestone rhyton were found. A similar lapidary's store was also found in the Late Minoan palace at Knossos. In it were large quantities of *Lapis Lacedaemonius*, several pieces of which showed signs of having been sawn.[3]

But the lapidary did not always use the lathe for turning his bowls. In the Ashmolean Museum is a bowl of hard diorite[4] of the first Late Minoan period which has not been turned at all but made simply by abrasion. It is very thin and exhibits not the traces of turning, in the shape of concentric striations horizontally round the sides, but rather the varied and unsystematic scratches and lines which indicate a rubbed surface. The rim of the bowl also is milled or notched, as with a file.

The lapidary could in fact use whatever tool he liked, though as a rule he preferred the lathe.

For convenience of classification I prefer to use the term lapidary only of those craftsmen in stone who made small ornaments and objects of use. The decorated steatite vases of Crete were turned by a lapidary and their designs cut by an artist or a sculptor. If the lapidary and the artist happened to be the same man the distinction of functions still remains

---

[1] No. Æ 962 in the Museum.   [2] Evans, *Palace of Minos*, II. i, p. 238.
[3] Ibid. iii, p. 269.   [4] No. 890 (from Palaikastro) in the Museum.

clear. For most lapidaries were probably not artists, and it is doubtful if many artists or sculptors wasted their time on the more elementary and less skilled work of the lapidary. In this connexion I should prefer to attribute the curious steatite cameo relief,[1] like a seal, which was found at the Harbour Town of Knossos to an artist or a gem-cutter rather than to a lapidary. This unusual object seems to be a trial or model for a gem which was to be cut intaglio in a harder stone. The 'trial' itself consists of a rough piece of steatite which has two gem-designs cut on one face and a third on the other. All three designs are cut in the soft stone with a knife blade and all three are animal figures of the types usually seen on gems of agate or chalcedony.

[1] Evans, *Palace of Minos*, II. i, fig. 134.

II

THE AGE OF TRANSITION

THE making of works of art of a sculptural kind either in stone or in bronze died out shortly before 1200 B.C.É. The instability of the times, the repeated attacks made upon famous cities by raiders, and the dangers of piracy to the coast towns, coupled no doubt with the poverty of princes, gave no chance to the sculptor to embellish buildings or to design votive or ornamental figures. The art of sculpture that began in the Cyclades, as far as Greek regions are concerned, had by the second Late Minoan period shown signs of collapse. By the third period it was as good as dead. The urban and military architect was more in demand than the adorner of shrines and cities. Mycenae, and perhaps Orchomenos on the mainland and Troy itself,[1] built about this time, or at least in the years between 1400 and 1200, immense fortress walls for the protection of their homes against outside aggression. The very Lion-Gate sculpture seems to have been removed from some earlier building and incorporated into a reconstructed wall and gate.[2] There is, in fact, no sculptured work of art which can be attributed to the closing years of the Mycenaean age.

From 1200 to 900 there was a period of such confusion and wholesale movement of peoples that art had to confine itself to collaboration with the crafts, and even this it did badly. Pottery designs and small ornaments make it hard to think that only a few hundred years before there had been made such masterpieces as the Lion Gate or the Chieftain Vase, the bronze Bull Jumper or the marble lioness rhyton of Knossos. Art was no longer wanted and craftsmanship had declined.

---

[1] Troy and Phylakopi alone of all the Aegean cities had been fortified at an earlier date also (Troy, II).   [2] *B.S.A.* xxv, and above, p. 30, n. 3.

It remains to see how much that had been learned in Minoan and Mycenaean times survived this period and passed the gap which the invasions of new peoples had made in Aegean culture and taste.

By 900, or in some places even earlier, a wholly new manner of minor art and craft had appeared. It had, perhaps, been foreshadowed by a curious change that had come over the later phases of Mycenaean art. In pottery design there is perceptible about 1250 B.C. a tendency to formalization and abstraction of design which implied that painters were thinking rather than observing, inventing rather than taking inspiration from things seen. In a word there had budded a tendency in art, liable to reappear in periods either of decadence or of infancy, which is usually described, rightly enough, by the terms 'formal', 'geometric', or 'abstract'.

Soon after the fall of Mycenae and the collapse generally of what is usually assumed to have been a Mycenaean hegemony or empire, controlled from the south mainland of Greece, there came into Greece a new people who arrived in several waves, all coming from north to south. Macedonia, Transylvania and Hungary, Bosnia and Illyria, all seem to have sent contingents at various times. In the centuries preceding their arrival these peoples in their homes had developed, each in their several ways, an art and a craftsmanship which was essentially of this 'geometric' or 'abstract' type. It can be no coincidence that the influence seen gradually penetrating Mycenaean culture about the thirteenth century B.C. was largely inspired by immigrants from northern regions and from central Europe. Nor is it a coincidence that central European types of weapon[1] appear at the same time inside the hitherto charmed circle of Mycenaean culture.

Granted that nothing worth the name of artistic production was active about 1200 to 950 B.C. we must look at the first appearance of the new styles in artistic productions of the

[1] Hall, *Civilisation of Greece in the Bronze Age*, pp. 254 ff.

tenth century. Sparta may, perhaps, serve as the key-site for the latest of the invading folk. For proto-Achaeans and for Achaeans there is an archaeological content,[1] tenuous and elusive, but definite. Within it there is no room for any of the arts and crafts except perhaps for painting. The 'Warrior Vase' from Mycenae shows at once the northern panoply, the survival of fine Mycenaean glaze-paint as a medium of painting, and that particular love of exact repetition and abstract conception of form which we shall see is the very soul of the 'geometric' art of the tenth, ninth, and eighth centuries.

But glaze-paint, itself a fine technical invention, survived the gap between 1200, when the 'Warrior Vase' was painted, and 950, when 'geometric' vases used the same paint exclusively for their designs. In some places, like Amyclae, it was improved by being given a metallic lustre, itself also a trick inherited from the Minoan world, for Kamares ware uses exactly the same kind of paint.

But there is no stonework which we can associate with proto-Achaeans or with Achaeans, unless we attribute to them the latest of the stelae from Mycenae (see above, p. 35). Nor do we find it in use again until the tenth century. In the earliest 'geometric' deposits[2] we find small seals both of steatite and of other stones hard and soft. Steatite, once so popular in Crete, has apparently not been forgotten. Its convenient softness has made it desirable for a generation of craftsmen who had little invention and limited tools. For the 'geometric' seal-stones that we find follow one technique and one only. They are from first to last cut with a knife, even when they are of hard stones, though in those cases the cuts become mere scratchings. 'Geometric' seals or gems are common enough. For the use of seals had not been forgotten, and the new invaders had found here and there[3]

[1] V. G. Childe, *The Aryans*, pp. 50 ff.

[2] Pendlebury, *Aegyptiaca*, 1930, p. 114.

[3] At Sparta, *Artemis Orthia*, pl. CCIV, B and C, and *B. M. Quarterly*, iv. 2, p. 34.

Scale 1/1.

a

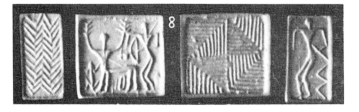

Scale 2/3.

b

FIG. 17. SEALS OF THE GEOMETRIC PERIOD

1 and 3. From the Argive Heraeum. 2. From Melos. 4. From Delos (?). 5. From Mycenae. 6. Unknown provenance. 7. From Attica. 8. Unknown provenance. Nos. 1 and 3 are in the National Museum, Athens. Nos. 2, 6, 7 are in the Ashmolean Museum, Oxford. Nos. 4 and 5 are in the collection of Sir Arthur Evans. No. 8 is in the Cabinet de Médailles, Paris.

old Cretan and Mycenaean seals which indicated to them the uses and advantages of sealing as a method and process. But the art of gem-cutting, as it had been known to Minoans and Mycenaeans, was completely and absolutely lost. We have but to look at 'geometric' seals,[1] good or bad, to see that neither the drill, the burin, nor the knobbed drill for the cutting of hollows was known. All these geometric seals are laboriously and in most cases unskilfully cut with an instrument no more formidable or elaborate than a penknife. The earliest seals are mostly of soft steatite and show the knife-cuts with unusual precision (Fig. 17A). The later groups (Fig. 17B) show how the purely geometric design is slowly being transformed into the Hellenic types and patterns of historic art. With this transformation we get at last the use of the simple boring drill, though the burin, which replaces the more primitive knife, is still more popular than the drill, and there is no means of cutting, nor any attempt to cut, the concave hollows which distinguish the flower of Minoan and Hellenic gem-cutting.

In a word the whole art of gem-cutting as perfected by Minoans has completely perished. The gem-cutter has had to start again from the crudest and most primitive beginnings. Stone-work, not being essentially a domestic necessity like pottery, has been forgotten. But pottery shapes and glazes and, in some rare cases patterns, have bridged the gap. In the earliest geometric strata at Sparta there are no stone bowls or ornaments or vases, and the earliest gems or seals are all of soft stone. But it was precisely this familiarity with soft material which gave the impetus later to the cutting of ivory, both at Sparta, at Athens (in the Kerameikos finds), and at the Argive Heraeum, which serves as a good type-site for the transitional period.

The very widespread trade-connexions with Egypt which are indicated by the extensive import of scarabs and other

[1] I have dealt in detail with the technique of a group of interesting geometric seals in *The Antiquaries Journal*, 1927, p. 38.

minor Egyptian ornaments[1] must have made the importation of ivory an easy matter. Scarabs are common on geometric sites from Pherae in Thessaly to Sparta and the Argive Heraeum. At Sparta the earliest ivories of all are small decorated instruments which are identified as kohl-needles.[2] They belong to the ninth century. The use of ivory increased rapidly, and it was in full swing by the early part of the eighth century.[3] It is not, therefore, surprising to find complete and well-executed ivory figures being cut at Athens in the eighth century.[4] The well-known figures from the Dipylon cemetery now in the National Museum at Athens constitute the first essay in sculpture in soft material in 'geometric' Greece, and, perhaps, in Greece generally. The knowledge of ivory and the cutting of it may conceivably have persisted through the cataclysms of the twelfth, eleventh, and tenth centuries B.C. Certainly the methods of rendering the human form in ivory did not differ in the Cretan ivories and the Dipylon ivories. The difference is entirely artistic, not technical. But artistically the difference is profound, for it is the difference between naturalism and formalism, two wholly distinct worlds of aesthetic.

In bronzework there seems to be a complete break with tradition, in every way as comprehensive as the break already seen in the methods of gem-cutting. I have elsewhere[5] already pointed out how geometric bronzes of the mainland types are made mainly by a process of smithing. The earliest bronze figures, childlike, bizarre, and crude, representing as they do simple human and animal figures, are almost invariably made from bars and strands of bronze

---

[1] Pendlebury, *Aegyptiaca*: Nos. 72–227.

[2] *Artemis Orthia* (1930), p. 203 and pl. 167 B. [3] Ibid., p. 203.

[4] In the National Museum, Athens. Nos. 776 (complete figure), 778 (upper part of a similar figure of the same scale), 777 (smaller complete figure), 260 (feet of a figure of the same scale as 777), and 779 (small complete figure). Cf. also E. Kunze: *Ath. Mitth.* 1930. Fig. 1. *Beil.* xl. and xli, and Pl. v–viii. Conceivably they are even before 800 B.C.

[5] *J.H.S.*, 1922, p. 207, 'Bronze Work of the Geometric Period and its relation to later art'.

which are twisted and beaten and welded. There is no trace at all of the solid casting of the Cretan type. Yet the one exception to the geometric method of welding and smithing their bronze figures is found in Crete. The curious but undeniably 'geometric' figures of warriors, dogs, cattle, horses, and even of a ship and its crew which were found in

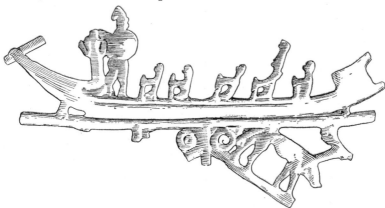

FIG. 18. MOULDED BRONZE OF THE GEOMETRIC PERIOD FROM THE IDAEAN CAVE. CANDIA MUSEUM.

the Idaean Cave[1] (Fig. 18), resemble in all respects the figures of the same objects found in the geometric levels of Sparta and Olympia. But whereas the latter are beaten and smithed, the former are cast in one process. Cretan moulds were clay-moulds or sand-moulds, the model being of clay or, as Evans has suggested[2] for the bull-jumper group, of wax, whereas these Idaean bronzes were made from a mould cut into the surface of some soft stone: the molten metal was simply poured into these cavities, leaving in the process the upper side of the bronze (away from the stone) smooth and flat as the molten surface of the metal hardened. The Cretan tradition of moulding bronzes may, perhaps, have influenced these 'geometric' artists of Crete to mould, where their friends on the mainland, who knew little or nothing of casting methods, preferred to beat and weld and model, probably in the cold metal.

[1] Maraghiannis, *Antiquités Crétoises*, I. xlii.   [2] *J.H.S.* xli (1921), p. 249.

It is evident, then, that the new Dorian or other invading settlers on the mainland, who must perforce be identified with the new style in art, knew little or nothing and cared less about the old Minoan methods of casting. They, like the geometric gem-cutters, had started entirely afresh. The gap had not been bridged in this particular branch of art.

There does appear to have developed in early 'geometric' times a rough method of solid casting of small animal figures which seems to have begun after the first process of welding and beating was used. The earliest figures of horses and other quadrupeds were cut out in a flat sheet of metal and then bent double along the back so that the figure could stand up.[1] Figures made by this 'sheet-bronze method' were superseded by more solid figures which were cast on the same general lines as these relatively perishable figures, but they were stockier and more solid. Miss W. Lamb makes the interesting suggestion that the solid cast figures were copies of terra-cottas, perhaps 'cast from the same moulds as the terra-cotta figures themselves'.[2] This casting process, like the figures, was primitive and crude and was in no way an inheritance from Crete. Nor, indeed, was it the earliest 'geometric' process for making metal figures. The earliest 'geometric' ornaments are always made by a process that involved the bending, twisting, beating, and hammering of the metal probably when cold. We can conclude without difficulty that all the 'geometric' methods of metal-work are the invention of 'geometric' peoples.[3]

Of human or animal figures in stone which can rank as sculpture proper we have no single example that belongs to the Geometric age. Geometric art is in its outlook, in its

[1] W. Lamb, *Greek and Roman Bronzes*, p. 39, fig. 1.

[2] Ibid., p. 41. An interesting example of a similar casting from Minoan or Mycenaean times comes from Phylakopi (*Excavations at Phylakopi*, p. 188, fig. 160).

[3] Or agree with Miss Lamb (p. 44) that 'one can find practically no points of contact with Minoan art'.

methods, and in its general character the true and natural forerunner of true Hellenic art, but stone sculpture proper does not make its appearance until the more or less uncontaminated geometric art of Greece and the islands had undergone a subtle change on encountering Oriental and other influences. Sculpture does not come down in the true descent from geometric bronzes, though the earliest forms of Greek sculpture and of those early bronzes are in many respects closely akin. Sculpture in stone begins suddenly and in many places in Greece and the islands (see below, p. 97). It was produced by different causes in different places and under different external stimuli. Geometric art had been slowly leading up to some wider, more artistic, and more ambitious form of art, but it had not necessarily been leading up to sculpture. The final weight that was placed into the balance and sent it down heavily on the side of sculpture as the main choice and ambition of early Hellenic artists was a weight that came from outside sources. Among the Greek towns of Asia Minor, to judge from the particular forms of their earliest statues, it was the sculpture of the Hittites and of the Assyrians that urged on the Greek to competition. In Crete and the Peloponnese it was rather intercourse with Egypt that led Greeks to conceive artistic forms anew in the light of the immense statues of stone which Greek travellers had seen in the Nile Valley. The very early intercourse with Egypt testified to by the numerous finds of Egyptian objects on Geometric and proto-Hellenic sites was an increasing intercourse. With the experiences of men like Solon to aid them, Greeks of the later times were soon fully versed in everything Egyptian. Naukratis alone would have served for the spread of Egyptian manners and methods.

The latent longing to carve the human figure which was seen in the ivory figures of the Dipylon cemetery needed the Asiatic and the Egyptian stimuli to make it bud and blossom And once in bud the harvest was soon reached.

Possible survival of pre-Hellenic wooden statues.

Before asking what were the earliest Hellenic statues it is essential to consider the possibility of the survival of Minoan or Mycenaean wooden cult-figures into a period when the cult and perhaps its furniture were adapted to later developments and to new worshippers. The survival of Mycenaean racial stock into the Hellenic period is probable and, indeed, to some extent demonstrable.[1] Although the manner of life and the customs of everyday existence had changed fundamentally with the arrival of the Hellenic invaders of the Mycenaean area, few would dispute that there survived in some places the old religious cults of the Minoan world.[2] Although the material setting of daily life was radically changed and the old styles of art forgotten, yet in the figures of old Minoan gods we may well expect to find the most persistent of all survivals. Their survival would have been aided by the care which could have been bestowed upon them by those of Minoan stock who still contrived to adapt themselves to the new conditions.

Certainly we have to explain two curious groups of facts that remain for explanation if we reject the hypothesis of the survival of Minoan cult-figures. The first group of facts consists of those which record the existence, often in the more inaccessible places of Greece, of a particular group of what the Greeks called ξόανα, which all have some kind of pre-Hellenic context or setting. The second group consists of facts recorded in literature which suggest activity in the Homeric period, that is to say, in the early post-Mycenaean epoch, in the making and preserving of sacred images of a very primitive type.

[1] A. Shewan, 'Ithakan Origins' in *Classical Philology*, 1929, p. 335. The author examines the literary evidence for the survival of Minoan people in Homeric times.

[2] Evans, *Palace of Minos*, iii, p. 524: 'That actual Minoan works of this class (i.e. like the conjectured colossal statue of a goddess from Knossos discussed in pp. 522–3) may have survived in ancient centres of cult in comparatively late classical times is quite possible.' Nillson, *A History of Greek Religion* (1925), pp. 24 ff.

There remains the question of what these images looked like. For this we have the slight testimony of the coinage of certain towns of Greece famous for their possession of well-known ξόανα. On these coins is struck the representation of the local ξόανον.

The facts which belong to the first group are numerous. We are told, for instance, by Pausanias[1] of the famous and ancient statue of Hera—τὸ ἀρχαιότατον Ἥρας ἄγαλμα, made of pear-tree wood and set up at Tiryns by Peirasos the son of mythical Argos. From Tiryns the statue was removed later by the Argives to the sanctuary of the Heraeum. Not only the site of the shrine where the statue originally stood but the name of its dedicator strongly indicate a non-Hellenic or pre-Hellenic origin for this image. A shrine of Hera was still active on the site of the old Mycenaean palace of Tiryns down to the fifth century B.C. It undoubtedly was a survival from the earlier and apparently more important shrine which held the image erected by Peirasos.[2] The development of the Heraeum as a new shrine of the mother-goddess, whose name became Hera, left Tiryns virtually abandoned, except for the bare minimum of service which an older shrine demanded from those who had superseded it. The pear-wood image may well have been one of the

---

[1] ii. 17. 5.

[2] See *Tiryns* (1912), i, pp. 2–46, and Blegen, *Korakou*, 1921, pp. 130 ff. The hypothesis of Frickenhaus is that a Mycenaean palace continued to exist down to about 700 B.C. It was then replaced by a Greek shrine, the builders of which were familiar with the appearance and architecture of the earlier building. But against this Blegen brings an array of stratigraphical and other arguments which suggest that the building identified as Hellenic by Fricken-haus is in fact a very late Mycenaean reconstruction of the larger and earlier Megaron. Against Blegen's view must be placed the solid fact of the discovery of a heavy deposit of sixth and fifth-century votive objects connected with a Hera cult. It may perhaps be wiser to reject the Frickenhaus-Blegen building altogether as a claimant and assume that the shrine of Hera was elsewhere on the citadel. Blegen admits that room must be found for it—'it is clear', he says, 'that a sanctuary stood somewhere on the site'. Where it stood is of purely academic interest for the purposes of the matter in hand: its existence is sufficient to make it possible that Mycenaean objects were taken over into Hellenic cult.

ritual figures of a small Minoan Palace shrine which was later transferred to a Hellenic shrine. The name Peirasos has a non-Hellenic flavour which is intensified when we see that another authority[1] declares this son of Argos to have been called Peiranthos.

Pausanias again tells[2] us that at Argos there was a ξόανον of Apollo which had been there from the time of Danaos. Danaos is dated by the Parian Chronicle to the beginning of the sixteenth century B.C. He also describes as outside the temple a relief of a bull-fight in which a girl is engaged, which was said to have been put up by Danaos himself. He describes the girl in the relief as 'Artemis'. It does not need much imagination to see in this relief a Minoan work of art comparable to the two bull-reliefs from Mycenae.[3]

We hear also of ξόανα in the Temple of Artemis on Cape Malea[4] which had stood there since the great invasion by the Amazons. This invasion was dated by the Parian Chronicle[5] to the thirteenth century. At Troezen also were statues of Artemis which belonged to the time of Theseus[6] and of another figure which was set up at the time of the sailing of the Argo[7] near Korone in Messenia.

At Thebes in Boeotia was a statue erected by Cadmus[8] and another said to have been made from the wood of his ships.[9] Of the Minoan associations of Cadmus we need have no reasonable doubt.[10] Two Cretan ξόανα of the birth-goddess Eileithyia were said to have been brought by Erysichthon from Delos to Athens.[11]

Daedalus, whose Cretan associations are vouched for by Homer, made a figure of Britomartis for the city of Olous in Crete,[12] not to mention other works in that island. Britomar-

---

[1] Schol. Eur. 932.   [2] ii. 19. 3.
[3] *Brit. Mus. Cat. of Sculpture*, I. i, Nos. A 56, A 57.   [4] Paus. iii. 25. 3.
[5] Marmor. Par. 36 (ed. Jacoby).   [6] Paus. ii. 31. 1.
[7] Id. iv. 34. 7.   [8] Id. ix. 12. 2.   [9] Ibid. 16. 3.
[10] Evans, *Scripta Minoa*, pp. 55 ff.
[11] Paus. i. 18. 5. He also notes that Eileithyia was born near Knossos.
[12] Id. ix. 40. 3, and Solin. *Coll. rer. memorab.* ii. 8, No. 3.

tis is a native Cretan deity, almost certainly of Minoan origin. He was also reputed to have made an image of Artemis Monogissa in Caria,[1] though the precise meaning of this attribution must remain obscure.

On the borders of Messenia and Arcadia were small ξόανα of Despoina and Demeter,[2] two deities whose pre-Hellenic origins are generally accepted.

In none of these instances would it be easy to argue that we are dealing with works of art or religious images made in the Geometric age. All alike suggest not only that pre-Hellenic cults are in question but that the actual cult-images are pre-Hellenic. It is astonishing that so many should have survived down to the time of Pausanias, when we consider the material of which most of them were made. Yet Roman woodwork such as the carved doorways of the fifth-century A.D. of the Church of Santa Sabina[3] at Rome and Romanesque wooden figures[4] have survived the vicissitudes of an even longer period, and such survival hardly borders upon the incredible.

In the second group of facts we have outstanding certain references in Homer which suggest that the habit of making rude images of deities still continued in the Period of Transition, that is to say in the period between the latest Mycenaean epoch and the earliest Geometric. We learn for instance that there was a temple of Athena at Troy[5] and that her priestess Theano 'laid a robe upon the knees of fair-haired Athene'.[6] This ritual act presupposes a seated statue.[7] There was a Homeric artist called Epeios, whose *chef-d'œuvre* was the Wooden Horse.[8] There is no reason to identify him as a non-Hellene, for Plato[9] calls him the son of Panopeus and

[1] Steph. Byz., s.v.   [2] Paus. viii. 35. 2.
[3] Made for Pope Celestin (A.D. 425).
[4] Cf. a large wooden Romanesque crucifix in the Brummer Coll., *Burlington Mag.* 1931, p. 208.
[5] *Il.* vi. 88.   [6] Ibid. 303.
[7] Strabo (xiii. 1. 41) was the first to point this out, but cf. Scott, *Unity of Homer*, p. 121.
[8] *Od.* viii. 492.   [9] Ion 533.

he may well have been a Boeotian. His name is Hellenic enough, and Euripides calls him a Phocian, for Panopeus was on the borders of Phocis and Boeotia. It would be tempting even to identify him as the Epios of Dictys Cretensis,[1] who came with a contingent from the Cyclades, the very birth-place (as we have seen, p. 15 ff.) of sculpture in stone!

In any case he seems to have had a real existence, for Pausanias attributed to him[2] two ξόανα of Aphrodite and Hermes respectively which were at Argos. They were the dedications of Hypermnestra, though this latter attribution would throw them back to the generation after Danaos and so make it impossible for Epeios to have made them.

That a statue of Apollo stood in his temple at Chryse may be inferred from the action of his priest who came

στέμματ' ἔχων ἐν χερσὶν ἑκηβόλου 'Απόλλωνος.

Fillets may possibly imply a statue from which they were taken.

Besides the works of Epeios and the temple-statues already discussed there were other statues recorded as being dedicated or worshipped in Achaean or Homeric times. The ἀγάλματα πολλὰ καὶ ἐσθλά which Eurylochus promised to dedicate[3] may possibly be statues. Odysseus was said to have set up a statue to Keleutheia, the patron saint of his slaughter of the suitors. The statue stood at Sparta and was seen by Pausanias.[4] He was also said to have dedicated a statue[5] of Poseidon Hippios which stood at Pheneos in Arcadia: the figure was made of bronze, and Pausanias, with his wide knowledge of craftsmanship and of archaic sculpture, hesitates to believe that such a bronze figure could have been made at so early a time. In this I willingly believe him to have been right. At Sparta also were wooden statues which were said to be as ancient as any in Greece.[6]

In Troezen was another statue said to have been dedicated

---

[1] *Bellum Troianum*, i. 17.　　　　　　　　　　　　　　　[2] ii. 19.6.

[3] *Od.* xii. 347. It is, however, uncertain if ἄγαλμα had yet acquired this meaning.

[4] iii. 12. 4.　　　　　[5] Paus. viii. 14. 5.　　　　　[6] Id. iii. 17. 5.

by Diomede,[1] and on the Larissa at Argos was a curious three-eyed ξόανον of Zeus. This monstrosity, whatever it was, was part of the loot brought back[2] from Troy and had belonged to Sthenelos. Nothing about it suggests the Minoan. In the same way Menelaos brought back ἀγάλματα of Thetis and Praxidike among his spoils from Troy.[3]

Outside this classification fall certain ξόανα like that of Artemis Orthia which was said to have come from the Crimea[4] or the ξόανον of Hermes in juniper wood which stood on Mount Cyllene and was 8 feet or more in height.[5] And there are others of the same kind.

What is, I think, significant is that so many seem to have survived in the hidden valleys and remote hills of the Central Peloponnese, in precisely the area which was passed uninvaded by incoming Dorians, and where old dialects lingered for a long time. Old cults and gods no doubt lingered too in Arcadia and Messenia. Certainly old statues seem to have survived the destruction of the invasions that swept over the lower plains and valleys.

Statues are extremely rarely mentioned in the Homeric poems. I have referred to all that can be found. Their rarity in the texts accords with what we might have expected from the history of the times. The ἀγάλματα πολλὰ καὶ ἐσθλά which were to adorn the temple of Helios at Ithaca remind us of what must have been the appearance of Cretan palaces. And it is no coincidence that a strong case has been made out for the identification of Scheria and Ithaca alike as two Minoan colonies among whose population the Minoan element was still strong in Homeric times.[6]

It remains to examine the material evidence as to the nature, technique, and appearance of these primitive ξόανα.

We learn first of all from Pausanias[7] that they were made of a variety of different kinds of wood. Ebony, cypress,

---

[1] Paus. ii. 32. 1.   [2] Id. ii. 24. 3.
[3] Id. iii. 22. 2.   [4] Id. iii. 16. 7.   [5] Id. viii. 17. 2.
[6] Shewan, op. cit., p. 344.   [7] viii. 17. 1.

cedar, oak, yew (μῖλαξ) and λωτός, which is usually identified as a North African tree which has a hard black wood. It is also known as the Libyan Lotus and is identified as the *Celtis Australis*. Another wood used was the θυία which had scented wood: it is also thought to be African[1] and is identified as a kind of juniper. Another wood called θύον was sometimes varicoloured.[2] It was of this wood that the statue of Hermes on Mount Cyllene was made. The Minoan wooden statue (see above, p. 9) of which the charred remains and bronze locks were found, seems to have been of local Cretan cypress-wood. Olive was also used.[3]

We have, in fact, only one detailed description[4] of what must have been a typical early Hellenic xoanon—that of Apollo at Amyclae, near Sparta. Pausanias says that, at a guess, it was 30 cubits in height—that is to say about 40 feet. It was 'not the work of Bathykles, but archaic and not made skilfully'. It had a face, feet and hands, but in other respects was columnar 'like a bronze column'. A helmet was on the head and a spear and a bow in the hands.

A Lacedaemonian coin of the third century B.C.[5] shows a figure which approximately corresponds to this description, and there appear to be features on the face. The body is slightly conical and certainly circular in section. The arms stretch out at awkward angles.

Later coins of the reigns of Commodus and Gallienus, struck for Sparta,[6] show the same figure with what is probably greater fidelity. The arms are in the same attitude but the body is shown as a conical (or rectangular) form in which the narrow part of the cone is at the base, whereas in the former coin the narrowing end of the cone came at the top of the figure. Also the later coins show a square base upon which the statue stands. A detail which tends to suggest that the later version is the more accurate is that the bronze plates

---

[1] There is also a variety that grows in Greece. Theophr. i. 9. 3.
[2] Strabo, iv. 6. 2.   [3] Paus. x. 19. 2.   [4] Id. iii. 19. 1.
[5] Gardner and Imhoof-Blumer, *Numismatic Commentary on Pausanias*, p. 59, n. xvi.   [6] Ibid. n. xvii.

which Pausanias describes as covering the body are suggested on the coins by what seem to be nails on the surface of the body.

The figure stood on an elaborate base made by Bathykles, who was an artist from Magnesia in Ionian Greece. Remains of the base which have been excavated show clearly enough that Bathykles worked in the Ionian tradition and in Parian marble.[1] He was contemporary with Croesus and had nothing whatever to do with the making of the xoanon itself. All he did was to enrich the base, as, indeed we are virtually told by Pausanias.[2]

From the coin-pictures of this figure we can be certain at least that Apollo was columnar up to the shoulders, that the right arm was bent at the elbow and the right hand raised, holding a spear, that the left arm held a bow outstretched, and that the head was helmeted. Both coins show that the face had features. It must not be forgotten that the accessories like the helmet, spear, and bow might well have been restored by Bathykles on the occasion of so important a reconstruction of a shrine as this. Conceivably also he covered the wooden core with bronze. We cannot assume from the words of Pausanias that the core was in fact of wood, but it is highly improbable that a bronze cover would have been fitted to stone. It is unnecessary to assume that the body was made either of cast or beaten bronze alone. Bronze castings were a local Spartan technique of which the Brazen House of Athena, made by Gitiadas, an artist contemporary with Bathykles, is the best known instance.[3]

The Apollo is thus comparable in some respects to the Knossian goddess of whose appearance we know at least that she had bronze hair separately attached and a body of wood. A possible comparison can also be made with the curious figure, identified by some as a cult figure, which stands in front of an altar in one of the panels of the painted sarcophagus of Haghia Triadha in Crete.[4] This painting dates from

[1] *Jahrb.* 1918, p. 107 ff.   [2] iii. 18. 9.   [3] Paus. iii. 17. 2.
[4] Bossert, *Altkreta*, 54. Hall, op. cit., fig. 293.

the end of the Middle Minoan or the beginning of the first Late Minoan period, and so is approximately contemporary with the Palace goddess. This strange figure in the painting stands rigidly in front of an altar with a ritual tree in front of or at the side of him. In front of the tree is an altar to which votaries approach with offerings. The figure assumed to be a statue of a deity has the curious characteristic of being smaller in height than the votaries and of being armless. The painting is damaged below the hips and it is impossible to say whether the feet were rendered as they are in the case of the votaries. Certainly a strong contrast is made between him and the votaries. The artist is especially careful to delineate their arms in full detail (Fig. 19).[1]

In many ways, then, it is possible to establish the working hypothesis that pre-Hellenic Cretan and some of the earliest Hellenic figures of deities shared the peculiarity of having plain or almost columnar bodies but realistic or, at least, partly detailed heads. The very fact that nothing other than the bronze curls was found with the remains of the burnt Knossian statue strongly indicates that the head was the only part of the figure rendered in detail. Whether the body was painted over the wood remains an unsolved problem, but if the painted figure of the Haghia Triadha sarcophagus is in fact a painting of a statue and does not represent a priest or a votary, then the garment which he wears (without

---

[1] H. R. Hall, in *The Civilization of Greece in the Bronze Age*, p. 224, assumes that the figure represents a dead man and not a deity. 'The concept', he says, 'is obviously inspired by the well known Egyptian scene of offerings being made to a mummy placed upright before a tomb.' But against this it may be said that there is no evidence for any mummification of the dead before the time of the Shaft Graves, and even here the evidence is but slight. Probably the dead were wrapped in thick shrouds, but there is no evidence at all to suggest that Minoans followed Egyptian customs as closely as this. The absence of arms supports both views equally, for there is no reason to think that Minoan statues had other details of anatomy than the head. The association of a tree, an altar and a shrine with a figure seem much more strongly to suggest that the figure is that of a deity than of a corpse. Innumerable cult scenes on Minoan rings bear this out. See Evans, *Frazer lecture for 1931*, figs. 5 and 13.

FIG. 19. SCENE FROM THE HAGHIA TRIADHA SARCO-
PHAGUS; statue of deity or of defunct person receiving offerings at
an altar.

Sacred tree and shrine are also shown.

Scale 1/2.

FIG. 20. PROTOCORINTHIAN ARYBALLOS, in the Ashmolean
Museum.

Athena, Aphrodite (?) votary, horsemen, and sphinxes.

Scale 4/5.

sleeves or arms) may have been either painted on the wood
or an actual garment worn by the statue. In this case the
features are clearly rendered and the curls of the hair, as
would have been the case with the Knossian figure. But it
is abundantly clear in the case of the Amyklaean Apollo
that the body is in no way sculptured in detail: it remained
a simple shaft of wood or metal or both.

Other representations of xoana on coins are rare. We find
the head of the olive-wood Dionysos on coins of Methymna,
a primitive statue which was reputed to have been dredged
from the sea,[1] and the whole statue can be seen represented
on the coins of Mytilene.[2] From these it seems that this
primitive statue was a terminal figure fixed to a square
basis. On the coins it is also shown as draped round the
term. There is no absolute certainty that this Mytilenean
figure was of great antiquity, but it resembles in structure
the Amyklaean Apollo as shown on the later Lacedaemonian
coins.

It might have been thought that bronze statuettes would
have preserved xoanon types at the earlier dates. But this
is not the case. There is no surviving statuette which shows
this particular columnar body, devoid of detail in quite the
same way. The earliest known geometric bronze statuettes
of human forms always have legs as carefully rendered as the
rest of the body. It is not till the sixth century that bronzes,
always of females, have rigid and hieratic bodies that suggest
comparison with the Amyklaean figure.[3] But the comparison
is fortuitous and reflects only the conventions of the day in
stone sculpture, which have an origin independent from the
conventions of wooden xoana. A curious terra-cotta figure
from the Argive Heraeum[4] seems to preserve the early

---

[1] Paus. x. 19; *Zeitschrift für Numismatik*, xx. 285; *Brit. Mus. Cat. Coins,*
Troas, p. lxxvi.   [2] Head, *Hist. Num.*, p. 562.

[3] See W. Lamb, op. cit., pl. xxvii *c* (Sparta) and xxv *b* (Boston) for two
characteristic examples.

[4] *Argive Heraeum*, ii, p. 27, No. 107, fig. 41. A similar comparison may be
made with the strange terra-cotta figures recently found in Lemnos. Here

Hellenic xoanon type with some fidelity. Its head and shoulders are carefully moulded, but the body is turned on the wheel and made quite cylindrical. The figure follows closely the type of the Amyklaean Apollo.

It is clear, then, that there was a similarity between Minoan cult statues, in so far as our knowledge of them can be built up, and the early Hellenic cult statues, as illustrated by the statue of Apollo at Amyklae, which was at once one of the oldest in Greece and probably far and away the largest—40 feet was an immense height for a cult statue at any period—and the Amyclaeans were justified in calling in Bathycles to repair their treasure.

Vase-paintings give practically no help in illustration of the earliest type of Greek cult-statues or xoana. Figures such as Palladia, on the other hand, but of seventh-century type, or even sixth-century in character, are not uncommon. But there is one notable exception. A Protocorinthian vase (Fig. 20) from Boeotia, now in the Ashmolean Museum, preserves what, if the identification is correct, is the earliest Hellenic representation of a cult statue. This vase, a small aryballos found at Thebes in 1896,[1] shows a scene of the greatest interest. The style of the drawing is Protocorinthian hardly emancipated from Geometric features and style. It must fall into the early decades of the seventh century. The scene shows two horsemen and between them three human figures. The first (from left to right) is a small figure with the arms raised in the conventional attitude of adoration. Next is a large figure dressed in a heavy chequered chiton or peplos holding a shield in the left and a spear in the

the arms are in some cases in the same attitude as those of the Amyklaean Apollo, while the body remains tubular. These figures belong to the seventh century. *Jahrbuch*, 1930, p. 141, figs. 17 and 18.

[1] *J.H.S.* xxiv. p. 295, No. 504. Johansen, *Vases Sicyoniens*, pl. xx. 1 *a* and *b*. H. Payne, *Necrocorinthia* (1931), p. 8, n. 1. Mr. Payne hazards the guess that the principal scene may be a copy of a geometric wall-painting in a temple. There is, of course, nothing to support this conjecture and there is no evidence to suggest that wall paintings existed in temples of the 'geometric' period.

right hand. The head is given a full and bristly growth of hair. Next to this is a figure of similar scale holding in the right hand what looks like a pomegranate. On the head is a polos and the garment is a close-fitting chiton, full in the skirt and narrowed at the waist. Johansen sees in this pair the two main Corinthian deities—Athena and Aphrodite— and he identifies the figures as those of xoana of those deities rather than as the deities themselves. The stiff attitude of both of them contrasts with the easy movement of the horsemen. But, on the other hand, the figure of the worshipper is equally stiff. Yet the worshipper would hardly be shown in the attitude of worship except before statues, and Johansen's suggestion seems to me to be sound. Further, a resemblance with the Apollo of Amyklae as rendered on the coins is at once evident. The attitude and stiffness are common to both.

Pausanias records[1] that at Titane there was a temple of Athena in which was an ἀρχαῖον ξόανον so that, if the identification of the vase-painting as that of a xoanon is accepted, it can be accepted with a certain background of history. Coins of Sikyon of the time of Caracalla[2] also show a xoanon which may be the same one. The figure identified as Aphrodite, on the other hand, cannot be associated with any literary reference. This is the only convincing vase-painting which may be identified as that of a really primitive Greek statue. Other vases have been cited,[3] but most can be explained on other grounds.

But of statues of a more advanced type there are clearer examples. Most interesting of all, perhaps, is a volute-crater of the fifth century,[4] found in excavations on the supposed site of Spina in the Po valley. On one part of the vase is a votary standing before nine small statues of a type which

[1] ii. 12. 1.   [2] Mionnet, Suppl. iv. 170. 1130.
[3] As in the case of a fourth century vase from Megara which Pervanoglou (in *Arch. Zeitung*, 1865, p. 68, pl. 199. 3) thought to be a figure of a xoanon of Athena Onke. In fact the alleged xoanon is a trophy, fixed on a pole.
[4] Prof. Beazley dates it about 430 B.C.

suggests the end of the seventh century.[1] These nine doll-like figures must be the nine Muses of Helicon. They suggest comparison with figures of the Auxerre type or with countless terra-cotta and ivory figures of Artemis Orthia from Sparta, figures in which the arms fall straight to the sides and which are clothed in close-fitting chitons. But as a general comparison for the Protocorinthian vase just described this volute-crater is interesting, since it shows a similar votary in a similar attitude in front of cult statues (Fig. 21).

Palladia are more common on vase-paintings. They often have their features clearly delineated and the features usually indicate the solemn countenances of seventh-century statues, not the smiling faces of the full archaic period.

It might have been hoped that the sanctuary of Athena Lindia in Rhodes would have provided some evidence of importance of an archaeological nature as to the character of an early cult image. The goddess Lindia, later called Athena by immigrant Dorians arriving about 900 B.C., was in origin almost certainly a pre-Hellenic and possibly a Mycenaean deity. Here if anywhere, one might have expected that a pre-Hellenic cult image would have passed on in succession to the Hellenic worshippers and have been taken over into their cult and worship. An island with so clear-cut a history as Rhodes serves indeed as a key-site where the transition between pre-Hellenic and Hellenic may be observed uncontaminated.

But our evidence as to the nature of the pre-Hellenic Lindia cult is tenuous in the extreme. Blinkenberg[2] thinks that the original image was a mere bole of wood placed in a sacred grove, the ἄλσος ἐν ἀκροπόλει of Pindar,[3] and so in no way as advanced a statue as the xoanon of the Knossian palace. This image, whatever it was, was taken over by the

[1] A. Colasanti, *La Necropoli di Spina, Rivista Illustrata del Popolo d'Italia,* Nov. 1928.

[2] *Lindos, Fouilles de l'Acropole,* 1931, vol. i, p. 10, and *L'Image d'Athana Lindia* (Copenhagen, 1917), p. 7.

[3] *Ol.* 7. 90.

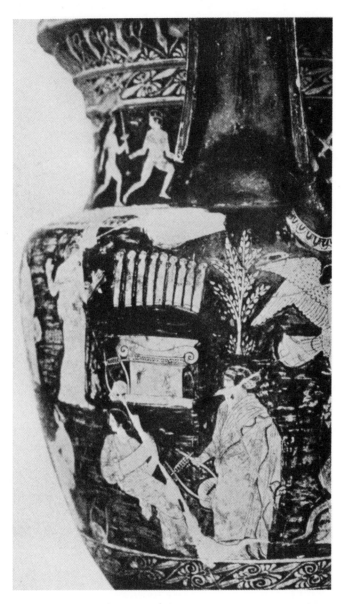

Fig. 21. VASE FOUND ON THE SUPPOSED SITE
OF SPINA, showing votary at an altar with small statues
of the nine muses in the background.

These statues are shown as small either because they were, in fact,
small, or else because they stood at a distance behind the altar.
In type they represent figures of the late seventh century.

incoming Dorians. I see no real evidence either way as to its character and appearance. Blinkenberg tacitly assumes that it was a mere tree-trunk, whereas it might equally well have been a more elaborate statue of the Knossian type. He makes the further unjustified assumption that it is not the same as the primitive statue which stood in the shrine down to the fourth century when a fire destroyed both it and the temple. This makes it essential to assume that the pre-Hellenic statue was either destroyed or superseded, and of this there is no scrap of evidence.

The question arises therefore whether the statue that lasted until the fire was the pre-Hellenic statue or not. We know at any rate something of the primitive statue in question. Firstly it must have been made before 690 B.C., for Lindian colonists went at that time to Sicily[1] and seem to have taken with them some knowledge or actual version of the cult statue of the metropolis.

Secondly, we are told by Kallimachos[2] that it was a λιτὸν ἕδος, a plain seated statue. This places it into a class of seated xoana established with some care by Strabo.[3] He gives as instances the xoana at Phocaea, Massalia, Rome, Chios, 'and many other places'.

Thirdly, the same passage of Kallimachos attributes this seated statue to the time of Danaos. As we have already seen (see p. 52), there was at Argos a xoanon of 'Apollo' said to have been there from the time of Danaos, as well as a relief by Danaos himself which we saw had every reason to be considered as a Minoan work. No doubt attributions of this kind were often as wild as they were numerous. But the curious fact emerges that the association of a statue with Danaos does seem to give it some kind of pre-Hellenic context. In any case there is no scrap of evidence to show that the oldest Lindian image of all was replaced by an early Hellenic version made not later that 690 B.C. There is,

---

[1] *La Chronique du Temple Lindien* (Copenhagen, 1912), C.56.
[2] Frag. 105 : καὶ γὰρ ᾿Αθήνης | ἐν Λίνδῳ Δαναὸς λιτὸν ἔθηκεν ἕδος. [3] xiii. 1.41.

indeed, nothing to prevent us from assuming that the statue which remained in the Lindian shrine until its destruction in the fourth century somewhere between 350 and 330[1] B.C. was that which had been there *before* the arrival of the Dorians. It was certainly a figure deeply revered, since Kleoboulos, the Rhodian equivalent and contemporary of Polycrates of Samos, Lygdamis of Naxos and Peisistratos of Athens, went to the trouble to rehouse it in the sixth century in a new temple.[2]

Blinkenberg's suggestion that we can see the statue reflected in certain terra-cottas found at Lindos[3] and in others from the Lindian colonies of Akragas and Gela, whither the type had been taken, is attractive but unconvincing. Terra-cottas in general afford but the vaguest clues as to larger works in stone or wood. There is no certain instance of an archaic terra-cotta repeating the type of a known statue with accuracy. The fact that the terra-cottas in question are of seated figures may suggest that the general attitude of the xoanon was copied. But the face and figure in general in each case are those of the sixth century, while, on Blinkenberg's own admission, the original wooden Lindia statue cannot date after 690 B.C., when the type of statue must have been totally different in detail.

The Lindian seated goddess must be associated with the seated Athena of Troy of which Homer speaks (see above, p. 53), but this statue seems to have been replaced by a later, though still primitive work. Strabo, with his critical mind, observes that the wooden statue of Athena to be seen in his day was upright, whereas that described by Homer was seated.[4] From this we can assume that the earliest statue had been replaced at an early date, for some reason which remains unknown.

But the existence at the very earliest times, Hellenic or pre-Hellenic, of seated statues seems amply attested. The

<hr />

[1] *Lindos, Fouilles,* &c., p. 17.   [2] Id., p. 14.
[3] *L'Image d'Athana,* pp. 27 ff.   [4] *loc. cit.*

Lindian figure recorded by the verse of Kallimachos, faintly reflected in the terra-cottas of a much later date and referred to in the temple-chronicles as being garlanded with a gold crown and decked with necklaces,[1] may have been the cult figure taken over by the immigrant Dorians. Certainly there is no evidence at all to show that the earliest cult was a mere tree-cult.

But there may be a gap in our evidence, and the decision as to whether this Lindian figure is pre-Hellenic or very early Hellenic must still remain open. But a little weight is added to the scales in favour of a pre-Hellenic origin by evidence from Samos. Athenaeus records[2] that a local Samian antiquary, Menodotus, believed that the Samian shrine was originally built by pre-Hellenic peoples. The passage of Kallimachos above quoted speaks of the Samian statue as being an ἄξοος σανίς, a description which recalls the simple log-shaped body of our hypothetical Minoan large-scale statues.

Unfortunately the excavations at Lindos have produced no small version either in ivory or in stone of any primitive statue. Indeed most of the small stone dedications seem to be Cypriote.

[1] *Chronique du temple*, C. 1 ff. (after an expedition under Kleoboulos to Lycia), C. 80 (after a similar expedition to Crete).　　[2] 15. 672 a.

THE EARLIEST HELLENIC STONE STATUES

I. SOFT STONES

THE name given by the Greeks to the earliest known statues was, as we have seen, ξόανα. But Pausanias adds[1] that they were also called δαίδαλα.

'People long ago called ξόανα by the name of δαίδαλα', he says, 'I believe they even called them so before Daedalus was born at Athens[2] and I think that the name Daedalus was a surname subsequently given him from the δαίδαλα and not a name given at his birth.'

Pausanias strictly limits the use of the word ξόανα to images of wood. Other writers, however, use it indiscriminately and widely in describing statues both of stone and of bronze, leaving to the word only the implication of age.[3] The lexicographers[4] explicitly apply it to works either of stone or of wood, deriving it from the verb ξέω. Pausanias seems to have been a purist in establishing a specific usage which contrasted with the general usage.

We can be certain, then, that the bulk of the descriptions in Pausanias of these wooden statues refer to works of high antiquity belonging either to early Hellenic times or to pre-Hellenic times.

For the date of the earliest large stone statues we have no literary evidence at all. We have only the statues themselves. Before considering them in detail it is essential to realize that they belong to an age of iron, when the simplest iron chisel or drill had an infinitely greater cutting and boring capacity than the tools of the Bronze Age. Iron swords of great cutting power and hardness are known in Greek lands

---

[1] ix. 3. 2.

[2] The best authorities make Daedalus an Athenian born. See Töpffer, *Attische Genealogie*, p. 165. Daedalus was a Metionid.

[3] The most succinct account of the usage of the word is to be found in Frazer's edition of Paus. II, p. 69 in a note to Paus. iii. 3. 5.

[4] Suidas and *Etymologicum Magnum*, s.v. ξόανον.

FIG. 22. FRIEZE OF HORSEMEN FROM PRINIAS IN CRETE

FIG. 23. ENGRAVED STELE from Prinias in the Candia
Museum. Woman holding distaff.
Limestone.
Scale 1/3.

from as early as the eleventh or tenth century,[1] and iron tools must have come into use very soon after that time. And yet, strangely enough, the art of sculpture derives no stimulus from this new and convenient material. As we have seen, the earliest Hellenic statues were still of wood, worked with almost equal ease either with bronze or with iron.

Our earliest stone statues seem to be those found in Crete. The astonishing series of relief carvings and of sculptured figures in the round from Prinias, a very early Hellenic settlement of which the ancient name is unknown, are of soft limestone. In shape they resemble in some degree what we have seen to be the simple schematic shape of the wooden ξόανον, as far as that shape can be reconstructed. That is to say, the upper part of the body is done in some detail and the lower part left in the main as a columnar shape. The Prinias figures have detail of dress and the feet made clear, but the substantial work is done on the upper part of the body from the waist upwards.

The Prinias sculptures,[2] derived from the lintel, doorway, and walls of a temple of very archaic type, consist of the remains of two seated figures of a goddess, two panels beneath them showing similar figures in relief, but standing, and a fine frieze of horsemen. There are additional sculptures in relief on the basis of the thrones on which the seated figures are placed.

The technical methods used in the fashioning of these sculptures are as follows:

The seated figures and the reliefs beneath the lintel. It is impossible to be certain how the primary work of blocking out these figures was done since the surfaces are everywhere at the final stage of craftsmanship. But it is clear enough that the final stages, that is to say the fashioning of hands, feet, features and detail of dress, was done with a flat chisel and

---

[1] Myres, *Who were the Greeks?* p. 399.
[2] *Annuario della Scuola Archaeologica di Atene*, i, pp. 19 ff.

with various forms of simple knives. Perhaps the divisions between the fingers was done with a rubbing instrument, but this is not certain. The reliefs of standing deities beneath the lintel are rendered in exactly the same way. The technique in fact differs in no respect from that of ordinary wood-carving in which the chisel and knife are the only tools used.

The horsemen relief-frieze and some other engraved reliefs. The horsemen (Fig. 22.) themselves are cut in precisely the same way as the previous works. But they have the peculiarity of being deeply outlined into the background: that is to say, the outline of each horseman was first drawn on the plain stone and then cut down to a simple outline which was deliberately incised into the plane surface of the back plane, thus giving each figure the increased clarity which a dark outline would afford.

This outlining process is of interest since it appears in other sculptures in Crete as the *only* process, a simple engraving of a design on a single-plane surface. Thus No. 235 (Fig. 26) in the Museum at Candia is a rectangular slab of soft lime-stone, heavily weathered, upon the surface of which has been incised, or rather engraved, a warrior with shield and greaves. The upper part of the relief is missing, but what remains shows the greater part of the warrior. A second slab showing a similar warrior is seen in No. 236 (Fig. 27).

With this engraved relief must be associated another relief in exactly similar technique, which shows a woman holding a distaff. It is No. 234 (Fig. 23) in the Candia Museum. The woman is rendered in the full Cretan manner. Some of the lines of the figure are engraved as in the case of the warrior stelai, others are in relief, the relief being achieved by cutting a slight groove on each side of the line, so throwing it into prominence.

A knife may have been used for some of this work, but the use of a chisel is more likely in most of the engraving, for in some places the starting-point of a line is clear and precise, and its finish blurred and sometimes run over past the point which it was intended to reach, a fault common in chisel work. This is perhaps made more clear by a drawing (Fig. 24) of two of the incised lines here shown:

FIG. 24. (From the right side of the peplos, below the knee.)

What is quite certain is that no rubbing instrument of the type seen in use in prehistoric times was here employed. The tools used are those of the carpenter and wood-carver.

The horsemen frieze from Prinias having been outlined by this process of pure engraving was finished with the knife and chisel also. Marks of the knife-blade are particularly clear on the rump of the third horse from the left. The outlining process is used again in outlining the legs of the riders against the bodies of the horses.

The beautiful architectural decoration consisting of a formal pattern that runs below the frieze of the horsemen provides definite evidence for the use of a tool which now appears for the first time in the history of Greek sculpture. Nor, as will be seen later, does it remain long in use (see below, p. 215). That tool can best be described as a cutting-compass and consisted of a powerful compass of which one leg ended in a point or spike and the other in a knife-blade. Its use can be most clearly seen in the delineation of the half-circles that form the upper part of the design in question. The holes made by the pointed leg can be seen at intervals of 9·8 cm. across the middle of the decorative frieze. This space of 9·8 cm. is also the radius of the inner semicircle described on the surface of the stone by the cutting leg. The cutting leg achieved both the inner semicircle and the outer semicircle in each case. The circles were not com-pleted, but from each end of the arcs there was run down a continuation of the two semicircles, cut free-hand with a knife. These continuations were then curved round into inturning spiral ends. The comparative clumsiness of the lower half of each semicircle is very plain. Equally clear is the way in which the compass-drawn semicircles sometimes went slightly beyond the limit of a semicircle and made it difficult for the knife-draughtsman to continue downwards from them. This can be seen in the drawing (fig. 25).

FIG. 25. Decoration below the frieze.

Other Cretan Sculptures.

The well-known statue on a small scale of a woman or goddess which is now in the Louvre[1] is universally accepted as being a Cretan sculptured figure of identical style and type with the Prinias figures. Its origin is remarkably obscure. All that is known about it is that it arrived at the Museum of Auxerre in France apparently without credentials and that it was duly catalogued with no detailed information beyond its number. (Fig. 28).

Fortunately its technical characteristics fully bear out its Cretan attribution. It is of soft yellowish limestone and has been fashioned in exactly the same way as the Prinias goddess figures. The knife and chisel are the only tools whose presence can be detected. The features, hands, fingers, feet and finally, the finely chased maeander-pattern down the front and sides of the peplos have all been done with a knife-blade.

[1] Collignon in *Mon. Piot* xx, pp. 6 ff. How the statue reached Auxerre is a complete and absolute mystery!

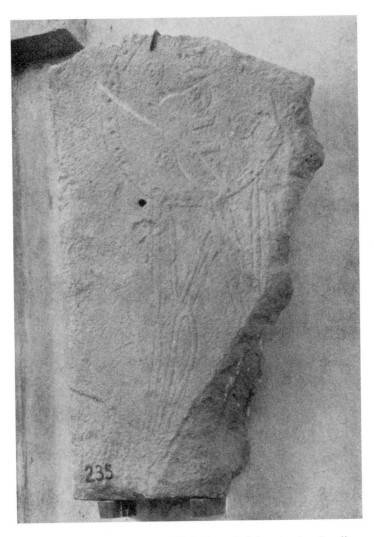

FIG. 26. ENGRAVED STELE from Prinias, in the Candia
Museum. Shield and legs of warrior, facing left.

Limestone.

Scale 1/2.

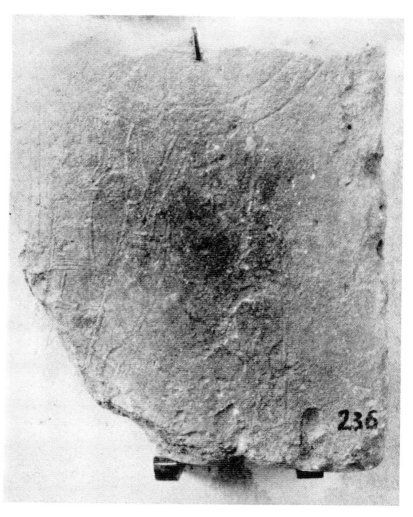

FIG. 27. ENGRAVED STELE from Prinias, in the Candia Museum.
Lower part of a warrior, facing left.
Limestone. In front of him a small figure.
Scale 1/2.

The chisel was probably used also for the roughing-out. The maeander pattern below and scale pattern above the waist, very lightly incised, were probably intended merely as a guide for the painter, since the lines are too light and sketchy to be considered as a final form of decorations. Slight incision of this kind serves the useful purpose of making a clear border between different colours and, by the fall of light on the incision, emphasizing the various outlines of differently coloured areas.

The lower part of a male figure in precisely this same Cretan style was found at Delos and is now at Athens.[1] It has exactly the same Cretan waistbelt as the female figures. But its legs and genitals are rendered with extreme care and skill. The rigid detailless type suggestive of the xoanon seems to have been reserved for the female figures.

The use of incision, as has already been seen, was already fully known and in use as a separate art in itself. The incised or engraved reliefs already discussed are certainly not later than the Prinias and Louvre figures. Conceivably they are earlier. It is, therefore, of no little interest to find incision here applied in detail to figure sculpture.

A second figure, in the Louvre, of far less merit than the Auxerre statue, is the small seated figure of a woman or goddess.[2] The pedigree of this figure also is vague and obscure, and there is no information which enables us to say that it came from Crete. It is of soft yellowish limestone. It does not bear at first sight a striking resemblance to the Prinias sculptures. It is poor work by a clumsy artist, but it seems nevertheless to bear the full imprint of Cretan handiwork. Nor has there been any attempt as yet to attribute it to any other origin.

The rather crude face and hair are clearly cut with a knife; the lines of the pattern on the dress are carelessly scratched

[1] *Mon. Piot*, loc. cit., fig. 11. and *Jahrb.* 21. p. 162, fig. 5.
[2] *Annuario della Scuola Arch. di Atene*, 1914, i, p. 109, fig. 63.   No. 3100 in the Louvre.

with a knife-point or with any pointed instrument, and the points of the eight-pointed flowers (which occur also in the Prinias figures) scratched in panels on the breasts and skirt are done with a simple auger. It thus bears a close technical resemblance to the Prinias works except in the fact that an auger is used. For at Prinias this instrument does not appear to have been employed at all.

No other Cretan statues of stone of this type and period are known. It is generally held that this group of works of art belongs to the third quarter of the seventh century B.C. It is thus possible to decide that the tools employed in the sculpture of soft limestone at this time were as follows: the flat chisel, comparable to a wood-carver's chisel, the knife, the simple boring drill or auger, the cutting compass with one leg consisting of a knife-blade, and perhaps a stone abrasive of pumice or emery, for detail on occasions and for general smoothing at the final stage, though this is not certain. It is also extremely probable, though not certain, that these statues were painted with a thick paste-paint. But of this there is no direct evidence: it is inferential from the presence of very light incisions on flat surfaces. There were no insertions of other materials either in the eyes or in any other parts of statues. The technique in general is that of woodwork.

The Attic limestone series.

The term 'poros', or in its usual Greek form πώρινος λίθος, was and remains an evasion of scientific accuracy of description. Its connotation, in so far as it has any connotation at all, is simply 'limestone' or any soft easily tractable stone which has no particular merit of surface or capacity for taking polish. Herodotus[1] uses it of the sculptures, now vanished, which the Alkmaeonidae replaced with other sculptures of Parian marble in the Temple of Apollo at Delphi. In the same breath we are told by Theophrastus[2]

[1] 5. 62. Herodotus speaks only of the façade of the temple, which I take to include all sculptures on it. [2] Περὶ τῶν λίθων. Ch. 15.

FIG. 28. CRETAN LIMESTONE FEMALE FIGURE.
Known as the 'Auxerre' figure. (Louvre.)

Fig. 29. HEAD OF FIGURE IN LIMESTONE, No. 55, in the
Acropolis Museum.

Scale 1/1.

that ὁ πῶρος ὅμοιος τῷ χρώματι καὶ τῇ πυκνότητι τῷ Παρίῳ, which suggests that the general change in the appearance of the temple was not so profound after the renovation. But in the same passage Theophrastus adds that the stone so named was remarkable for its lightness of weight (κουφότης). Pausanias uses it to describe the rather hard grey limestone of which the Temple of Zeus at Olympia was made. He calls it ἐπιχώριος πῶρος.[1] The κρηπίς of the Altis at Olympia also was of this stone.[2] The term was, in fact, loosely used and comes to mean any soft or moderately soft limestone, which might vary according to the locality in colour and texture.

We can, however, be quite certain that it does not refer to any particular kind of soft stone. It can include sandstone, limestone, volcanic tufas, and calcareous stones. Such in fact is the variety of stones used in antiquity for fashioning statues and sculptures of different kinds.

Almost without exception students of and writers on Greek sculpture describe the archaic series of limestone sculptures found on the Acropolis at Athens as being made of 'poros'. The particular stone which is indicated by this term is in fact the dark yellowish limestone which is the natural formation of many parts of the Athens district, particularly at Peiraeus and Munychia. It is sometimes almost bright yellow in colour and is of a soft texture, in strong contrast to the very hard blue limestone of which the Acropolis and Areopagus are made. Fresh from the quarry it must have been even softer and almost as cuttable as a hard tufa.

Without exception the large series of early sixth-century sculptures in the Acropolis that are not in Pentelic or Hymettan marble are of this soft yellow limestone. The sculptures of this series are so numerous that they afford ample evidence of technique. Since, also, all of them are derived from architectural settings there survive far more unfinished surfaces than would be the case with single votive statues that were destined to stand in isolated positions.

[1] v. 10. 2. [2] vi. 19. 1.

The chronological sequence of the whole series has been more or less satisfactorily fixed by Guy Dickins.[1]

The so-called 'Hydra Pediment' is dated by Dickins as the earliest and assigned approximately to 570 B.C. It is, as he says, 'a drawing on stone with the background cut out'. The method by which the background was so cut was that of the flat chisel and knife, the former for the main and heavy work, the latter for the detail. The whole composition is made up of six slabs of limestone which differ considerably in quality. The four left-hand slabs are coarse and full of shells. The fifth is of a finer grain. As with almost all the 'poros' sculpture these defects of material were intended to be hidden by a thick wash of paste-paint. In this pedimental relief-sculpture the colour survives to a considerable degree. No less than four colours can still be made out.[2]

It is not, of course, possible to draw useful technical conclusions in the case of each of the limestone series in the Acropolis Museum. I shall confine myself, therefore, to those only which exhibit indisputable evidence of technique.

The pedimental group usually known as the 'Introduction of Herakles to Olympos' has much to tell us. It is made of limestone of good quality with few defects due to shell and cavities. The inner parts and base of the throne upon which Zeus is seated show numerous cuts made by a narrow-bladed flat chisel. A similar chisel was used for the beard and hair of the Zeus and for the beard and hair of the Herakles. The embroidered patterns on the garment of the Hera may have been made with a chisel, but they could equally well have been cut with a knife as in the Auxerre statue. The clearly marked chisel-cuts on the Zeus were made with a chisel which measured less than half an inch in cutting width.

Marks of other tools cannot be clearly distinguished, and it can at least be safely said that the bulk of the cutting and

[1] *Catalogue of the Acropolis Museum*, vol. i, pp. 18, 29 and *passim, sub num.*
[2] Dickins, op. cit., p. 57.

FIG. 30. HEAD OF 'PROTEUS', No. 35, in the Acropolis Museum.
The eyes are compass-cut, the remainder is done with knife and chisel.
Scale 2/3.

Fig. 31. HEAD OF SERPENT IN LIMESTONE, in the Acropolis
Museum.
The eyes are cut with a cutting-compass, the other incised patterns with a
knife.
Height 35 cm.

detail in the final stages was done with the same tools as those used in the Cretan limestone figures, with the exception of the cutting-compass, and, perhaps, the auger. Certainly if the auger was used at all it was not used for primary work or for any subsequent work of importance.

The pedimental sculpture known as the 'Troilos Pediment'[1] shows clear marks of the chisel in the cutting of the ashlar wall of the building which occupies the centre of the pedimental scene. The olive-branches are also incised on this background of wall with either a chisel or a knife. The small figure of a *hydriaphoros* and also the figure of a man which Buschor has assigned to the group both show signs of rubbing in garments and hair, for in both are grooves which could not be chisel-cut. But for the rest they are ordinary chisel and knife work. The beard of the man, in particular, shows clear chisel-lines (Fig. 29).

The well-known Hekatompedon pedimental group in limestone usually known as 'Blue Beard',[2] shows exactly the same technique as all the foregoing. The chisel is the main tool and is used also for all surface-lines. Its use is best seen on the extreme left of the background. The hair shows signs of chisel and knife, and the finger-divisions have been chisel-cut. The eyes are cut with a cutting-compass, 1·2 cm. in diameter (Fig. 30).

The pedimental serpents Nos. 39 and 40[3] (Figs. 31 & 33) with their intricate and involved scale-markings are, on the surface, almost entirely the work of a knife. Similar are two other serpent's heads, not specifically assigned to buildings, nor described by Dickins. It would be almost impossible to do a large series of semicircular scales as in No. 39 or of parallel but wavy lines as in 40 with the aid of so uncertain a tool as

---

[1] It was previously known by the name of the 'Erechtheium pediment', an erroneous and misleading title. Dickins calls it more simply 'Pedimental relief representing a building with olive trees'. Its present title is due to Buschor (*Ath. Mitth.* xlvii, p. 80), who seems to have identified its subject correctly.

[2] Dickins, p. 78.   [3] Id., p. 74.

the chisel. A chisel cannot be controlled for the entire length of its stroke: it may go too far or not far enough after the first drive. A knife would, in fact, be both safer and quicker on soft and easily handled material like Attic limestone than a chisel. To cut it with a knife would be even easier than to cut wood. These scales, and with them the feathers of birds' wings of which there is a large number of fragments in the museum, are all alike knife-cut. So also are the scales on No. 36, the pedimental group of Herakles and the Triton.[1]

From the remaining works in limestone from the Athenian Acropolis no further evidence can be gleaned. There remain, however, two curious pieces which cannot rank as sculpture proper since they were never intended as serious work. These are the two grotesques Nos. 11 and 12[2], both in the same Attic limestone. They are rightly classed by Dickins as what might be called 'lunch-hour masterpieces'. They are simply rough sketches or even caricatures cut out hastily with a knife in a few minutes by some high-spirited mason. One (No. 11) even has a dash of paint on its lips. Their sole value is that they show clearly the marks of the tool with which they were cut. And that tool is a knife.

The Spartan limestone reliefs.

Of great interest is the series of small limestone reliefs which were found at Sparta during the excavations of the shrine of Artemis Orthia.[3] They have a particular importance partly because they can be dated on archaeological evidence that has an absolute validity and partly because, though small-scale objects, they appear to have a direct connexion both with the technique and with the composition of large-scale sculpture.

These little carvings are numerous and, though resembling the two Acropolis grotesques described above in some respects, differ from them in that they fall for the most part

[1] Dickins, p. 82.   [2] Id., p. 72.
[3] *The Sanctuary of Artemis Orthia* (1930), pp. 187 ff.

into a definite class of votive objects, as can be safely inferred
from the inscriptions which some of them bear. As votive
objects they may be considered as dedications of the work-
men employed on the building of the later temple. Some
few may perhaps be regarded simply as 'lunch-hour masterpieces' like the Acropolis faces. The fact that they vary in
quality from being mere scratchings (e.g. Nos. 53, 56, 57, 58)
to almost perfectly finished reliefs (e.g. Nos. 13, 46) is hard
to explain. Those that can be certainly identified as dedications are No. 23, a relief of a horse's head offered to Artemis
Orthia by one Theokormidas, No. 28, a horse in relief offered
by one Epanidas, or No. 33, a horse's head in relief offered
anonymously to Ϝροθασία. All three are clumsily cut and
unbeautiful. Perhaps it would be wiser to interpret them as
the simple offerings of mere masons who were, perhaps
light-heartedly, endeavouring to emulate the examples of the
sculptors whose work was being done before their eyes.

There is a small group of figures in the round. Some, like
Nos. 1, 3, and 7–11, were certainly never intended for serious
contemplation; others, like Nos. 4, an unfinished ?male
figure wearing a polos, or 5, a fragment of a small xoanon
figure, are intended as, and might have succeeded in being,
works of art.

The bulk of the remainder are reliefs. Of these some, like
Nos. 12–16, are in the manner of the Spartan ivory plaques,
and show figures which have been achieved simply by a
process of cutting away a background round a line-drawing
which was the first step taken by the sculptor with his plain
stone slab. The various stages of this cutting away of the
background can be seen in No. 38, a horse in relief, where it
has just begun, and No. 24, where the process is completed,
save for the final smoothing of the background. In both alike
the marks of the knife-blade are plain beyond cavil and the
marks of a chisel are nowhere apparent.

No. 16, a queer and clumsy figure of a man holding a spear
or staff, bears a striking resemblance to the equally clumsy

figure of a man from a stele from the Shaft Graves at Mycenae (see above, Fig. 14). The process of cutting round was the same in each and the figure finally achieved has in each case reached the same standard of unloveliness. Scratching of detail with the point of the knife is plain enough in Nos. 17, 28, 32, 39, and 40, to choose the most obvious examples. There is also a tendency here and there to that outlining of form in low relief which we have already seen at Prinias in Crete and in other Cretan works (above p. 68). Nos. 14 and 23 show this outlining more clearly than many.

But in addition to the groups of figures in the round and of plain low relief-carvings there is another small group which is technically of very great interest and importance. No. 17 shows a horse (Fig. 32), partly damaged, which is unfinished. Its process of manufacture is described.[1] The carver first drew his horse in outline on a plain slab, as in the case of the low reliefs. But his next process was to cut away the background, not to make relief but to remove it altogether and produce in the process a horse in three dimensions, of which the back and front would be the two sides of the slab and the other dimension derived from the thickness of the slab. Having outlined his horse he then pared off the slab round its outline. But he did not pare *right up to* the outline[2] because he needed a little extra beyond the outline in order to make the transition to the other surface provided by the thickness of the slab. This particular example shows us the horse just at the stage when it was on the point of acquiring its third dimension. It was in fact a short cut to sculpture in the round and as such a most instructive example. For it is no isolated phenomenon. The best example of this 'biscuit sculpture', as it might well be called, is seen in the pedimental relief in marble of Herakles, Apollo, and the tripod on the front of the Treasury of the Siphnians at

---

[1] *The Sanctuary of Artemis Orthia*, p. 190. It was presented to the British Museum by the Greek Government in 1923. See *Brit. Mus. Cat. of Sculpture*, 1.   [2] As indeed the editor, Prof. Dawkins, suggests, p. 190.

FIG. 32. UNFINISHED LIMESTONE FIGURE OF A HORSE,
from the Sanctuary of Artemis Orthia at Sparta.
Scale 4/5.

FIG. 33. SERPENT IN LIMESTONE, in the Acropolis Museum.
Missing portion near head restored in plaster. The eye is compass-cut and the
remaining surface carving is done with a knife. The jaws are painted red and
the body is painted with vertical stripes in indigo and red.
Height 23 cm.

Delphi.[1] The Nikandra dedication from Delos, a full-scale work, may to some degree also be looked on as a work of this type.

The Sphinx, No. 68, is an even better instance from these Spartan carvings. Here, by the use of the flat slab, the face of the Sphinx has been forced back into the same plane as the wings, unlike its bronze contemporary equivalent,[2] where the face properly projects. The Sphinx of limestone is virtually finished. Its face is done with skill and in some detail. Dowels for the attachment of a second wing appear at the back. It is indeed a work of no little art, and has been achieved by this fret-work process, which seems to have been an adaptation of relief work so as to transform it into round sculpture.

An exact parallel for the way in which the head of this Sphinx is forced back into the single plane of the relief is to be found in full-scale relief-sculpture in the seventh-century metope of a Sphinx from Selinus[3] and in the companion metope of Europa and the Bull, where both bull's head and the head of Europa are kept rigidly within the limits of the flat surface. Had the Selinus Sphinx had the background cut away and the edges smoothed off it would have emerged as a precisely similar work of art to this small Spartan sphinx. The methods of cutting in the Selinus metopes also accord with the methods of the Spartan reliefs.

A group of reliefs showing heraldic lions, poorly and rapidly cut, (Nos. 41–46) have a special interest in so far as they are thought to be architect's sketches for a possible pedimental group.[4] This is at any rate presumed for the two triangular reliefs of pedimental shape Nos. 41 and 42. No. 45 also is derived from a relief originally triangular in

[1] Modern instances are seen in the work of Mr. Eric Gill. See J. Thorp, *Eric Gill*, pls. 2, 6, 11.

[2] *The Sanctuary of Artemis Orthia*, p. 202, fig. 116.

[3] Della Seta, *Italia Antica*, p. 130. Compare also the later sphinxes from S. Mauro (ibid., fig. 131), which follow exactly the same technique.

[4] Op. cit., p. 23.

shape. But in view of the certain knowledge we have that many if not most of the other limestone plaques are votive it might be equally well assumed that these triangular slabs are also votive, being copies of the standing sculptures of the temple. Against this it may be argued that none of the lion-reliefs have inscriptions. In any case, the technique of this lion-group is identical with that of the horse reliefs. All alike are carved at the same period and by the same kind of artists.

Almost exactly similar in technique to these Spartan reliefs and small sculptures are certain small figures in the round that were found at Naukratis and Kameiros. All are in the British Museum. No. B. 457 is the upper half of a female figure made of fine yellowish limestone. Its present height is 0·145 mm. It is described in the catalogue[1] as 'unfinished', the eyes, ears, diadem, and parts of the head being incomplete in detail. It is of course possible that it is in fact complete and that it was originally heavily coloured with paste. The catalogue refers to the fact that 'chisel marks remain everywhere', but the marks are really those of a knife-blade. This can be seen with particular clearness on the lotus flower which the woman holds in her right hand. No chisel could possibly have been used for such cuts. Similar marks are also visible on the breasts.

No. B. 453, of white limestone, also unfinished, shows the same cuts, and on B. 455 of dark grey limestone, they can be clearly seen. Both are female figures and all three are dated to the second half of the sixth century.

Nos. B. 338 and 339 from Kameiros, both male, show similar knife-markings.

Other Sculptures.

There remain to be considered those figures in hard limestone which are our chief record of large-scale sculpture of the close of the seventh century. All alike seem ultimately to be derived from the Cretan style seen in the Prinias

[1] *Brit. Mus. Cat. of Sculpture.*

sculptures, since this Cretan style can be dated earlier than any other sculptural style in Greece (see pp. 84–5).[1]

Summary.

The technical examination of these earliest Greek statues leads us to conclusions of importance which are both positive and negative.

We find first of all that, on the negative side, sculptors seem not to have employed *for sculptural purposes* either the drill or the punch for the final stages. Unfortunately no half-completed figure of the seventh century survives, and we cannot tell exactly what the primary processes of making a statue were. It seems probable that the block of stone was first sawn into approximately the shape required and then, by a secondary process, chiselled and cut into its final form. The claw-chisel was not used at all at any stage, as is clear at least from the evidence of the Attic series where many unfinished or partly finished surfaces occur on pedimental groups.

On the positive side we can be certain that, after a preliminary sawing of the block of stone destined to become the statue, the detail was chiselled out with a fine chisel and helped with knives of various dimensions. The use of stone-rubbing instruments seems to have been very rare indeed. It can be detected only on some of the Attic figures and only once or twice in the earlier Cretan examples. The use of a rubber seems to have come in for work in soft stone only later, when much work was being done at the same time in marble, and the technique of marble work found its way into poros work. Nor would the stone rubber have been used for anything except detail, since there was no necessity in these soft-stone works to produce a fine surface-finish. Every indication shows that all statues in soft stone were completely covered with paint, either in the shape of a soft wash that just tinted the stone or else as a thick paste that filled up all its inter-

[1] Beazley, *C.A.H.* iv, p. 593

stices. The nature of the stone probably decided the method of painting. While the Prinias statues would probably have been covered with only the lightest of washes, the Attic series, made of coarse stone which was pitted with holes, would have necessitated a thick paint. And it is such a thick paint that in fact survives in many instances in the Attic series.

The only detail that seems to have called for more intricate tools was the detail required on faces and sometimes in decorative detail. The cutting-compass is the only instrument which can be identified in this connexion. But it was widely used. It is seen in limestone sculpture employed for the eye of the Lion No. 4[1] in the Acropolis Museum, for the eyes of the serpents referred to above, for the eyes of the three-headed monster of the Hekatompedon pediment. But it was only used in Crete apparently for architectural detail, as in the border of the horsemen-frieze at Prinias.

The cutting-compass seems, at least on the mainland, to be an instrument taken over from other crafts, chiefly those of the potter and the ivory-carver. The priority of its use by other crafts is proved conclusively by the remarkably clear evidence of the excavations at Sparta, where ivory 'spectacle-fibulae' were found in the geometric strata and then continuously to the strata that dated to the close of the seventh century. The eighth century seems to have been the period when they were most in use. Consequently we can be certain that the use of the cutting-compass antedates in ivory-work its use in stonework, for all spectacle-fibulae of ivory are cut primarily with this instrument.

In ceramic the use of the instrument cannot be proved for certain at a date earlier than the Prinias statues, but it is best seen on contemporary and later terra-cotta architectural fragments from the site of Artemis Orthia.[2] Here a compass that would be better described as an 'incision-compass' is used to describe the double semicircle scales that make the

[1] Dickins, op. cit., p. 76.   [2] Op. cit., pls. xxii–xxiv.

body of the pattern. The radius of the semicircles so described varies from 1·2 cm. to 2 cm.

The instrument used in these architectural ornaments must be a simple development from the compass used in the painting of the concentric circles of Geometric pottery, where one leg of the compass was a point that left its mark on the vase and the other was a pen or brush which described its arcs and circles. The early origin for the compass in ceramic before it developed into an incision-compass is assured and we can without much demur agree to the general assumption that the sculptor did not invent it for use in his own art. The sculptor's cutting-compass was carried on into use in hard-stone sculpture and will be discussed in that context below (see p. 215).

In general, then, it might be said that the earliest Greek stone sculpture uses throughout the technical methods of other materials. Its tools are chiefly those of the wood-carver, with the exception of those additional helps which were provided by the tools of the painter. Soft stone was thus considered simply as if it were hard wood. The old wooden xoana were produced in another material, and the advance from wood to stone was not at first accompanied by any such change as might seem to herald a new era in the art of the sculptor. In fact the sculptor, as the word is properly understood, did not really exist until the advent to fashion of hard stone as a medium. The workers in soft stone were merely developing the craft of the wood-carver and elaborating it with the aid of those advantages of superior tractability and cohesion which soft stone has over wood.

An intermediate stage where all the tricks of wood-carving can be seen in full is found in the very early series of Spartan bone and ivory xoanon figures in miniature. They probably stand for miniature copies of the various larger xoana of Artemis Orthia which stood at Sparta. They show a simple bone cylinder like the section of a tibia, which has been adapted with the aid of a knife and nothing else to the simple requirements of the xoanon type. They illustrate the process of wood-carving being translated into a much harder material. From ivory-carving it was a logical advance to stone. But the material advanced in quality and the technique remained static.

II. HARD STONES

There is no hard and fast chronology for the use of material in the history of Greek sculpture. Indeed, the well-known statue dedicated by Nikandra of Delos, itself immediately derivative from the Cretan style, can be dated certainly to the seventh century by its inscription alone. It is the earliest example of marble sculpture on a large scale that is known in Greece, and its marble is island marble, hard and crystalline, almost certainly that of Naxos. This strange and hieratic figure, resembling the Prinias figures but differing from them in its more primitive or provincial character, does not yet introduce us to the full methods of hard stone technique. The figure must almost certainly have been sawn from a rectangular block of marble. The back of the figure—one face of the block—remains roughly dressed, and it is perfectly clear that the punch was never used to prepare this surface. It looks rather as if it had been hammered with a flat-headed hammer, or else the rough surface at the back may be the actual cleavage surface of the marble. The front of the figure, on the other hand, is smoother and has been finely dressed, but there are few, if any, traces of a process of abrasion with stone tools.

The inscription on the side is clearly cut on a rough surface with an ordinary chisel-blade, and traces of a large blade, perhaps even a plane, are seen on the right and left shoulders and arms. Such paring off of the stone must have given much trouble and required a powerful blade. In effect the whole statue is in a sense transitional from work in soft stone to work in marble, for the tools employed in its cutting are in the main those of the woodworker. There is no trace of systematic punching of surfaces, none at all of the claw chisel, and but little of abrasion and the use of stone instruments. Hence inevitably the character of the statue takes on the nature of flat relief. In effect it is a statue blocked out in relief and thrown into three dimensions by the same process that produced the 'biscuit sculpture' of Sparta. We have not yet arrived at the stage of full three-dimensional sculpture, conceived as such by the artist from the outset.

Two other works of the seventh century of full scale survive—the Dirmys and Kitylos twins from Tanagra and the bust from Eleutherna. But both are in poor preservation and provide us with all too little evidence as to their construction. The Dirmys and Kitylos is made of a rich brown stone full of minute holes, hard and firm, but still classifiable as 'poros' and a little softer than marble. Clear traces of a chisel are seen in the inset corners and on the top of the base between the feet. No other tool seems to have been used for the final processes. There is no trace of a claw chisel. The Eleutherna bust is also a softish limestone, but still not so soft as the sixth-century Attic poros. The hair of the Eleutherna bust at the back has clearly been divided into its rectangles by means of a blade and not a stone tool. It thus falls into line with the Prinias group.

It will thus be seen that marble and hard stone were not, when first used in the seventh century, immediately treated with the technique best suited to such material. There was a definite period of technical transition. Soft stone does not necessarily precede hard stone in date always. It is true enough that most of the earliest Greek sculpture extant[1] is in soft stone, but when hard stones came into fashion they did not oust soft stone from popularity. Indeed in some places, such as Cyprus, the use of soft limestones continued throughout the whole history of sculpture. Even in the

---

[1] There is, of course, an exception in the shape of the Cretan head closely resembling the Prinias and Auxerre heads, which comes from Selinus. It is in white marble, and is on a marble lamp. See E. Gabrici: *Daedalica Selinuntia*, II. 1.

mainland of Greece, where marble was plentiful, its rise to popularity did not drive out of fashion the softer limestone which had been in use generally in Greece. The Attic poros sculptures described above post-date some fine marble sculptures. Poros was even in use at a time when the prevailing Ionic fashions from east Greece had converted Attic artists not only to their own peculiar style of art but also to their favourite material—Parian marble.[1] There is, indeed, every reason to think[2] that the earliest known Attic sculptures were cut in marble. Certainly there are no works in poros from Attica which belong indisputably to the seventh century, whereas there survives at least one splendid example of marble sculpture which belongs perhaps to the end of the seventh century, and certainly to a date hardly later than 600 B.C. This is the impressive head in island marble found in the Dipylon cemetery (Figs. 34–5). It is of a scale slightly larger than nature and is derived from a kouros figure.

The technical processes by which this head was made mark a complete break with the processes by which the soft-stone sculptures either of Crete or of Sparta or of Attica were made.

This Dipylon head is a masterpiece from more points of view than one. It is a masterpiece of abstract art. It is a masterpiece of sombre loveliness, pondered solely in the mind of its maker. But it is also a masterpiece of laborious and painstaking technique of a type new in Hellenic Greece. For almost every detail of this head, except the hair, is achieved by a slow and intricately thought out process of abrasion.

The head is constructed from a rectangular block of Pentelic marble. The frontal view is narrow and slim. The cheeks and side view, on the other hand, are of surprising broadness.

A glance at the outline of the jaw against the neck will show

---

[1] Dickins, *Acrop. Mus. Cat.* No. 50 and p. 88.
[2] Id., Introd., p. 16.

FIG. 34. MARBLE HEAD FROM THE DIPYLON,
National Museum, Athens.

Seventh century. Island marble. The facial curves and
hollows and the eyes are done by abrasion with stone tools.
Scale 1/3.

FIG. 35. PROFILE OF THE DIPYLON HEAD, in the National
Museum, Athens.

The hair-globes are done with a punch only. The ear-grooves and the
eye-grooves are hollowed with abrasive. The line of the jaw is also
abraded. The fillet and necklace are done with a flat chisel.

From a cast.

that it is rendered by a fine broad sweep of line. Close inspection shows that this fine curve is a rubbed curve, the neck having been removed, but only to a slight depth, from the plane of the face by steady abrasion. The face has been perfectly smoothed, but this smoothing could not reach the area between and just below the forehead and temple curls, consequently the line that marks this difference of surface is faintly seen. In the same way the groove of the eyebrows is a groove which has been achieved by a steady process of rubbing with a stone rubber shaped roughly like a pebble. This particular form of hollow groove beneath the eyebrow, above the eye and under the eye is peculiar to Attic work. It is first seen on this head, but lasts almost to the end of the sixth century. It can be seen most clearly in the Berlin Kore,[1] in the Berlin 'portrait' head,[2] in the Attic head in the Louvre,[3] in the Sunium Apollo,[4] in the Moschophoros, and, in reliefs, most noticeably in the 'Hoplite' relief from the Kerameikos,[5] to mention but a few instances. On the other hand, its occurrence in sculpture from other districts is extremely rare.

The Attic artists, in fact, used their abrasive stone on this particular feature in a way which soon became established as a fixed local convention that can almost be used as a criterion by which to distinguish Attic work.

The hair of the Dipylon head, on the other hand, is achieved almost exclusively with the aid of a punch. I can detect no chisel-marks at all among the numerous hemispheres which make up the very conventional hair of this splendid head. Each bulb is carefully picked out with pointed tools. The eyelids seem to have been rubbed into the clear ridges that outline them, though the chisel may have been used for picking out the main lines.

The sides of the nose are, in effect, made by a continuation of the grooves above the eyelids. These two grooves are run

[1] *Antike Denkmäler*, 1929, 11–18.   [2] No. 308, Altes Museum.
[3] No. 3104, Louvre.   [4] No. 2720, Nat. Mus., Athens.
[5] No. 1959, Nat. Mus., Athens.

in a curve downwards to the nostrils. The only certain use of the chisel in the final phases of this head are to be seen on the ribbon that passes round the hair. The flat surface of this ribbon shows the unmistakable marks of a steady flat chiselling.

There is no sign either of drill or compass. The final dull polish of the surface is the polish of abrasion, not the 'dragged' surface characteristic of the late fifth-century sculpture where a metal file was largely used in the last phases of the finishing process.

The ears, extraordinarily formalized into a pattern, which is repeated again in the Sunium Apollo, are simply a pattern made of grooves cut out by a stone tool similar to that which cut the eyebrow grooves.

With this head must be grouped a whole series of small rigid and xoanon-like figures in Pentelic marble, found on the Acropolis. They must all belong either to the last years of the seventh century or to the first of the sixth. They are Nos. 582, 583, 586, 589, and 593, in the Acropolis Museum. All alike are versions of a primitive and simple type of statue, xoanon-like in its simplicity and in its absence of detail from the waist down. Dickins dates them all to what he calls 'the earliest period of Attic art' in sculpture, and this, as we have seen, must belong to the late seventh century, at least in part, and to the early years of the sixth century.

There is little resemblance between these Attic figures and the Cretan statues. There is, perhaps, a similarity of hieratic stiffness, but there the similarity seems to end. All the Attic series are small statues, mostly about half natural scale, with the notable exception of No. 593, which is full scale, and in extremely good preservation as regards surface, although the head of this, as indeed in the case of all the others, is missing. From a technical point of view much can be learned from this full-scale figure, and what is so learnt is more or less confirmed by the other examples, even though they are badly weathered.

FIG. 36. BELT END ON THE TORSO,
Acropolis Museum, No. 593.
From a cast: scale 1/1.

All except No. 589 are of Pentelic marble, from which it may rightly be inferred that Pentelic quarries provided the material for many of the earliest Attic sculptures. The Dipylon head, however, is like the kouros from Sunium, of Island marble.

The exception No. 589 is of island marble and is the work of an Attic artist on imported material.

No. 593 is the figure of a stiff and formal Kore. She holds a pomegranate in the left hand and her right hand holds a ring or wreath. In this there is a marked resemblance, which may nevertheless be fortuitous, to certain early Cretan representations of women holding such wreaths.[1]

The bulk of the surface detail was achieved by a steady process of rubbing with a variety of differently shaped stones so as to achieve the various grooves required.

Specific proof of the use of still another type of abrasive tool is found in the peculiar cross-line pattern at the girdle end that hangs loose on the right side. Here (Fig. 36) the cross-hatched lines have been made with a pencil-shaped stone, pointed and firm in action. The lines cut are hollow grooves, *not sharp incisions*; they have been rubbed, not cut. To make this distinction absolutely clear one has but to compare them side by side with the incisions made, say, on the front of the peplos of the Auxerre statue. Knife-cut and abraded lines will thus be seen to be totally distinct.

The rest of the detail of this torso is achieved almost entirely by similar processes of abrasion. Even the cross-cuts on the locks of hair are so done, and not with either file or chisel.

How the main features that are prominent were achieved is another problem. The pomegranate and the wreath were probably punched out in the rough and then rubbed down to a good surface, detail being added partly with the chisel, partly by abrasion. But in any case these last assumptions are mainly hypothetical, in the sense that they are not capable

[1] E.g., *Ath. Mitth.*, 1906, pl. 23.

N

of final proof, whereas the details of drapery and embroidery are clear beyond dispute. In fact this torso, together with the Dipylon head, can rank among the finest examples extant of sculpture in which the process of abrasion is responsible for the bulk of the final work and so for the artistic skill and effect of the whole.

Following directly on from this early group, which mostly belongs to the late seventh century, or at least about 600 B.C., comes that splendid masterpiece of craftsmanship, the Kore, acquired in 1924 by the Berlin Museum and known to have come from Attica. Here again we see the characteristically deep eyebrow grooves, neatly and perfectly scooped out by abrasion, the hollows under the eyes and the moulding of the face rendered in the same way. Most marked too is the groove of the upper lip which has been rubbed to a sharp edge, the rubbed surface being pressed far into the cheek in an almost disconcerting way. The vertical grooves of the hair are likewise fashioned by a process of vertical rubbing.

It is, in fact, evident that in Attica, perhaps more than in any other place, this technique was used to its full extent in the seventh and early sixth centuries. Unfortunately the gaps in our knowledge of the history of Greek sculpture are so serious that we are unable to explain how such mature and relatively sophisticated masterpieces as the Dipylon head have no antecedents in stone that are as yet known. For they have no parallel except the figures in ivory (see above, p. 46), also from the Dipylon. The latter are earlier in date, but they throw no sort or kind of light upon stone technique, since the manner of their making belongs to the craft of carving in soft materials. At some time in the seventh century in Attica this method of finishing a statue in all its final detail—the main work of the sculptor, that is to say, after the blocking out— almost entirely by the aid of rubbing tools of stone, became the technique of Attic sculptors. Work like the Dipylon head should normally be expected to have had a reasonably long ancestry in stone sculpture. But of that ancestry no trace remains.

Summary.

While the earliest Greek statues are in soft stone there is no certain reason for thinking that there may not be works in marble which have yet to be found which are as early. For there is no hard and fast chronology of material, and soft stone continued in use when marble technique was fully perfected.

The technique of fully developed marble statues is totally and fundamentally distinct from that of soft-stone statues, whose method of manufacture is identical with that of figures carved in wood. The Nikandra figure is almost alone in exhibiting a confusion of the two kinds of technique.

The primary processes of manufacture of the earliest marble figures cannot be fully demonstrated, but it is almost certain that the point or punch was the principal tool employed after the preliminary trimming with a hammer. Various punches would have been used and then the bulk of the detail was carried out by a detailed and intricate use of abrasive stone instruments. All the facial and body refinements and mouldings were so abraded: features, such as eyebrows, ears, jaw-lines, nose-furrows, and drapery were executed solely with abrasives. Detail of drapery that in soft stone had been done with knife or chisel, was done in marble with fragments of emery shaped according to the hollows required. Where in soft stone lines were engraved with the knife, in marble they were engraved with an emery point or pencil, just as, to some extent, they are to-day. Sharp incisions or lines were studiously avoided and broad general effects were magnificently achieved by this laborious and exhausting process of abrasion, partly because greater certainty was attained by means of rubbing at right angles to the stone and partly because longer sweep of line can thus be more adequately achieved. Detail of hair, on the other hand, was almost always done with the punch, and the flat chisel was only used for the most superficial occasional detail, and even such detail was not well executed. The earliest marble statues thus show no trace of claw-chisel, drill, or gouge, and only a minimal use of the flat chisel.

IV

MARBLE SCULPTURE IN THE ROUND
FROM 600 B.C. TO ABOUT 540 B.C.

SOME of the Attic marble figures dealt with in the last chapter certainly belong to the early part of the sixth century. But in type they are derived essentially from seventh-century figures. The Berlin kore, it is true, has a smile in the true sixth-century manner, but her shape and the technical methods by which the detail of her clothing was achieved belong essentially to the earlier period. The absence of fine chisel-work or of occasional gouge-work for detail and the very wide use of abrasive tools in the finishing of all the main detail associate her essentially with work like the Dipylon head.

The primary processes by which works like the Dipylon head were cut are not absolutely certain since we have no unfinished works of the same period by which to judge. But it seems likely that the processes of ordinary sixth-century work of the full archaic period were mainly employed. What these primary processes were has been most fully and accurately explained by Carl Blümel and it is unnecessary to do more than restate the general nature of those processes here. They were as follows:

(1) The block of marble, fresh from the quarry, was first trimmed with a trimming-hammer (see Fig. 56) and then reduced to within a narrow margin of its final surface by the aid of the punch. Various punches were used, starting with a heavy punch and finishing with a finer and lighter one.

(2) This roughened but more or less level surface, which had reached very near the final version, was then carefully worked over. A claw-chisel was used at this stage and also a *boucharde* to a limited extent. But whether the

claw-chisel and *boucharde* were used in the early part of the sixth century involves a chronological inquiry which will be dealt with below (p. 128). Probably only punches were used at first. Later the claw and *boucharde* replaced them.

(3) The statue was now virtually in its final state minus only the detailed carving and the smooth final surfaces which should be devoid of tool-marks. This final surface was achieved by a process of rubbing with stones, first pumice, then harder stones like emery.

It must be assumed in subsequent discussions herein that these three stages of the general process of sculpture were those employed in almost every instance in sculpture of three dimensions from the beginning of the sixth century.[1] Relief sculpture is another matter and will be dealt with separately below.

Blümel has not, however, described the very first stages of statue-making in any detail, and it will be convenient to explain them here as a preliminary to subsequent discussion.

The block of marble was sawn out in the quarry with metal saws, either in the shape of wires or blades, or else dislodged by means of wooden wedges and then sawn on the principles and by the methods which had been in use from the early Bronze Age. The process of the removal of blocks of marble from a quarry can be inferred from the extant traces still visible on the matrices in the quarry-beds in various places in Greece. The process throughout history seems to have been always the same. The *cipollino* quarries of green marble at Karystos in Euboea,[2] the *verde antico* quarries on Mount Mopsion near Larissa in Thessaly,[3] and

---

[1] Regrettably enough there is no phrase in the English language by which conveniently and accurately to describe sculpture in the round. *Rundplastik* excellently satisfies the need in German, *ronde bosse* more ambiguously in French.   [2] Lepsius: *Griechische Marmorstudien*, p. 41.

[3] I visited these quarries in 1917. Pillars of *verde antico* were roughed out in the quarry itself.

FIG. 37. BACK OF THE TORSO OF ATHENA, from the pediment of the Temple of Apollo Daphnephoros at Eretria (now in Chalkis Museum).

The surface finished with a small punch can be distinguished near the shoulders from that worked with a claw-chisel. On the top of the shoulders the clawed surface is rubbed smooth to the final polish with abrasive. *From a cast.* Scale 1/3.

the red-veined marble quarries of Skyros[1] all alike show how marble used in Roman times was removed from its bed. The much more ancient quarries of Naxos[2] show similar evidence for an island marble which was popular only for a limited period in the sixth century.

How far a block of stone from the quarry was sawn into shape in the studio by the artist is another matter. The Dipylon head, as its rectangular structure strongly suggests, looks as if it had been roughly sawn to shape before the final processes were brought to bear upon it. But of this there is no proof, only the suggestively rectangular shape of the head itself which prompts the theory.

But one instrument certainly belongs to the earliest stages of all, when the rough block was being worked into the general form of the statue which it was destined to be. This was the ordinary 'carpenter's square'. The evidence for this is conclusive enough and belongs to what might be called 'descriptive' as contrasted with the 'inferential' evidence of tool-marks. A curious relief carved on the native rock in the hidden Cave of Vari on the south-western foothills of Hymettus shows a 'Selbstbildnis' of the sculptor holding two of the instruments of his art. (Fig. 55). In his right hand is a trimming-hammer and in his left a 'square'. Both are the tools of the first stages of manufacture. The portrait is presumably that of Archedemos of Thera, whose numerous and entertaining inscriptions, all datable to the early years of the fifth century, adorn the walls of the cave.[3] Other sculptural work presumably by him can be seen in the cave, notably a seated kore or goddess in such high relief that it can be considered as a statue in the round. In fact only its back joins it

---

[1] I examined the Skyriote quarries in 1920. They are at the north and south ends of the island.

[2] Blümel, op. cit., pls. 1 and 2.

[3] *A.J.A.*, 1903, pp. 263 ff. At first the 'square' was thought to be a chisel. This identification failed to detect the lower limb of the square. The hammer is a typical trimming-hammer of the type used at all periods by stonemasons and sculptors.

to the native rock. From this as well as from his relief portrait it is justifiable to infer that he worked in a style that was essentially archaic and more akin to the styles of the sixth century than to those of the fifth.

The square would have been used for establishing the frontal and side planes suitable to archaic work and for maintaining the general rectangular masses of the composition. The trimming-hammer was used for the very earliest stage after the final sawing had been finished in the quarry. If there was any sawing of the figure to shape by the artist after the block had reached the studio, it would, on the other hand, probably have been done *after* the trimming.

Blümel's evidence for the main processes of the sixth century is unassailable and, in quantity, more than sufficient to prove his assertions. Nor has any criticism been levelled against his main contentions. The unfinished works of the sixth century speak for themselves, needing only the explanatory annotations given by Blümel.

It remains to consider the main groups of three-dimensional sculpture from different parts of the Greek-inhabited area in order to discover what were the processes by which the ultimate detail was achieved, that is to say Stage (3) of the three stages referred to above (p. 94). The exposition given above of the first two stages is here accepted *in toto* as being the universal practice of Greek sculptors in the sixth century. In Stage (3) the artist had full scope for precisely those variations in detail by which his own regional or personal style was to be made manifest. Once the main technique of sculpture in marble was established in the sixth or perhaps in the seventh century, Greek sculptors adhered to its rules with remarkably little deviation. But as time went on some among them discovered the advantages of using tools not hitherto employed for sculpture; others seem to have invented tools that were altogether new, and others still invented new ways of employing old tools. Added to this there was always scope for sculptors to invent new details for their sculpture as well as to conceive of new forms. Indeed it might be said that the middle of the sixth century, and from then for at least thirty years, sculptors were engaged almost exclusively in the invention of new detail, that was so alluring a task in itself that, in the end, it became almost an obsession. The close of the century marked a brusque move away from this inventiveness in detail to a deeper inventiveness of conception; new forms and attitudes, new compositions and characters were sought for with indefatigable enterprise.

The following discussion will therefore aim at establishing in order of time the new fashions in the execution of detail and the introduction of new tools in the order in which they are introduced. Ancient historians of art were mainly engaged in establishing the various inventions, aesthetic and technical, for which specific individual sculptors were responsible; their pages were paragraphed with 'Primus hic . . .' or πρῶτος ἐξευρών . . . almost ad nauseam. But this venerable cliché reveals the fact that the ancients looked upon a history of art as a process of explanation of the continuous and systematic inventions of artists. And it is precisely that method of inquiry which still can prove most fruitful in our examination of the technical side of Greek sculpture. For by learning what they invented and when, we can get some insight into the aesthetic changes that were going on inside their minds and get some hint of the astonishing fecundity and imaginative power that was behind their work. For technical inventions may revolutionize the whole outlook and capacity of an artist. By the aid of a small invention he may suddenly find that a whole universe of power is opened to him.

The seventh century and the early sixth were a period of calm and slow development from an unknown start. But the second quarter of the sixth century led suddenly to a vivid growth of new vigour both in conception and in execution. Some of this vigour was undoubtedly due to the ability of artists to put old tools to new uses and to adapt conventional technique to innovating style and execution.

The Sculpture of the East Greek Mainland and of the Islands of Naxos and Samos.

It will be seen later that the sculpture made of the peculiar marble found only in the island of Naxos falls directly into the group of works cut in Miletus and Samos and in some other parts of the Ionian mainland.

The earliest works that belong to this group are a series of rather hieratic figures which were found near Miletus. The bulk of them are in the British Museum, but some are elsewhere.[1] With them must be classed a figure, almost identical, recently found near the Heraeum at Samos and the well-known statue of Aiakes.[2]

Of the ten figures of this type in the British Museum found at Miletus one is distinctly earlier than the rest [3] and belongs to about 570 B.C. Eight of the remainder fall into the period 550–530 and the tenth to the close of the century.[4] The new examples from Samos must be classed with those that fall to about 550 B.C., and the two at Istanbul belong to the end of the series.

It will be obvious at a glance that these curious seated figures are in no way so advanced or developed as was contemporary sculpture in the mainland of Greece or in Attica. This is, of course, primarily a question to be discussed by the stylistic experts. But it has some bearing on the technical problems, since it shows that the sculptors of the East were out of touch with the new developments of the West and more hide-bound by Assyrian, Hittite, and Babylonian hieratic influences.

It is not, therefore, surprising to find that they show no trace at all of technical inventiveness. The scope of their technical devices is a bare minimum. Their construction involves the smallest amount of sculptural work (in the sense of such work being a removal of matrix in order to reach the

---

[1] Nos. B. 271–80. See *Brit. Mus. Cat. of Sculpture*, I. i, p. 104. Two are in Istanbul. See Mendel, *Catalogue*, i, p. 570, Nos. 248–9.

[2] *Ath. Mitth.* xxxi, pl. xiv.   [3] No. B. 271.   [4] No. B. 280.

underlying shape) that could be reasonably expected. They have, in short, precisely the hall-mark of that particular form of indolence which was always said to be characteristic[1] of Ionian Greeks.

Unfortunately all are weathered and it is difficult to detect traces of actual tool-work. But it is clear enough that the square block of stone has kept its squareness. The arms and frames of the chairs or thrones on which these ceremonious figures sit involve but a few simple adaptations of the rectangular form of the quarry-block. Punch-marks are particularly evident in the unfinished sides, especially in the case of No. B. 280 from Miletus, where the sides are not even half completed. Most of the detail that goes to any depth is also punch-work and not chisel-work. Signs of the trimming-hammer and also of the heavier punches such as were used in the earlier stages are visible round the edges of the bases.

The long sweeping lines of drapery, sparse and economic, are achieved in the main by abrasion, and the use of a pointed burin-shaped tool of abrasive is definitely indicated by the long parallel striations placed close together which delineate the thin undergarments in Nos. B. 272, 274, and the Samian example. In the others a few widely-spaced lines above the feet, rendered by the same tool, give a more perfunctory suggestion of a soft under-chiton.

In two examples, Nos. B. 275 and B. 277 and to some degree in B. 274 also, the processes by which the panelled sides of the thrones were cut can be very clearly seen. It is important to realize that after the panels had been worked roughly into shape with a punch, or with several kinds of punch, the surface so reached was not smoothed with the claw-chisel but with a flat chisel. The marks of the flat chisel are clear in each case and there was no process of final rubbing with stone. Nor was the claw used even in the latest of the series, No. B. 280. Here the statue remains definitely unfinished and without any final stage of rubbing.

[1] Herodotus, vi. 11, 12.

The marks of a small punch can be seen on the side of the left knee, on the left arm, and on the sides. On the right side the area treated by a small punch can be clearly distinguished from that treated with a large punch. But there is no trace of a flat chisel, perhaps because the final state was not reached at all. The other nine of these seated figures follow very closely one simple system as far as technique is concerned. After the primary processes were achieved with hammer and punch, the final detail seems to have been done on the relief panels at the sides with flat chisel and the body surfaces with a rubber of stone. The implications of this flat chisel work will be dealt with below (p. 127). The face is preserved in the case of B.271 only, but is too weathered to give any clear indications. Possibly the chisel was used on it, but this is not certain.

Statues other than the seated figures of Miletus which throw a considerable light upon the technique of this regional group are as follows:

From Samos (from the excavations at the Heraeum in 1928–30). (*Neue Deutsche Ausgrabungen*, 1930, Pl. 6 and 7=1 and 3 below):

1. A reclining figure leaning on a cushion. From the Heraeum at Samos. In splendid condition.

2. A standing female figure whose right hand clasps part of her chiton; with her feet side by side (Fig. 38).

3. A similar figure to No. 2 with the hand clasping the chiton in the same way but with the left foot slightly forward.

4. A figure similar to Nos. 2 and 3 but very badly weathered.

From Samos (from earlier excavations).

5. The Hera of Cheramyes now in the Louvre, from Samos. In Naxian marble.

From the Acropolis of Athens.

6. No. 677 in the Acropolis Museum. A bust in Naxian marble from the Acropolis.

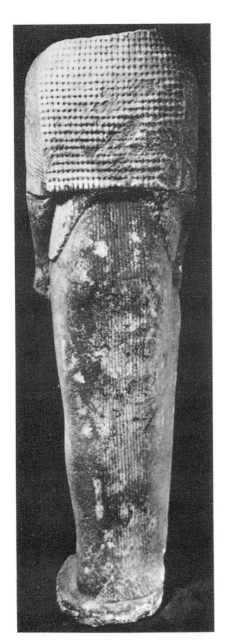

FIG. 38. FIGURE FROM SAMOS

FIG. 39. STRIATIONS ON THE SAMIAN FIGURE, No. 619,
in the Acropolis Museum.
This is characteristic drapery rendered by abrasion.
Scale 1/1.

7. No. 619 in the Acropolis Museum in Naxian marble, which closely resembles both the Cheramyes figure and Nos. 2–4 above.

8. A tripod in Naxian marble, No. 592 in the Acropolis Museum. The bowl of the tripod was supported by three small figures resembling Nos. 2–7 above in appearance, but simpler and rather more hieratic.

This group is a particularly close one. The statues have a most marked and individual style and, even at a cursory glance, a similarity of technique that at once strikes the eye. Leaving discussion of style to others, let us concentrate upon this remarkable identity of technique.

As in the Miletus type of seated goddess, the technique is simple and arresting. But it is infinitely more successful from an artistic point of view. The general effect is one of swiftly-cut sweeping lines of drapery of very great elegance. These are undoubtedly all works of art of a distinguished type, bearing the imprint of a kind of clear-cut abstract treatment of line and mass that is quite unusual. It is important to see exactly how this effect was arrived at.

In this group one is struck at once by the fact that here the style is largely controlled by, if not indeed created by, the technique. An artist or a group of artists of great inventive ability discovered that the cutting of bold striations in clearly marked groups was a powerful aid to a particular style. That particular style was one of sweeping lines and bold effects. Minute chisel-work of the type seen in so many of the Attic korai of the latter part of the sixth century would create a wholly different effect. Here, on the contrary, a simple technique created a simple but strong effect and so achieved a style.

The presence in the group of several examples in Naxian marble, which was an unusual marble in the sixth century, gives us the necessary hint as to the origin of the technique. Naxos, as we have seen (p. 19), had been in prehistoric times the centre of a lively trade in marble sculpture in which the only tool employed was abrasive stone, emery. Naxos had also been from time immemorial the centre of the export trade in emery-stone for all purposes. Naxos was also itself a producer in the sixth century, and perhaps at an earlier date also, of colossal as well as large-scale marble statues, cut in the Naxian marble. The existence of the unfinished colossi at the quarries of Naxos or of the Naxian Sphinx, also in Naxian marble, dedicated at Delphi by Naxians and bearing their name, is sufficient evidence for this.

It remains to see whether the incised striations which we have seen to be peculiar to this group are effected by a chisel or by abrasion. In the Hera of Cheramyes, the Acropolis torso (No. 7 above), and the new statues from the Heraeum at Samos (Nos. 1–4 above), these striations are almost always uniformly placed and spaced. They are also of very great length compared with the drapery-lines on statues from other regions. In nearly every case they extend from the waist to the feet without much deviation from the straight. In the Cheramyes figure they avoid curves with particular attention. But even where, as in the case of a seated figure No. 1, from the Heraeum, the lines are almost entirely curved, the curves are as open and as sweeping as possible.

Now to cut long straight lines over a metre in length by means of a chisel alone is an almost impossible task, if the line is to be perfectly straight. At the best the groove so cut will suffer from a series of uneven edges (see Fig. 66 and p. 140) and at the worst from actual accidental slipping of the chisel. The chisel might, indeed, be used to cut the outline very lightly, and the main cutting could then be done with an abrasive. But it seems to me much more probable that the lines were, in the case of the straight vertical lines, first drawn or faintly scratched on the surface of the marble with the aid of a ruler, and then engraved firmly along that line, with a sharp burin of emery-stone.

Light pressure at first would give the general course which the line was to follow; gradual increase of pressure would deepen the line or groove to the required depth without the smallest risk of unevenness of edge or of accidental slipping. The maximum of safety and the maximum of precision, both qualities very dear to the heart of a Greek craftsman, would so be obtained, and I cannot think it possible that a chisel could have been used. Moreover, any native-born Naxian would naturally use his native emery in the traditional way for stone-cutting, since it would be infinitely cheaper than metal tools and vastly more effective. For emery cuts more quickly than iron.

In short, I detect in these conventional striations of the Naxian and Samian figures a technique peculiar to these two islands which must have been invented in the first instance by the craftsmen of Naxos. The association of this technique, itself a technique of pure abrasion, with the marble of Naxos, and the association of the requisite emery-stone with the same island which had produced the marble seems to me to be a coincidence which is far too striking to be mere accident. Nor can it be accidental that Naxos was renowned in remote antiquity as being the home of marble-cutters who used emery-stone for the cutting of their island marble.

Here, in brief, is the origin and genesis of a technique which, as technique, moulded a style. Its importance is therefore considerable, since the order of control is nearly always the reverse.

Sculpture of the Peloponnese and the West.

Western sculpture in Greece prefers the male to the female form, at least in the early part of the sixth century. This preference naturally led sculptors away from the alluring intricacies of drapery and from the schematic arrangement of the figure which a preference for drapery would make attractive. Peloponnesians, by their early interest in Olympian athletics, were early predisposed to the nude male form.

Consequently, in contradistinction to the work of the Naxian-Samian group, it will be *a priori* likely that form will control technique rather than technique form.

And this, in fact, proves to be the case.

A representative group of early Peloponnesian or western marble sculpture can be selected as follows, for the purpose of a technical inquiry:

1. The head of the cult statue of Hera from the Heraeum at Olympia.
2. The Corfiote pediment.
3. The twin statues of Kleobis and Biton from Delphi.

It is not possible to add to the number, since relief sculpture will be dealt with separately below and it is from relief sculpture that most of our knowledge of early western work is derived. It may be argued that the Corfiote pediment is really relief work, but a glance at the figure of Chrysaor will show that, in the main, the whole pediment is conceived in terms of three dimensions, with a powerful tendency to frontal design which tends to transform what is in effect a series of complete figures into a very high relief group against a background.

The head of Hera is by some placed back into the seventh century, but even though this may be so, it has the qualities of the advanced style of the early sixth century and is not retrospective in character. Most recent views, indeed, tend to place it at the turn of the century, almost at 600.[1]

This strange and compelling head shows with exceptional clarity how far from realism was this early work in the Peloponnese, and yet not so far removed as the Samian and Naxian statues previously discussed. For Peloponnesian artists were, perhaps, the first to use their eyes. At the same time there is nothing about the Hera which suggests a realism in the sense in which that word can be used later.

The stone of which this head is cut is a very hard blue limestone which must rank as marble. Hard limestones are

[1] H. Payne, *Necrocorinthia*, p. 235.

but the unmetamorphosed material which, under great
pressure, might anywhere be transformed into marble. The
lower levels of Mount Pentelicum or of Mount Pangaeum
alike show the material which at the higher levels turns into
fine crystalline marble.

This head, with its wide staring eyes and flat facial surface,
falls into line with the Chrysaor and the Kleobis heads. The
mouths are straight and insensible, the eyebrows uninteresting and scamped in comparison with the finely grooved
Attic brows. But it is of no little interest to find that the
eyeball is cut with a cutting-compass. This tends at once to
place the conception of the face, as these Peloponnesian
sculptors saw it, more on a level with pattern-making than on
that of a realistic conception. For the Attic poros faces are
in some small degree quite definitely representational. In
contrast the Peloponnesian artist is not interested in faces as
individual things but only in faces in general in so far as they
contribute to design. This fundamental characteristic of
western Greek sculpture is perceptible for a long period in
the development of Greek sculpture as a whole. And, in the
same way, the hair is patternized and there is no attempt in
the mouth to express individuality. Attic sculpture even in
the seventh century had patternized its faces, most notably
in the Dipylon head, yet there remained, even at that early
date, some feeling of distinction, some aiming at expression,
which marks out the earliest Attic work from this less lively
Peloponnesian style.

The cutting-compass is, indeed, used in Attica both in the
poros series and also in a hard-limestone head of great beauty
from the shrine of Apollo Ptoïos near Thebes.[1] But it does
not deflect Attic sculptors from their principal aim—individuality.

[1] *B.C.H.* 1907, pl. 21. This small and lovely Attic head is now in the
Museum at Thebes. Its eyes are compass-cut, but the face is so individual
that the tendency to pattern-making does not destroy its charm. In all probability this head is a dedication by one of the Alkmaeonidae or Peisistratidae,
both of which families have left inscriptions at this shrine.

In the Hera head the eyes are large and staring and expressionless. They recur, cut again with a compass, in the Chrysaor of the Corfiote pediment. Here, too, is the same mouth and the same eyebrows, rapidly cut and without much care. The mouth is heavy and expressionless and ends abruptly against the cheeks at each corner.

In the Kleobis and Biton twins the same features again recur, though the actual facial surface does not allow one to judge if the eyes were compass-cut or not. The same eyebrows and mouth are here, but instead of the heavy and staring face of Chrysaor or the stern hieratic features of Hera we have a more human conception.

But all three alike are peculiar in avoiding those surfaces which require the mouldings which only abrasion can give. The final processes of abrasion seem to have been limited to a mere smoothing of the stone surface, and there has been no inventive use of the burin or the pebble-shaped rubber so as to get subtleties such as we see on the face and neck of the Dipylon head or the Berlin kore. There is no love of sharp ridges to catch the light and give clear-cut lines such as are so evident in the two Attic works. The western sculptors, on the other hand, exhibit a roundness and solidity of form both in face and in body, a squareness and structural magnificence which is essentially the quality of great sculpture. But this quality is so uppermost in the sculptor's mind, he is so obsessed by the main sculptural objective that he is after, that he neglects those joys of detailed invention that were to be the great achievement of Attic and eastern art later in the century.

But western art led to the sculptures of the Olympian pediments, while Attic art had to draw fresh inspiration from the Peloponnese before Pheidias could win his fame.

It is sufficient to note, then, that western art avoided those tools that in the east cut with such ease and controlled style with such fatal facility. The Peloponnesian, Corinthian, Eleian or Corfiote—whoever he may have been who carved

Fig. 40. KORE, No. 679, in the Acropolis Museum.

these works, used the greatest of all the sculptor's tools—the punch—to the greatest possible effect, and cut the detail, such as it was, mainly with a chisel. Nor must it be forgotten that Naxian abrasives were more easily come by in the east and among the islands along the Attic promontory than in the west.

The hair of Kleobis and of Chrysaor alike is mostly done with the chisel rapidly and with little interest, and then the artist lavished all his genius upon the swinging rhythms of the body. For this his punch and *boucharde* and hammer served to bring out the rounded masses[1] and the solid strength of the male athletes that interested him.

The use of abrasive stone tools was so incidental in these sculptures that it is worth while to observe exactly for what detail it was employed. The abdominal lines of the Kleobis are lightly but firmly engraved with a stone burin. More noticeably the grooves between abdomen and thighs that join the pubic hair at an angle are rubbed in an unequivocal way, and, more strikingly still, the groove that divides the thighs beneath the genitals is as clearly abraded as is the groove between the legs of a Cycladic idol. In clear contra-distinction the mouth, formalized to a geometric pattern, is cut only with a flat chisel. This can be seen in the accompany-ing diagram, where the corners are seen to be simple triangles and the lips themselves flat surfaces. So, too, with the mouth

Mouth of Kleobis   Mouth of Hera

of the Hera, which is in all respects identical except that it has a fuller lower lip and a curve which contrasts with the straight line of the mouth of Kleobis. The mouth of Chry-saor is less lively and heavier and can be considered as a blend of the other two in type. The perpetuation of this heavy style of mouth in Peloponnesian sculpture is seen at

Cf. Blümel, op. cit., pp. 4 ff.

the end of the century in the face of the warrior recently found at Sparta.[1]

Of other tools the simple drill is used for the centre of the forehead curls of Kleobis. But the thin lines on the hair seem to have been engraved with a burin after having been blocked out into locks with a chisel. The vertical lines on the polos of the Hera are likewise done with a burin.

In the Corfu pediment there is no consistent use of abrasive, and it seems to alternate with the ordinary flat chisel for detailed work without any clear preference. The sandal straps of the Gorgon are worked by means of rubbed grooves, while the maeander pattern is as clearly chiselled by the flat chisel as is the maeander on the Auxerre goddess. The fine curves of the sandal-wings, on the other hand, are done by pure abrasion, while the edge of the drapery near them is chiselled. The artist clearly enjoyed working equally with both tools.

A very clear contrast may be made by comparing side by side the Kleobis figure with the colossal kouros from Sunium. The Kleobis has vigour and life and movement in his body, but a face that is dull and uninteresting. The Sunium figure has immense gusto but fewer sculptural qualities, except in the face. The Kleobis is tense and living, as far as so archaic a statue can claim these qualities; the Sunium figure stands a little awkwardly and seems to be bodily self-conscious, but his face is quick and lively and his clear brows, cut in that fine Attic technique of sharp grooves, gives his face an interest and an arresting quality.

This contrast shows in brief the precise difference between the two main groups. It was a difference which was brought about mainly by the different importance attached by the artists to the tools they used. And so ultimately the difference is one of technique.

Sculpture in Attica.

We have already seen how Attic sculpture in marble made its début suddenly in the seventh century and continued the

[1] *B.S.A.* xxvi, pls. 18–20.

methods and style so formed into the sixth. But the avidity of Attic artists for advance and development soon heralded a change. New ideas were germinating, even among the sculptors of the poros pediments on the Acropolis. Ionian influences of the kind that produced later the Assos pediment, and eastern influences generally, were permeating Attica. An odd head in poros has been rightly singled out by Dickins as an example of almost exclusively eastern fashion in the poros period.[1]

The earliest, and in some ways the most impressive, of the sixth-century korai, apart from No. 593, indicate a clean break with the seventh-century traditions that controlled the style of the Berlin kore, and of such of the earliest marble figures that still reflected seventh-century style.

An interesting group is seen in Nos. 611,[2] a torso; 617, a head; 624, the 'moschophoros' dedication of Rhombos; 678, a fine figure with its head intact; and 679, perhaps the flower of all the korai figures of the Acropolis.

It is as important at this stage of our inquiry to see what tools are omitted as to see what are used.

All these statues alike are Attic to the core, but it is interesting to find that all except 624 are in island and not Pentelic marble. 624, curiously enough, is in grey Hymettan and not Pentelic marble.

The foreign marble, imported to Attica for Attic artists, suggests an influence from eastern regions, presumably from the islands. However this may be, the main structure and appearance of the statues is Attic, in so far as we are able to isolate a definite character distinctively Attic. More clearly, we might say that the style already perceptible in the Berlin kore and in the earlier poros figures is here merely developed and not drastically changed.

No. 679 gives us the clue to the technique of the whole group. It is a statue in perfect condition, as far as an ancient statue can be. It lacks but one arm and one foot and other-

[1] No. 50, p. 88.   [2] Dickins Catalogue under these numbers.

wise is in what might almost be called mint condition. Probably it stood under cover after its dedication, and the eighty years or so during which it was seen and admired before it finally was buried in the rubbish cleared from the Acropolis after the Persian catastrophe, seem to have done it no harm. It has hardly any traces of weathering, and its lines and details are as fresh as when they were first cut. I know of no more perfect example of an ancient statue to serve for a technical analysis (Fig. 40).

The structure of the statue is rectangular and reminiscent of quite ancient forms. This may, perhaps, be looked on rather as a personal preference of the artist than as any definite tradition, for earlier korai of the type of No. 593 are not so rectangular. The tools used in the final and most intricate processes are as follows:

The flat chisel. This has been used for the facial detail, as far as can be seen, for eyelids and mouth.

The gouge. Three distinct types of gouge have been used. Their dimensions were as follows:

A   B   C

Gouges A and B were used for cutting at right angles against the stone on the back hair. The zigzags of the locks falling down the back are so cut (see Fig. 41).

Gouge B was used for the lines on the surface of the locks of hair which fall over the shoulders in front. The locks themselves may have been blocked out with a chisel, but the striations of hair are done with this very small gouge, with the utmost care.

(Gouges B and C are of a type more commonly used in wood-carving. For a gouge must have a very open curve in stonework or else it easily breaks in use. Gouge B has therefore been very lightly used for merely paring away the surface. Gouge A has been used for quite heavy work and used boldly.)

Fig. 41. HAIR AND LEFT EAR of No. 679 in the Acropolis Museum.
The arch-shaped locks of hair on the right of the photograph were cut with a
gouge. This tool was used to cut the hollows of the arches, more or less at right
angles to the marble.

Scale 1/1.

FIG. 42. LOWER PART OF THE UNDER-CHITON of No. 679
in the Acropolis Museum, with fold of the peplos.

The wavy grooves here are cut with a 'bull-nosed chisel' not with a gouge. This
is plain from the nature of the striations of the grooves.

Scale 1/1.

The 'bull nosed chisel' (see below, p. 192). This tool was used for the ripples of the under-chiton, where it shows below the peplos by the feet (see Fig. 42). Its dimensions can be estimated roughly thus ⌒⌒.

The simple drill. A large and strong drill has been used for structural purposes in the dowel of the left forearm and right hand. A very small drill has been used to bore the lobes of the ears. Otherwise there is no drill-work at all for the finishing of the statue. It is as yet a tool which has no artistic use.

Abrasive tools. These have clearly been used for designing the sharp frontal folds of the peplos, and for the folds along the sides. The general surface effects are wholly abraded on the smooth faced garments.

But most remarkable of all is the way in which the girdle is rendered. The falling girdle straps are done by a careful process of rubbing away at the sides of the strip which was to stand out as the girdle end (Fig. 43). It is thus thrown into false relief by paring away the true surface on each side. This process we have already seen in the case of certain knife-cut primitive reliefs in soft stone (pp .35 and 68 above) at Prinias and Mycenae, and again at Sparta. It is a method which any artist may invent at any period, but it is not a widely-used method at any time. Among the korai it is rare.

These are the places where the certain use of these tools can be inferred. No doubt they were used in other places as well, but it would be wiser to limit ourselves to the known areas.

The rest of this group follow the technical methods of this splendid statue, though in some respects the Moschophoros dedication of Rhombos has some unusual qualities, to which Dickins [1] has already called attention. Thus the eyes are rendered in a way which suggests the influence of an Egyptian convention. That Egyptian style and subject were practised

[1] Dickins, op. cit., p. 159.

at Athens at this period is clear from the two statues, Nos. 144 and 146, both in Pentelic marble and both contemporary with this group. The eyes of the Moschophoros furthermore are hollowed for insertion of other material, a practice not met with in Attica until the close of the century. But the main technical qualities of this group are seen in the way in which the back of the calf is carefully abraded and in the very clear eyebrow grooves which we have already seen to be characteristic of early Attic work in hard stone. Many surfaces of the Moschophoros exhibit traces of the tools used before the final smoothing. The hollows of the legs of the calf show very clear punch marks made by striking at direct right angles to the stone. The back of the calf shows chisel-marks. But nowhere, even on the basis, are there any traces of a claw-chisel.

The next group, in chronological order, from which it is possible to make important technical deductions is the largest of all. It consists of those korai which Dickins classified as of the 'full Chiot style'. Another basis of classification is that which isolates the group on grounds of general structure and treatment of drapery. The group is not definitely limited to a fixed number of works, but the following can be taken as representative of the whole: Nos. 594, 613, 670, and 675. The group can be largely increased, but I have selected these particular examples because they illustrate the technical processes with greater precision and clarity than the remainder.

No. 594 is a torso which Dickins describes as 'of the period of greatest Ionian delicacy and elaboration'.[1] No. 670, one of the finest and best-preserved of all the korai, is said by Dickins to belong 'to the period of direct Chiot importation'. No. 675, perhaps the best preserved of the smaller korai with a surface almost as fresh as if it had just been cut, is said by Dickins to exhibit 'all the characteristics of Chiot art' and to be 'one of the clearest instances of direct importation'.

[1] He also remarks that 'the drill is used throughout'; but this is not so.

FIG. 43. BELT-ENDS from No. 679, in the Acropolis Museum.
The striations of the abrasive which was rubbed on each side of the belt
are here clearly seen.
Scale 1/1.

However this may be, we are clearly in the presence of a homogeneous group so that we are in a position to establish technical inferences as to the whole of the group.

The first important fact, upon which Dickins largely relies for his theory of importation, is that all are in island marble. But the most important quality they all have in common is a negative one—the complete absence of drill-holes for sculptural purposes. This at once brings them into line with the earlier Attic series in which the drill was not used, the series of which No. 679 is the criterion. But this later group differs from the other in advancing in the direction of complicated drapery cut in much higher relief. The earlier group had an affection for flatness both of drapery and of figure (a tendency which reappears in great vigour in the early fifth century). And in flat treatment of drapery the use of a drill is unlikely; there is little that it can do to help. But in these more advanced figures the drill might in many details have been of great advantage especially in the case of No. 594. But it is not in fact employed at all. This is of the greatest importance, since it shows that the drill had not yet come into fashion in Athens as a sculptor's tool by the time these figures were made. Accepting Dickins's dating, we should date them to the period 540–530, when the Ionic tendencies of Peisistratus and his love of importing foreign influences were most marked.

While the drill is not used in the sculptures of this group there is, on the other hand, recourse to other tools such as the gouge and the flat chisel for the rendering of all sharp detail on the edges of drapery and on hair, as well as in the facial features. The main sweeping lines of drapery, on the other hand, are still most manifestly done with the older methods of abrasion. There is no change in the uses to which abrasive tools are put. Indeed it seems that every ingenuity was employed to take the fullest advantage of the varied purposes to which abrasive could be put. The advantage of stone tools is that they can easily be selected or shaped to the purposes in view. Metal tools can only take certain shapes, and those shapes can only be changed with considerable labour. Fragments of worked or unworked emery or other abrasive can, on the other hand, be chosen to suit the precise intention of the sculptor.

A second group of this more advanced period consists of Nos. 671, 672, 674, 676, 683, 685, and 687. This group also has the common quality of dispensing with the drill for sculptural purposes. The group is, however, distinct from the other group in that Pentelic marble is often used instead of island marble. Thus Nos. 671, 676, are of the local material, and no single example in the group can be singled out for such specific classification as 'Chiot' or 'imported' on grounds of style. All alike, though they vary enormously in character and appearance, have the one common quality of seeming to be local attempts by Attic artists, whether in imported or in local material, to achieve the more finished style of the 'Chiot' sculptors. Nos. 676 and 683 are notable instances of this 'copyist' tendency; in these two cases, indeed, it is the only possible basis upon which to explain their unusual, and in No. 683, definitely ugly, appearance. Their technique is excellent, their appearance unimpressive. Surely so bizarre a combination is exactly what one would expect in the work of a sculptor whose training was perfect but whose inspiration was derived from the work of other artists greater than he.

Now in all the statues in this group the drill is sedulously avoided and the main surface detail and general moulding done in the same traditional way with the aid of flat chisel and abrasives.

The justifiable inference from this is that the drill did not come into use at the time when the 'Chiot' sculptors of Attica were cutting their greatest masterpieces. The dating of the korai of the Acropolis is still open to dispute, but few would, I think, venture to date the more finished masterpieces of the 'Chiot' group much later than 530 or 525, and

the second group of the 'copyists' would be roughly contemporary. It might perhaps be safer to say that the drill is
not a sculptors' tool in Attica, in the sense that it is regularly
used together with their other tools, until after 520 B.C. And
this is an important conclusion.

But before we can ascertain the place and time of the
origin of the use of this instrument, it is essential to look at
other sculpture outside Attica of the same general type and
in the same style as the 'Chiot' group. Unfortunately there
is all too little to serve for comparison, for the bulk of the
available comparisons are in relief and, as will be seen later,
relief cannot serve finally as the criterion by which to judge
of the technique of sculpture in the round.

Three archaic korai from Eleusis, Nos. 24, 25, and 26 in
the National Museum at Athens, must, of course, rank as
Attic work. Their comparison is useful. In No. 25 there is
no trace at all of underdrilling of the drapery, which is
relatively flat. In No. 24, which is the only one of the three
in which the head is preserved, the lines of the lower
drapery are very evidently rubbed both with grooves and
with thinner incised lines. In each case the work is abrasive
work. In No. 26 the under-chiton is shown by a series of
wide grooves, each carefully gouge-cut: between the grooves
is a ridge caused by the leaving of the original surface. This
ridge is in turn carefully incised with a chisel, in long lines
which are not very steady. This method of rendering soft
drapery is not uncommon in works of this period. There
is no trace of the drill.

In other regions the korai from Cyrene [1] and two others
from the Marmara coast near Perinthos [2] have their drapery
so remarkably flatly rendered that there was no scope at all
for drill work.

The frieze of the Siphnian Treasury at Delphi is in such

---

[1] *Notizie archeologiche sulla Tripolitana*, 1915, No. 4, figs. 59, 60.

[2] Pelekides, Θρᾳκικά, 1928; Μνημεῖα τῆς Θρᾴκης, pp. 5 ff., and *Jahrb.* xxiii,
Beibl., p. 145 (Kalinka).

high relief that some comparisons can be made with the
Attic groups which it resembles in style. Here, however, the
drill makes its début. It is used with extreme caution and
very rarely. It is used for the undercutting of the drapery
folds of the Artemis and again on the pedimental relief in the
same way in the drapery of the Herakles.

The winged figure found at Delos, often associated with
the name of Archermos, is, of course, earlier than our second
group of Attic korai and perhaps contemporary with the first
group, of which No. 679 is the type example. This figure was
achieved without any recourse to the drill and with the minimum of decorative adjuncts.

From an examination of these groups it is reasonable to
come to the following conclusions:

1. The earliest Attic marble korai of the sixth century,
with the Berlin statue as the best instance, avoid detailed
drapery and adhere closely to the technique established in
the seventh century.

2. The next group, with No. 679 as the standard type, is
more inventive and puts the accepted tools and methods to
more intricate uses. The approach of influences and new
ideas from the island schools is felt rather than expressed.
It is seen in a diminution of that sombre and more hieratic
appearance which distinguishes the works of the seventh and
early sixth centuries, and in a certain elegance and, as in
the case of 679, exquisite simplicity which is new to Attica.
None of the earlier group can conceivably be described as
'exquisite'. Most of the group associated with 679, with the
notable exception of the Moschophoros, can certainly
claim that the term should in some way be applied to
them.

3. The increase of detail and of an absorption in it stamps
the 'full Chiot' group as being inspired with a wholly new
feeling. But, as yet, there is no trace of new instruments or
new technique. They have simply developed the old methods
to perfection. The gouge, as we have seen, and the flat

chisel and 'bull-nosed' chisel, were in full use when No. 679 was cut. The same tools are employed more and with greater assiduity in the 'full Chiot' group, but in no new way.

4. The Attic artists, native born, attempt to emulate the island artists, sometimes with success, sometimes without. They, too, use exactly the same tools and methods but lack something of the inspiration of the island sculptors.

5. Elsewhere, less invention is seen than in Attica in the works of island and east Greek artists. Drapery seems flatter and less entertaining. But at the close of the period when island artists seem to have been active, the drill was brought into use for very minor detail of drapery.

6. The chronology of technique over this period must of necessity be without exact precision. But it seems that somewhere about 530–525 the drill began to be used. During the ensuing quarter of a century its use increases, as will be seen later. The claw-chisel remains a difficult tool to date. Its traces are not seen on unfinished areas of works of the first half of the century and, while instances to the contrary may be discoverable, it seems likely that it was not much employed before the middle of the century. Indeed, it is possible that it accompanied the drill and came into use at the same time. The sculptor of the Moschophoros did not use it at all.

In effect, from 600 to 530 sculptors merely developed the technique already used in its broad outlines in the seventh century.

7. Here, as in the Samo-Naxian group of sculptures, the style is largely controlled by the technique. The extensive use of stone abrasives and the minimal use of the flat-chisel, originated in the seventh century and developed with greater elaboration in the early sixth, has tended towards flattened surfaces and smoother mouldings of the main structure. No. 679 is typical of the fullest possible and most successful development along these lines. In its combination of suaveness and severity this particular mode of surface treatment can

be considered as one of the most effective and beautiful ever invented by the Greek sculptor. In effect, as we have seen from previous chapters, it is a normal development from what in origin are the methods and technique of the Stone Age, perpetuated and adapted to the needs of a perfected and sophisticated culture. To-day there has been no supersession in sculpture of these Neolithic methods. Their effectiveness has not yet been surpassed by any of the inventions of a mechanical age.

But in the sixth century, after a time, there arose a demand for greater complexity in ornament and drapery in the carving of statues. Sculptors and their customers discovered in the intricacies of Ionian garments a new source of pleasure, perhaps to the detriment of invention in the larger sense of new attitudes and new compositions. For a decade or so after 550 we find a concentration of interest in the drapery detail of statues which leads in turn to a gradual increase of relief and an abandonment of the flatness of the preceding technique. But at first the older methods were still used and the higher relief was achieved merely by an elaboration of the old technical processes. The last group dealt with above was achieved without recourse to any new tools.

But now the new demands for higher relief and new effects at last introduced a new tool—the simple drill. This instrument we can consider as having four possible forms, all of which were known to Greek lands from the Middle Minoan period at least, though only for structural purposes in sculptural stonework or as the tools of the gem-cutter.

These four forms are as follows:

(1) The auger-drill, used like a bradawl by hand-pressure and hand-revolution. Small shallow holes could be rapidly cut by it.

(2) The carpenter's drill, or brace-bit. This was so used that the pressure came from the weight of the body, the user leaning or pressing against the knobbed end. The revolution of the drilling point was done by turning at any pace

required the metal crank which joined up the drilling point with the knobbed handle against the chest. The action was simply that of the driving crank of an engine of a ship, the drilling point corresponding to the propeller-shaft and propeller.

(3) The bow-drill. There might be several variants of this, but the principle is that which revolves the 'propeller shaft' of the drill not with a crank, but by means of a wheel or its equivalent which was structurally part of the main shaft itself. Round this wheel, which was grooved, there was run a string or strand of gut attached to a bow. By holding the bow in the hand and pulling it backwards and forwards, the gut would revolve the wheel of the 'propeller' and so the drilling end would turn backwards and forwards at a very great speed, so giving an enormous penetrative power.

A competent artist could either use the bow in one hand and hold the drilling point on to its objective with the other, so working the bow at will, or else he could concentrate all his energy on directing the drilling point and leave the manipulation of the bow to his assistant. Gem-cutters, since they used relatively small bow-drills, could control both processes at the same time. A good example of such drilling operations can be seen on an early Greek gem (Fig. 81).

There need be, of course, no limit to the size of such drills short of what could be actually man-handled. They could vary from the great pole with which Odysseus bored the eye of the Cyclops, his men working the 'bow-string', down to the minute drill with which the eye of a stork was cut on a gem of the fifth century.[1]

(4) The single-handed bow-drill. There is no definite evidence to show that this was in use in antiquity, but its construction, being a simple common-sense variation of the construction of the double-handed bow-drill, involved

[1] As in *Brit. Mus. Old Cat. of Gems*, No. 121, *New Cat.* No. 553.

no difficulty to an ingenious mind. This type of drill is to-day largely used by gem-cutters and metal-workers

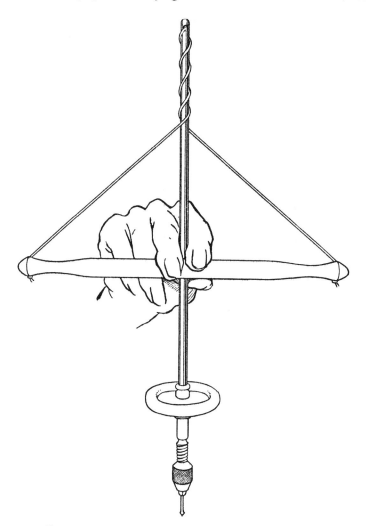

FIG. 44.   MODERN SINGLE-HANDED DRILL

(Fig. 44). It is used in one hand, while the other is free to hold or move the object drilled. The revolution of the strand which revolves the drill is obtained by a vertical movement of the hand on the drill shaft. This drill was known as a sculptors' tool in Italy in the 13th century.

It remains then to examine those archaic sculptures of the sixth century in which the drill now appears as a tool essential for the cutting of detail which was itself an integral part of the design and composition.

V

MARBLE SCULPTURE IN THE ROUND FROM ABOUT 540 B.C. TO ABOUT 475 B.C.

Early use of drill. A large and interesting group of the korai of Attica can be assembled in which the use of the drill can be seen, not merely for occasional undercuts or incidental detail, but for the main construction of the detail of drapery. Nos. 615, 680, 681, 682, 684, and 694 are the best examples, though by no means the only korai to exhibit the use of this tool.

Of these No. 682 is certainly the earliest. It is in the full style of the island sculpture. It is also one of the largest of all the korai. A study of its technique is the more important.

A drill has been used thoughout with very great care and diligence, but only for the undercutting and the folds of drapery and sparingly even for that. Possibly more than one drill was used, but the only drill that can be safely reconstructed from the extant drill-holes measures in diameter about 2·5 mm. thus [1]: ●

Nos. 615, 680, 684 are all of the class called by Dickins 'Attic-Ionic', that term indicating a greater adaptation by native Attic artists to the new style suggested to them by the island artists. As such this class belongs to the period 525–500.

No. 681 is the famous Antenor kore, datable almost certainly to the decade 510–500, since it is improbable that an artist employed by the Alkmaeonidae would have worked in Athens under the régime of their enemies the Peisistratidae. Nor is it likely that Antenor would have carved a group of Tyrannicides if he had been a protégé of the tyrants. The

---

[1] It must be remembered that the drill-hole is inevitably larger than the drill in diameter, and further allowance must be made for the axial swing of the drill, used by hand, which tends to make the drill-hole conical in shape. The diameter of the end of the hole is alone a criterion by which to estimate the diameter of the drill.

Fig. 45. KORE BY ANTENOR, in the Acropolis
Museum.

FIG. 46. DRAPERY ON THE RIGHT FRONT OF THE KORE
BY ANTENOR in the Acropolis Museum.

The drill-holes for undercutting folds of drapery are large and numerous.

Scale 4/5.

further probability that he was concerned with the execution of the Delphian pediments, which seems most probable when the style of the pedimental statues is compared with that of this kore, suggests that he was indeed in exile from Athens before 510.

In the 'Attic-Ionic' group the drills employed are sometimes as small as or even smaller than that used in the purely island kore No. 682. Thus in No. 680 it is a trifle smaller and used only for undercutting. In No. 615 it is small and skilfully employed. But in No. 684 it is larger, though not as large as that used in the Antenor kore. The chisel and gouge are used no less and no more than in the full Chiot period. In No. 680 the folds on the shoulders are clearly cut with a chisel; in No. 684 a small gouge is used for the three lines immediately below the waist.

Full use of drills. Antenor's kore No. 681 (Figs. 45–7) shows not only a very extensive use of the drill for every conceivable place where a drill could be used in the drapery, but it shows that the drill was as large as a sculptor's drill conveniently could be. It measures no less than 8 mm. in diameter thus: . In No. 684 the drill is not so large, but it is at the same time as extensively used. There are, indeed, no other archaic statues in which the drill is so evidently used by the sculptor as these two. No. 684 can hardly date much before 510 and may indeed be as late as 500.

In No. 694, a torso of Nike, which can be considered as still in the tradition of the korai, we find the use of the drill carried over into the fifth century. The drapery is flatter than in the Attic-Ionic series, and the drill both smaller and less used.

It remains to see how the drill was employed in sculptures of the same period from places other than Athens and Attica.

The smallest drill, which, as we have seen, coincides with the earliest type of drill to be used, has already been noted as very sparingly used on the frieze of the Siphnian Treasury and on the pedimental relief of that building. But the type of drill used in the Attic sculptures of the last quarter of the sixth century is something new in the répertoire of sculptors' tools. It is a large and heavy instrument that is used on all possible occasions. With it were used, no doubt, a series of smaller drills as well.[1]

The most notable example from outside Attica of sculpture in which the same type of heavy drill is used as that seen in the work of Antenor is the group known as Theseus and Antiope, and the torso of Athena from the pediments of the Temple of Apollo Daphnephoros at Eretria.

In the Athena the drill is used extensively on the drapery on the left side of the figure, particularly for piercing underneath folds. The mouth of the Gorgon's head on the Gorgoneion is cleared by the drill at the corners and, incidentally, it appears that the drill was used rather clumsily, for the side of the Gorgon's tongue is pierced with a drill-hole. The drapery on the right arm also shows heavy drilling.

In the Theseus and Antiope marks of the drill can be seen in the ears and also generally on the drapery.

The pedimental archaic figures of the kore type from the Temple of Apollo at Delphi all alike show intensive use of a very large drill. This strengthens the attribution made on other grounds[2] of these works to Antenor or his school.

The kore with transverse folds of drapery across the breast[3] has every fold of drapery heavily underdrilled. In one there are extant twelve large drill-holes of approximately this diameter ● . The holes are conical, suggesting that the drill had a fairly sharp point. The diameter of the holes is almost identical with those on the Antenor figure, and in no other archaic kore yet discovered are similar holes found.

---

[1] The central Ω fold at the back of the Antenor kore has been hollowed out with a smaller drill measuring 5 mm. in diameter. Three holes made by it are clearly seen inside the fold.

[2] Hinted but not stated by Poulsen, *Delphi*, p. 154.

[3] *La Sculpture grecque à Delphes* (Picard et de la Coste-Messelière, 1929), pl. xiv (right).

The drapery lines, as in the Antenor kore, are done by strong and clear abrasion and not with the chisel. The locks of hair which hang over the shoulders are filed across horizontally with an abrasive stone (or possibly, though not probably, with a heavy metal file). This again brings it into close analogy with the Antenor kore, which has precisely the same locks rendered in the same way.

The other Delphian pedimental kore,[1] which is better preserved and more complete, has the same drill-holes and exactly the same filed hair-locks.

Both in common have their under-chiton rendered in long sweeping lines as in the Antenor kore.

The acroterial figure,[2] which was winged, shows the use of a fairly heavy drill in the drapery folds, but the drill is not so large as that used on the preceding two figures or in the Antenor kore. The hair is filed in the same way as the other two, but the grooves are smaller. The rest is abraded. The differences, in fact, are differences of degree rather than of quality. All three are certainly in the manner of the Antenor kore.

Decline of use of drill. After the turn of the century, the drill, so extensively used from 510 to 500, seems to fall out of fashion. Why this is so it is difficult to say. The tendency towards a flatter style in drapery and the loss of interest in drapery as such, which is evident in works like the Nike No. 694, made it hard to find opportunities for using the drill at all. It was the change of style which excluded the use of the instrument—a reversal of the situation in the Samo-Naxian school, where it was the technique which conditioned the style.

Consequently draped figures of the kore type which belong to the period 495–475, avoid the use of the drill completely. The Euthydikos kore, No. 686, the similar smaller kore No. 688, and the recently discovered flying figure from Eleusis, sometimes called Persephone, all alike

[1] Ibid. (left).   [2] Ibid. (centre).

avoid the drill. Their drapery is simple, smooth and flat, a reversion in style to the drapery of the earliest Attic work in island marble of which No. 679 is typical. A figure of a kore type of about 475 or even later, probably made in Sicily and now in the Barracco Collection,[1] also falls into this group.

But if the drill was definitely abandoned for a time, as a reaction perhaps against its excessive use at the close of the sixth century, its value is not forgotten. The group of works which can for convenience be associated with the school of Kritios and Nesiotes seem to have used it in the most careful and eclectic way. But its use is relegated almost back again to its old status of a structural instrument. It is used solely in the hair for incidental purposes. Thus it is very slightly used on the hair-rolls of the Kritian youth, No. 698 in the Acropolis Museum. It is also used for piercing the centres of forehead curls in the Este head.[2]

The same use for forehead curls continues into the Olympian pedimental sculptures, where it is so used on the head of the Lapith bitten by a Centaur[3] and on the curls of Sterope and on the Apollo. It is also used on the beard and hair of the Seer (Fig. 48). On the whole I am inclined to think that this usage of the drill is more frequent with Peloponnesian sculptors than with Attic, for there is no trace of such drill-work in head No. 698, which is contemporary with the early work of Kritios.

Claw-chisel. The use of the claw-chisel is a question which demands a certain scrutiny. From Blümel's researches it might be supposed that it was in regular use from the earliest archaic times. But in fact the earliest unfinished work which Blümel himself describes does not show its use. Thus his No. 2, an unfinished torso of the beginning of the sixth century, has no trace of the claw and was worked solely with

[1] No. 76 in the Museum.

[2] *Jahrb.*, 1920, Pl. v. I have examined this head in detail and feel convinced that it is an original and not a copy.

[3] Blümel, fig. 16. This was, of course, a very ancient practice; it is seen on the Kleobis head, to mention only one early instance.

FIG. 47. DRAPERY OF THE KORE BY ANTENOR

The drill has been extensively used for undercutting the drapery. The vertical lines of drapery, on the other hand, are rendered by simple abrasion; the 'fading-off' of the lines at the top is characteristic of this technique.

Scale 1/5.

FIG. 48. THE HEAD OF THE 'SEER' AT OLYMPIA
The central points of each curl are drilled.

punches and abrasives. Nor has the colossal Kriophoros from Thasos any trace of claw-work (Fig. 59). It is punch-worked. This I believe to have been the universal method of the early archaic period. The claw is nowhere used in soft-stone carving, mainly no doubt because the traditions in such work were those of the carpenter and woodworker. But it comes into use fairly early in the century, perhaps before the drill. Its characteristic marks are seen in Blümel's No. 3, a bust from Miletus, now in the Ottoman Museum at Istanbul. It is also clear enough in the case of the unfinished head at Munich, of unknown provenance, Blümel's No. 6. Both these belong, I think, to the middle of the sixth century, and both are east Greek in style. The claw is also used extensively on the parapet edges of the Sphinx tomb, B. 290, in the British Museum from Xanthos, but it is not seen in the earlier Branchidae figures. It may prove that the claw is a tool of east Greek origin, since its appearance at Athens or in the Peloponnese cannot yet be established for a very early date. At the same time this may be due to the lack of sufficient examples of unfinished work. At Athens the earliest indubitable instance of its use that I can discover is on the marble Hekatompedon pedimental figures, the Athena and the Giants, which can hardly antedate 520 B.C. But here the claw-work is considerable and detailed, and it is used with experience and knowledge that presuppose some years of use. More than one type of claw was used. The following marks show both the width of the teeth of two claw-chisels and the width of the chisel blade. Others may have been used, but these are the only two of which I can be absolutely certain.

a   b

It will be evident that the two tools indicated by these marks are both larger and finer than most of the claw-chisels used to-day. I know of no modern sculptor who uses a claw so finely toothed as b. The claw most commonly used by Michelangelo is more like a. His numerous unfinished works enable one to see very clearly what his tools were. His medallion of the Virgin and Child, now in the Diploma Gallery of the Royal Academy, shows the use of two claw-chisels, of which one had teeth each about an eighth of an inch wide and the other a sixteenth of an inch. The second would have been not unlike b above, but not quite so fine. Still it is of no little interest that Michelangelo employed, unknowingly, the Greek method of using two claw-chisels.

So far as any generalization is safe in the matter of the claw-chisel, I should feel inclined to say that it did not come into use until shortly after 550 B.C., but that, once in use, it was never at any subsequent period discarded for working on sculpture in the round. Within a few years of its discovery it was found that more than one claw-chisel should be used, the coarsest coming first and the finest last. The finest of all produced a surface which it is difficult at times to distinguish from a roughly abraded surface.

Influence of bronzework on stone. Abrasion as one of the most important processes in the making of a statue is still universal. But the broad wide areas of abrasion which formed one of the principal features of the early sixth-century sculpture were abandoned at the beginning of the fifth. I think that the growth of bronzework and the making of statues on a large scale in bronze affected the style of stone sculpture. The hair, for instance, of all male statues of the period 520–475 is cut carefully with a chisel in parallel striations. There is no more of the subtlety of the island korai. The chisel alone is used on hair, whereas in the korai the hair is often rendered with a chisel used in several ways, aided by a gouge and helped at times by an abrasive stone. The Peloponnesian styles of the decades each side of 500 B.C. tend to use the flat chisel only. An instance is the 'Strangford Apollo', where the hair is typical chisel-work. A more austere note has crept into sculpture, and the *finesse* of previous generations is abandoned in favour of a larger and more sculptural devotion to form and mass—a concentration of interest which in a very short space of time flowered into the masterpieces of the Olympian pediments. The hair of the 'Strangford Apollo' and similar figures suggests the influence of the bronzeworker's burin and solid gouge (see below, pp. 230 ff.).

Rash generalizations about the supposed influence of bronzework on stone sculpture should, however, be avoided. Undoubtedly the great popularity of bronze-casting at the end of the sixth century B.C. helped stone sculpture to expand and extend its attitudes. Marble-cutters clearly attempted to rival bronzeworkers in the new freedom of attitude which bronze allowed, though they could never hope to attain to the freedom and extension of limbs of statues like, say, the Harmodios and Aristogeiton and the Artemisium Zeus in the fifth century. But undoubtedly bronzework enabled marble-workers to get out of the rut of the rigid standing or seated figure and led them to experiment.

It is often asserted that the curls on the forehead of the type seen in the heads of the Aeginetan pediments, or, to take a good instance, on the Eretrian Theseus, round and rather conical in shape, are derived from bronzework. The best instances in bronze are to be seen in the frontal curls of the bronze bearded Zeus from Olympia,[1] or of the Piombino bronze in the Louvre. But it would be extremely hazardous to say which was derived from the other, or whether, indeed, both were not simply examples in two materials of a common fashion of the time.

Support for the bronze origin of this type of curl may be obtained from the analogy of thirteenth-century Siamese bronze heads of Buddha. For the stone heads copy with immense labour what had been much more easily done by a highly specialized and admirable bronze casting. The small

[1] Athens Nat. Mus. No. 6440.

cones that cover the bronze heads, as curls of hair, are meticulously rendered in the stone, and it is most unlikely that a stone-carver could ever have devised so unnecessarily difficult a fashion of hair had he not followed after the workers in bronze. But in the case of the Greek curls there is nothing like the intricacy of the Siamese work, and it was no matter of great difficulty for the Greek sculptor to do hair in this manner. Nor is this cone-curl necessarily plastic in type, and so derivative from a clay and bronze original. That it could be independently devised at a time when there was no bronzework at all in large sculpture is clear enough from the instance of the angel at Rheims whose forehead is fringed with cone-curls, lightly drilled in the centre, of a type almost exactly similar to those of the Aeginetan heads of the Eretrian Theseus.

As far as I can see the direct influence of bronze is confined almost entirely to the careful imitation in stone of the hair striations that radiate from the crown of the head, a manner of hair treatment which is fundamentally the result of copying the burin-engraving on the heads of bronze statues. In effect what was taken from the bronzeworker was not his plastic effects, based on work in clay, but his engraved details, done on the cold bronze and so belonging to the realm of cutting rather than of moulding.

Greeks were too good artists to confound their media, and it is the more interesting to find that where the technique of carving is influenced by that of the moulder it is in precisely those things in which the moulder was for the moment turned carver.

The cutting of grooves. At this point it is important to realize the part which abrasion and the flat chisel respectively take in the cutting of deep grooves of drapery, such as are particularly evident in the larger korai that fall into the beginning of this period.

The best examples of the deep drapery grooves that belong to the close of the sixth century are those seen on the Antenor kore itself, and perhaps even more clearly those on the lower part of an otherwise very fragmentary kore, No. 147 in the Acropolis Museum (= Dickins, No. 1360).   This figure, of which little survives, was reconstructed by Schrader in 1907. The part that concerns us, the lower left leg, is in excellent surface condition. The drapery over the leg, which was held up by the left hand, falls in almost vertical folds which are rendered with very deep and careful cuts.   The remaining folds are lightly marked on the surface and contrast vividly with the more shadowed grooves of the other manner. Here, in short, are the two techniques of drapery typical of this period (Fig. 80).

The statue No. 147 itself is dated by Dickins to the 'Full Attic Period', which in our chronology would be equated with the period of Antenor. Schrader was particularly struck with these deep vertical folds of drapery, and remarks of them[1] that they indicate the use of a saw, aided by abrasive sand. He notes also the use of the drill in other parts of the figure.

We must at this stage differentiate between deep narrow folds like those on this figure and wide open folds such as are found on most of the korai at all periods and on the Antenor figure in particular.

Wide open folds can be cut in two ways:

(a) By long and laborious abrasion only. That this was done in any except the earliest periods is most improbable. It was a wasteful and unnecessarily tedious method. But it was a common one.

(b) By using the flat chisel to block out the main hollow of the required fold and then, after preliminary work with this tool, the sculptor would use his abrasive after the heavier work had been done with the quicker-working

---

[1] *Archaische Marmorskulpturen*, fig. 21 and p. 26. Dickins, p. 282, follows Schrader.

instrument. This method is best understood from the following diagram:

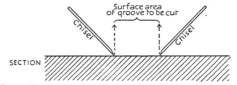

SECTION

Stage I. Beginning of preliminary chisel-work.

Stage II. Groove roughed out by chisel.

Stage III. Grove finished, deepened and smoothed by abrasive.

In Stage I the flat chisel is used at right angles to the fall of the groove, not along it. Working from both sides, the sculptor is thus able to cut out a rough hollow. Most sculptors to-day, when cutting grooves, invariably follow this method. After this blocking-out process is over the sculptor then gets to work with an abrasive stone and rubs up and down the chisel-cut groove; while the chisel-cutting is against the groove, the rubbing is with it. Consequently, every modulation of the surfaces of the groove can be carefully controlled. Lighter pressure and heavier pressure can be alternated so that the groove may diminish or increase in depth. The chisel-work has served as a guide and the hollow removed by the chisel has saved much time.

There is no possibility of fixing this particular method in time. It must have been used at almost all periods down to the fourth century.

The deeper narrower grooves such as are seen on the figure referred to above, No. 147, are done in a different way. Here there is no chance for the time-saving chisel-work. The grooves are all very close together. The chisel would be far too dangerous a tool to use because it would tend to break the thin walls between grooves. Schrader therefore suggests a saw. The mason's saw was probably a semilunar instrument, a simple blade of metal, untoothed (see above, p. 31) and about an eighth of an inch in thickness. It might have been used, with emery, as Schrader suggests, for the central parts of these grooves. But it is difficult to see how it could have been made to reach up into the top corner where all the lines of drapery converge. It is possible to see here a comparison with the striations of the Samian statues and to presume the use of a stone only. For a stone could penetrate easily into the top corner without any risk of overrunning the mark. And its cutting power, assuming it to have been made of emery, would have been far greater than that of a saw. Once the line had been traced out, perhaps with the aid of a ruler, the rest would follow easily. Stone is invariably a better and more reliable cutter than metal.

We have thus established two distinct methods of cutting drapery folds—that common to all periods, where the chisel was used in conjunction with an abrasive and that where only abrasive was used. The latter method seems to have come into use in the beginning of the sixth century, and it lasted long. It illustrates how on occasions the abrasive stone could do heavy work which no metal tool could do better. The extreme symmetry of the folds on this particular figure show how very successful the stone tool could be in the hands of a skilful sculptor.

Use of drill in the early fifth century. As time went on, however, and, in the early years of the fifth century, as sculptors began to experiment with the new tools which had been introduced in the sixth century, they discovered a new way of cutting grooves which was destined to last to the end of the fifth century. The drill, which had been used until 500 B.C. solely for undercutting drapery and for occasional incidental work (as in the mouth of the gorgon-head on the Athena from Eretria: see p. 124) was, as we have seen, further used for detail in hair. Soon the discovery was made that it could be used as an alternative to the punch or the flat chisel for the removal of moderately large areas of stone just as the tubular drill had been used in Mycenaean times. The hollows of eyes, in cases where an eye of coloured material was to be inserted, were often probed out by drilling a large number of holes into the socket. This can be most clearly seen in the eyes of the so-called Leonidas, the Spartan statue recovered from the Acropolis of Sparta in 1927.[1] The date of this work is generally agreed upon as about 500 B.C. Another similar example is the head of a similar type and date found at Olympia,[2] and there are many other instances in works of this period.

The use of the drill for such work was of course virtually structural. The drill was usually a small one and was found more convenient because it could penetrate into places where the use of a chisel would be hazardous and the punch inadequate or slow. This usage led sculptors without much difficulty to the discovery that long folds of drapery can be roughed out even more conveniently and quickly with the aid of a drill than with a flat chisel. A series of drill-holes can be made along the line of the groove or hollow required and then these holes can be transformed into a continuous groove by removing the partitions which separate them. This process has already been recognized by some students,[3] and it is thought to be the last stage in the use of the simple drill before its use as a running-drill came into fashion. This, however, is improbable since the same rows of drill-holes can be found on works on which the running drill also is used (see below, p. 206).

The following diagram illustrates how a groove can be made by a simple drill:

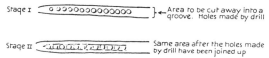

In Stage I the drill-holes are seen arranged in a row along the line of the area marked out for the transformation into a

[1] *B.S.A.* xxvi, pls. 18–20.   [2] Treu, *Olympia*, 3; Furtwängler, *Aegina*, 347–51.
[3] Ashmole, *J.H.S.* 1930, p. 102.

Fig. 49. DETAIL FROM THE SCENE OF LAPITH WOMEN AND CENTAURS AT OLYMPIA

The drapery-lines are worked with an abrasive tool.

Scale 1/2

hollow groove. In Stage II the partitions between the holes are removed with a small chisel and there remains a rough but definite groove which can be used as the starting-point for a larger groove which is later to be finished with an abrasive.

The sculptor was thus using a method of breaking down stone which went back to that used on the Lion Gate Relief at Mycenae, where the drill was a tubular drill employed for the same purpose and with the same labour-saving intention.

This use of the drill in the fifth century is not hypothetical, but is seen in many instances. The earliest instance known to me is the delightful little Athena No. 140 in the Acropolis Museum. It is dated by Dickins to a time shortly before 480. But this seems too early. It was not found in a pre-Persian stratum and seems to belong more probably to the period 470–460.

Although in heavily-draped works the chisel and drill were playing a much more fundamental part in the early fifth century, in lighter drapery the older and, to some sculptors more satisfactory, methods of abrasion seem still to have persisted. The flatter drapery of the Lapith women on the Olympian pediments as well as on the metopes is largely done by abrasive methods, mainly, I think, with an emery pencil. A close examination of the lines of folds will show that a groove ends, as a rule, in a narrow line that resembles in appearance the lines on the drapery of Samian figures. The groove is not sharp, as it would be if cut by a flat chisel, but rather a rounded furrow. While the chisel was indeed largely used on the Olympian sculptures, the softness of drapery grooves shows that abrasives had played a considerable part in their construction (Fig. 49).

The contrast between these earlier Greek methods and those in vogue when the flat chisel was the primary tool is best seen by comparing the drapery of the latter and restored corner figures of the west pediment with that of the original sculptures. The uncertainty of line in the later figures contrasts strongly with the precision and clarity of the drapery lines in the earlier.

VI

SCULPTURE IN RELIEF

RIGID distinctions and classifications in Greek sculpture are notoriously difficult to make. Nor should I pretend that any which I have made hitherto in this book will stand the strain of too close an application. Yet some kind of classification must be essential to serve as a basis for research, and I shall at no time demand from any which may be made here a greater certainty than can be claimed for any working scientific hypothesis, for in the long run that is all that a classification can be.

Relief-sculpture will be, for the purposes of this book, classified into 'low relief' and 'high relief', itself a venerable distinction whose age is no necessary proof of validity!

By 'low relief' I mean such relief as may rise from its background to a height that does not much exceed 6 cm. I have no doubt that there will be exceptions: that some reliefs, essentially in the manner of a relief that has a height of perhaps 1 cm. only may, in fact, while retaining the characteristics associated with such low depth yet rise in places to a height even above 6 cm. But in the main it will, I think, be found that low relief rarely exceeds 6 cm. at any point, and indeed usually falls below it, while high relief practically never emerges within so narrow a limit of planes. It is, therefore, essentially a working hypothesis, but it is one which it is essential to make if a proper analysis of technical methods is to be achieved. For the technique of low relief seems to me to differ profoundly from that of high relief, nor indeed are the aesthetic assumptions of the artist the same in the two cases.

Perhaps the classification may be made in another way and the division established on a basis of the artist's intention, between reliefs which are intended to look *flat*, no matter how high the relief-carving may reach on occasions, and those which are intended to be protuberant in their main features. The former will of necessity produce an effect of strictly lateral movement, the latter one of more diverse movement.

But the distinction is best made clear by examples. The Laconian stelai, of which the example at Berlin is both the best preserved and the most interesting from a technical point of view, are essentially what I have here classed as 'low relief' even if, in fact, their most prominent parts extend from the background or 'drop-curtain' to the surprising extent of 3·5 cm. But they are intended to give an impression of flatness, without the faintest suggestion of *ronde-bosse*. On the other hand, the bulk of the frieze reliefs from the Siphnian Treasury at Delphi, although often in quite exiguous relief, are intended to stand out with brilliant contrast of light and shade. The artists here aimed at vigorous movement, sometimes abandoning the usual convention of lateral movement to which almost all Greek relief was addicted, and experimenting in movement which was from back to front. This quality is more evident in the east frieze than in that on the west, where one detects the hand of an artist more accustomed to a 'flat' style. The north frieze again is in the rounder more protuberant style, and it is here that one can find instances of movement from back to front which are more likely in 'high' relief and never found in 'low' or 'flat' relief. The lion in the Gigantomachy turns to seize a warrior who is really in front of him; the lion's face is frontal to the spectator. The fallen bodies of the slain intensify this inclination to depth. Contrast them with the proud horses, heads raised and tails waving, of the west frieze and the difference is clear. Here the wings of the horses are deliberately used to flatten out the whole scene, by stating explicitly a front and a back plane, whereas the lion and warriors of the Gigantomachy are rounded and realistic.

Formal artists, I think, preferred the 'flat' style: realists (using that term in the most relative sense) preferred the rounded.

Now this distinction—which, I must emphasize again, should never be pressed too literally—is either based on or goes parallel with a technical distinction of great importance. 'Flat' reliefs are almost always cut with a flat chisel, not merely in detail but in their entirety; nor is this true only of the earliest periods: it goes right through the sixth century and perhaps penetrates well into the fifth. It is, I think, no mere coincidence that the balustrade of the Nike Temple, like the Parthenon frieze, is almost wholly chisel-work, while Parthenon metopes are achieved by the use of all the tools of the sculptor.

The distinction will, perhaps, be made more evident by the following list of relief-depths in a small group of well-known works:

Maximum depth of relief.

Lamptrai Basis (Nat. Mus. Athens) . . .	0·2 cm.
Athletes Basis (Nat. Mus. Athens) . . .	0·6 cm.
Teichiussa Dancers relief (Brit. Mus.) . .	1·3 cm.
Hermes and Nymphs relief (No. 702, Acrop. Mus.)	2·5 cm.
Aristion Stele (Nat. Mus. Athens) . . .	2·7 cm.
Sphinx Tomb from Xanthos (Brit. Mus.) . .	2·8 cm.
Hydra Pediment (Acrop. Mus. Athens) . .	3·0 cm.
Laconian Stele (Berlin)	3·5 cm.
Sunium Athlete (Nat. Mus. Athens) . . .	3·5 cm.
Spartan four-sided stele (Sparta) . . .	4·0 cm.
Harpy Tomb (Brit. Mus. London) . . .	4·0 cm.
Hoplite Runner stele (Nat. Mus. Athens) . .	4·2 cm.
Sikyonian Treasury, Cattle Raiders (Delphi) .	7·0 cm.
„ „ Argo (Delphi) . . .	19·5 cm.
Siphnian Treasury frieze (Delphi) . . .	7·2 cm.
Treasury of Athens metopes (Delphi) . .	12·0 cm.

It will be evident at a glance that in this series a definite change of style occurs when the relief exceeds the height of 6 cm. It can no longer adhere to the flat planes and neatly-cut edges of low relief. The Sikyonian reliefs mark, I think, the transition, for here, at least in the Cattle Raiders, if nowhere else, there is still a tendency to step the edges of relief and not to round them. The figures have not emerged into a freer and more mobile world. In the curious scene of the horsemen and Argo the great extension of relief is due to the experimental cutting of two frontal horsemen, the heads of the horses protruding prodigiously. Here the figures have wholly left the tradition of flat relief. The artist in a sense is working in the two modes, and so is essentially an artist of transition. But it must be remembered that the transition is one of feeling and outlook and not of development in time.

The Siphnian Treasury, at least certain portions of it, must be definitely classed as high relief, and the Treasury of Athens finally cuts clear away from all 'flat' tendencies. Other reliefs, such as the Perseus and Kerkopes of Selinus, the Corfiote pediment and, of course, the Olympian metopes, so greatly exceed even the highest dimension in this list that they automatically fall into the class of high relief.

Clearly the artist was here controlled by his technique. The lower the relief the more he is compelled to use flat chisel instead of punch; the higher the relief the more he must carve with the full series of the sculptors' tools, since he is approaching nearer to sculpture in the round. A relief as low as that of the Athletes Basis could not be achieved with a point, however fine, since the depth accessible is less than the depth given by the moderate stroke of a mallet on the butt of a pointed punch. And it must be remembered that the depth of the carvings on the three sides of this relief is mostly below the figure given in the above list. The use of a flat chisel seems to have been compulsory in this kind of work, on purely technical grounds. On rare occasions the sculptors' love of the punch persisted even in low relief. Thus the warrior's hair on the Aristion relief is pointed with a punch.

These conclusions are based on inferences from the existing facts, not on hypotheses as to the nature of relief. They contradict in a sense Blümel's wider thesis—that early archaic work was cut without recourse to the flat chisel[1] except for detail. For here we find whole reliefs cut with no other tool but the flat chisel at a time when sculpture in the round avoided the flat chisel as far as it was possible to avoid it. The fact is that Blümel's main thesis is perfectly correct if applied only to sculpture in the round. It fails in the matter of relief.

Examine some of the reliefs above referred to. The Hydra pediment is chisel-cut, though its surface preservation is not good, and this is not easily detected. The Laconian stele at Berlin, on the other hand, shows on a great part of its surface the unmistakable signs of a small chisel. There is no claw-work, no pointing or punch-work. The Athletes Basis,[2] with its almost perfectly preserved surface, shows at all points the marks of a flat chisel. On the lines of drapery this is evident in an uncertainty of line, a slight shakiness in the straighter-cut lines of drapery. The Cat and Dog group shows this with particular clearness (see below, Fig. 66). A smooth surface cut with a chisel is less easy to detect, but once detected cannot be mistaken. A flat chisel, held and struck correctly, describes on the surface that it cuts a very slight parabolic curve. The end of its drive, in consequence, is marked by a sharp indentation where the chisel digs into the marble at the end of its run. A chisel-smoothed plane surface therefore is bound to show a series of these 'digs', unless, of course, it has been subsequently smoothed with a stone. The plane surfaces of the Athletes Basis have never been smoothed with a stone and their carved surfaces likewise are unrubbed. Almost any square inch of the plane surface of the background shows these

---

[1] Op. cit., pp. 12 ff.

[2] The claw was used in the preparation of the surface before the carving began and its traces can be seen on the upper framework of the reliefs. This is true of all low relief of the second half of the 6th century. The claw chisel was used for preparing the ground, but not for any part of the actual sculpture. The Aristion Relief shows this very clearly.

unmistakable chisel-marks, just as the use of the chisel is
equally clear in the drapery lines. A clear but cruder instance
of a chisel-cut background is seen in the Laconian stele at
Berlin. Here a narrow chisel has been used roughly. The
background is heavily indented. A better instance of a chisel-
cut background, comparable to that of the Athletes Basis, is
seen in No. 702 in the Acropolis Museum, the relief of
Hermes and the Nymphs.

A claw-chisel used for producing a plane surface leaves
the definite striations of its teeth and, from the manner of its
use and structure, does not dig into the marble at the end
of a stroke. The dimensions of the flat chisel used on the
Athletes Basis are reasonably large, about 2 cm., but that
used on the Laconian stele is much smaller, perhaps 1 cm.
only in diameter. The former, being fine marble in almost
perfect preservation, has left almost all the tool-marks visible
(see Figs. 65, 66 below). The latter, slightly weathered, is
not so good or clear an instance.

On *a priori* grounds one would have liked to assume that
flat relief in marble derives from flat relief in soft stone, and
both from wood-carving. There is no direct evidence that
this is the case, but the fact that in the flat and lowest reliefs
there is no trace of a rubbing-stone and no abrasion, even
of the plane surfaces, strongly suggests that the artists were
those mainly employed on woodwork, or at least that the
tradition of woodwork was strong in that artistic tradition
which was concerned with low relief. There seems no other
explanation of this neglect of abrasive processes. But it must
be noted that not every low relief does avoid an abrasive
finish.[1] For the influence of the sculptor of statues was
bound to make itself felt upon some of the relief-cutters and
there is no inherent reason why low reliefs should not profit
from a final smoothing with stone. It is indeed remarkable
that the Athletes Basis, made at a time when marble-cutting

[1] The 'Hockey Basis' is also chisel-cut throughout, but the whole surface
has been finished by careful and subtle abrasion with a stone.

was the dominant art and when every trick of abrasion was used, should still have adhered to the mannerism of wood-work. It is a masterpiece of an artist who knew both the power and the limitations of the flat chisel.

Very high relief in soft stone, such as that of the Troilos Pediment and the Introduction Pediment, does not, of course, follow the traditions of work in marble. Like the low reliefs it is achieved mainly by the aid of a flat chisel. This, as has already been pointed out (p. 83), is because all work in soft stone is in the tradition of wood-carving, and perhaps carried out by the very artists who worked in wood. The distinction is not so clearly observed to-day, but it is worth remark that Eric Gill, whose work in wood is of a high order, works in soft stones and only rarely in hard stone. He employs the flat chisel almost entirely. Frank Dobson, on the other hand, whose principal tools are the point, the *boucharde*, and abrasives, has done nothing in wood at all. Apart from his work in bronze and plaster he confines himself to hard marbles like Parian and the harder of the non-crystalline stones. In the case of other living artists the distinction of style and technique is not always so clear.

Once it is seen that flat relief in Greece was carved mainly with a flat chisel it becomes apparent that, unless the relief exceeds 6 cm. in depth, there is not much scope for the use of other tools. The drill cannot be used for any artistic purpose. No trace of it can be found on any flat relief of the type of the Laconian stele or the Athletes relief. Even on the Siphnian reliefs, with their relatively high-standing figures, it was little used; but here, as we have seen, it was not used for the simple reason that at the time when the reliefs were made the drill had hardly come into use even in sculpture in the round. Even in the metopes of the Treasury of Athens at Delphi, which belong to a slightly later period, the drill is no more extensively used.

The claw-chisel, on the other hand, seems to have been used for plane surfaces and even, perhaps, for the earlier stages of the main figures as soon as high-relief develops. The Xanthos Sphinx tomb in the British Museum shows its use on areas outside the sculptured panels, but it does not seem to have been used in the panels themselves. The Xanthos reliefs, which are low and flat, are the work of a flat-chisel. As was explained above, it was also used in preparing the uncut surface of the Athletes Basis.

The running-drill is not seen on reliefs, high or low, until the fifth century, perhaps about the middle of the century. It is used, for instance, to divide the fingers of the central figures on the Boston Counterpart of the Ludovisi throne.[1]

Files, saws, and rasps are by their nature difficult to manipulate on low and flat relief. Traces of their use are not therefore common, though in high relief they occur from time to time.

The aesthetic intention of the artist of a low relief was to make sharp but light transitions of surface and plane and to collect the light and shadow on his design more in the manner of a sharply-outlined drawing or engraving than in the manner of a heavily lighted and shadowed painting. Sharp-edged chisel-work without graduations of outline or smoothed transitions would thus create the desired effect. To rub his work over, therefore, would be to spoil the sharpness of his composition and fail in the 'engraved' effect aimed at. With relief as low as a fraction of a centimetre the lines had to be hard and to some extent sharp, or even harsh. The Laconian stele is, like the others of its group, a work that stands out clear and defined at a distance with all its formalism evident. Formalism has been described as 'that element of a composition which survives both in space and time.' Low relief is thus more formal aesthetically than high relief, since its detail and general design is more evident at a distance, while its sharp lines remain longer in the memory than the more

---

[1] G. M. A. Richter, *Sculptors*, p. 145. General mention only is here made of its use on this sculpture. I am assuming that the reference is to the finger-divisions, which appear to be so worked.

expressionist effect of a sculptured relief that has a pronounced system of hollows and cavities and graded shadows. You will remember more easily the design of a sculpture like the Athletes Basis than you will a metope of the Athenian Treasury; its lines are easier to fix. So, as you recede in distance from the more rounded metope, you lose its sense of composition more easily. The spatial and temporal value of formalism are considerable.

Such knowledge was, I think, in the minds of the makers of relief-sculpture in Greece. Those who favoured the hard clear design as such with a fine calligraphic effect would naturally incline to the fashion of low and flat relief. Vase-painters may well have worked also as relief-carvers in this style. The relief of a potter, whose name is preserved only in the unenlightening last three letters,[1] is in this flat style, with a maximum depth of relief of 4·5 cm. He may conceivably have carved the relief himself. Were the inscription preserved intact perhaps we should know for certain. The Athletes Basis has already occasioned more comparisons with the work of painters than with that of sculptors.[2] Here, and here only, it seems to me can be established a firm and sure comparison between the work of these two very different classes of artists. For, throughout history, the sculptor and the painter have followed divergent paths, except, perhaps, during the Middle Renaissance in Italy when sculpture was largely subservient to the rules and inspiration of the painters. For even when a sculptor draws or paints there is a world of difference between his work and that of the painter who is a painter only. One has but to glance at the drawings of Rodin, of Maillol, of Alfred Stevens, of Gaudier or Frank Dobson or, indeed, of any fine sculptor, to see how his drawing implies a solider form and a greater realization of solid masses than do the drawings or pictures of painters. Greek vase-painting can be compared always with low-relief carving,

---

[1] No. 1332 in the Acropolis Museum. Dickins, p. 272. Pamphaios is suggested as the potter's name.
[2] Della Seta, *Dedalo*, 1922, fasc. 4; *Liverpool Annals*, x, p. 61, &c.

FIG. 50. STELE FROM NISYROS, in the Ottoman
Museum, Istanbul.

The whole figure has been carefully outlined on the marble.
Early fifth century.

FIG. 51. UNFINISHED PART OF THE FOURTH FRIEZE OF THE NEREID TEMPLE

The relief, which is low, has been blocked out with a punch and the background prepared with a claw-chisel.

Scale 1/2

sometimes with profiles of statues in the round, but it cannot bear a general comparison with sculpture as a whole or with works in high relief. Art-critics to-day make the mistake of judging the merits of a sculptor by the standards suited to a painter. The confusion is wholly unnecessary.

A further point which painters and sculptors in low relief have in common is the emphasis of outlines. The more flat a relief the greater the tendency of the sculptor to give it a clearly drawn outline. The most emphatic instance of this is in the case of the low relief of an athlete, dating to about 460, found in the island of Nisyros and now in the Ottoman Museum[1] at Istanbul (Fig. 50).

In this relief the whole of the figure is carefully given a moderately deep outline that will catch a lateral lighting and clarify the composition. The lowest parts of the relief barely rise above the surface of the background and would, owing to the non-archaic nature of the figure, tend to merge into the back and be lost. To prevent this the artist has cut a careful groove round the figure—itself a standing youth holding a spear in his left hand—and the groove is more emphatic at those points where the relief is lowest. The right shoulder and neck, the left leg (which is the inner leg, and so only just in relief), and the left arm all show this groove more clearly than in the rest of the figure. The same desire to emphasize what might be otherwise lost in the background leads many centuries later to a violent abuse of the same process with the aid of the running-drill. In late Roman sarcophagi, where the design is in moderately low or very low relief, the running-drill is used, like a stylus, and traced round every important element and sometimes quite unimportant details of the design. The result from close at hand is deplorable, but from a little distance gives a surprising vigour and graphic strength to the design and composition.[2]

[1] Halil Edhem and M. Schede, *Meisterwerke der Türkischen Museen*, 1928, pl. VI.
[2] For very clear examples of this practice see G. Rodenwaldt, *Der Klinen-*

It was an almost universal custom in late Roman times when painting and mosaic work largely controlled the style of the sculptors of tombs and sarcophagi.[1]

Outlining as such can be traced to the very earliest periods of Greek sculpture. The horses on the frieze from Prinias are all outlined with a deep groove into the background. In fact, outlining by itself as a single and final process, as exemplified in the engraved reliefs described above (p. 68) in the Candia Museum, was the particular form of art from which the trick of outlining sculpture no doubt developed. At any rate at Prinias we see the two phases side by side, the simple engraving, to be filled out with colour, and the coloured sculpture in low relief outlined for emphasis. Fainter outlining is seen both in the Athletes Basis and in the 'Hockey players' basis', on all three reliefs of each basis.

In the fourth century the distinctions made above between low and high relief seem no longer applicable. One of the friezes of the Nereid monument has portions which are unfinished (Fig. 51). These show that the design was first drawn on the unsculptured surface and then the sides of the figures in the design were cut away, not with a chisel but with a punch. The surfaces so punched away between the figures were then smoothed not with a chisel, as in the sixth century, but with a claw. The clawed surface is everywhere perfectly plain. The depth of the relief is here only 3·8 cm. and the relief should rank as low relief, but its technique is that of high relief. The Gölbashi reliefs, on the other hand, were probably chisel cut, and their dependence on painting is obvious. But their condition precludes certainty for a technical diagnosis.

Hitherto the distinction between high and low relief has never been made quite clear. It will, I hope, have been made clear from the above that the point at which the distinction

sarkophag von S. Lorenzo, Jahrbuch, 1930, fig. 31 (a flat design) and other instances in figs. 33, 34, 35. It is not used in high relief of the period: see fig. 55.

[1] A very striking instance is in the reliefs of the 'Mausoleum' at St. Remy.

can be made coincides with the point at which the technical processes change. As has been seen, the change usually takes place after the height of relief has passed the fifth or sixth centimetre.

This conclusion must be taken as applying to the sixth and early fifth century only. The distinction is clear even at a later date—as notably in the case of the Parthenon frieze as compared with the Parthenon metopes—but by the time the manufacture of Attic grave reliefs had begun on a large and commercial scale it is doubtful if artists maintained the contrast of style and technique in the two types of relief.

VII

BRONZEWORK

I SHALL deal here mainly with full-scale bronzes. Consequently this chapter will be a short one, since the number of full-scale original bronzes of the sixth and fifth centuries is small.

Bronzes, not being the direct product of man's handiwork, but the result of a mechanical process which removes them one stage away from the artist's touch, illustrate only at second-hand the methods used in their making, except only in certain details. Ancient bronzeworkers almost always worked carefully over certain parts of their statues with special tools after the casting. Before considering this we must admit that there remain certain problems which are unsolved. These can be summarized under the following headings:

1. *Primary surface.* No certain evidence of any sort is forthcoming as to the way in which the artist dealt with the surface of his bronze immediately after he had received it from the furnace. A bronze, fresh from the casting, is always more or less black and its surface is in places uneven or marred with bubbles. Actual cracks or faults or bubble-blisters were dealt with by patching (see below, p. 162). But what we do not know is exactly how the *primary* cleaning and polishing was done. Burnishing was invariably employed in the later stages of cleaning (see p. 150), but how the actual 'fire-skin' was removed is uncertain.

2. *Final surface.* We are equally ignorant of the character of the final surface achieved by the artist. As we have them to-day, all bronze statues are patinated to a colour that varies from cobalt-blue or malachite green to a cuprous red. These variations are due to the chemical compounds in the various soils in which the bronzes were found. All forms of patina

alike, however beautiful, are the work of nature and do not
indicate the intention of the artist. Indeed in a sense they
obscure it, especially where the patination is uneven. There
is, however, some indication that the surface of a bronze was
in some cases treated with a preparation. The whole question
indeed as to whether a patination was artificial or natural was
raised by Plutarch.[1] In his essay on the Pythian Oracle a
discussion arises about the patina of a bronze group in the
sanctuary. One of the disputants observes that the surface
of the bronze is a glistening blue—ʾΕθαύμαϛε δὲ τοῦ χαλκοῦ
τὸ ἀνθηρόν, ὡς οὐ πίνῳ προσεοικὸς οὐδὲ ἰῷ, βαφῇ δὲ κυάνου στίλ-
βοντος. Clearly enough, the contrast here is between the dark
corroded surface which a metal might be thought to acquire
through use and exposure and a vivid shining bluish colour.
It seems certain that what the speakers were looking at was
a group which had stood for some five hundred years, since
the monument was erected to commemorate the battle of
Aigospotamoi. In that time a bronze will acquire a completely blue surface which is smooth and sometimes with a
dull polish. The copper roofs and cupolas of Tudor mansions
in England are by now almost exactly that colour. There was,
indeed, no basis at all in the alternative view of the disputants
that it might be artificial. The contrast between πίνος[2] or
ἰός and the lovely blue patina was merely a contrast between
a newly tarnished surface of bronze, such as the speakers had
seen on the surfaces of their domestic bronze furniture and
objects of use, and a surface which had undergone a chemical
change during several centuries. The former would be black
or dull, the latter coloured and bright. But the discussion,
pointless though it may be to us, led to the further inquiry

---

[1] De Pythiae Oraculis, 395 B. Quoted and discussed by G. M. A. Richter
in Catalogue of Greek, Roman and Etruscan Bronzes in the Metropolitan Museum,
1915, Introduction, p. xxix.

[2] There is some reason for thinking that in Roman times a patina was
considered part of the charm of an archaic bronze. See Dion. Hal. περὶ
Δημοσθ. 39: διαφαίνεται δέ τις ὁμοία κἂν τούτοις εὐγένεια καὶ σεμνότης ἁρμο-
νίας τὸν ἀρχαῖον φυλάττουσα πίνον.

as to whether ancient masters deliberately used any preparation as a patina for their bronzes. The argument in the end decides against this suggestion.

From this most interesting passage we are entitled to conclude that artificial patination in the centuries before Plutarch was not a practice sufficiently widespread to be known to the ancients. For here it appears as a mere conjecture, an hypothesis in an argument. On the whole we should be justified in saying that the practice did not exist at all.

There is, however, a passage from Pliny[1] which suggests that some preparation in which bitumen played a part was used for giving a shine or polish to bronze figures. Pliny, however, qualifies it by saying that it appeared to be a Roman custom and not a very ancient one at that. This wash or 'varnishing' of a bronze statue was, I think, merely a protection against natural chemical patination, rather than a definite artificial patination in itself. It appears to have given the statue a certain brilliance or polish but was not necessarily intended to do so. It was a protection pure and simple.

The general view here put forward is that there was no such thing as a deliberate attempt on the part of ancient bronzeworkers to make an artificial patina. This is borne out by an inscription[2] from Chios which ordains that the ἀγορανόμοι shall see that a certain statue is kept free of corrosion and bright (λαμπρός). From this we can infer that the bronze in question, either gilt or in the untouched metal, had to be polished and cleaned and kept free from all chemical change. In similar cases, though not in this one, no doubt the bituminous preparation above referred to would have been employed.

In strong contrast to these methods modern bronze-workers almost invariably give to their bronze statues an

[1] Quoted by Richter, op. cit. and excellently analysed by her. I am much indebted to her discussion of this question.
[2] Richter, loc. cit. ὅπως δὲ καθαρὸς ἰοῦ ἔσται ὁ ἀνδριὰς . . . ἐπιμελεῖσθαι τοὺς ἀγορανόμους.

artificial patination. This is done in a variety of ways. Many
artists have their own special concoctions while others, less
interested, leave it to the cruder methods of the foundry.
Sometimes a patination is obtained by means of chemical
fumes, sometimes by an acid bath. The French sculptor
Barye may be considered as the first artist in bronze to invent
a great variety of different patinations—and, fine artist
though he was, he never succeeded in inventing one which
was attractive or even tolerable. Very few sculptors to-day
attempt to use the lovely colour and surface of the metal for
its own sake. They seem, for the most part, entirely unaware
of the beauty of bronze.

Curiously enough, brass is to-day the only metal which is
invariably kept bright and polished, and from a long domestic
habit of keeping brass shining, a predilection for polishing
brass when used for a statue is evident among some few
modern artists in England, such as Underwood or Dobson.
But bronze still remains the ugly sister of the metal-workers.

Unfortunately there is no evidence to tell us what a Greek
bronze statue looked like when it had emerged from the
studio of the master. The native colour of the bronze could
be anything from a pale rose-red to a dull brown. In any case
a few days' exposure to the elements would at least tarnish
the surface, just as a little use tarnishes the glowing red of a
bronze penny to a dull surface. Such, I think, must have
been the colour of the average Greek bronze statue, in effect
almost the colour of sunburned skin. That, no doubt,
explains why bronze was the material most favoured for
athletic male statues, while Parian marble was the material
used for the feminine nudes of Praxiteles and his successors.
It was the old tradition of sixth-century vase-painting,
or perhaps the even older conventions of Minoan fresco-
painting, still exercising their influence—brown men and
white women, or else the plain fact that in Greece men were
probably more sunburnt than women.

But it is quite clear that, after a few years' exposure, bronze statues would tend to get that vivid blue or green corrosion, unless they were tended and cleaned and polished. Our evidence does indeed suggest that statues were, or at least should have been, so polished. If only a tithe of the care spent on the great chryselephantine statues of the larger sanctuaries had been spent on the bronze figures they could have been kept clean. Probably this was in fact done, for, if the statue of Zeus at Olympia was handed over to the charge of the descendants of Pheidias who were named the 'Burnishers of the Statue',[1] it is highly improbable that the statues in the rest of the sanctuary were allowed to go green with age and neglect!

The actual patinations we see on ancient bronzes are due to chemical change, and these changes vary according to the composition of the soil in which the statues have been found.[2] The fullest patination may be as deep as 0·1 cm. in some cases, the depth consisting of a corroded or changed surface of the bronze rather than of an *addition* to the original surface. In effect the metal is changed down to a certain depth into a non-metallic compound. It is thus evident that the difference between marble and bronze statues that have come down from antiquity is that, in the marbles, we have the original surface that was handled by the sculptor, which can have suffered no chemical change at all, but at the worst a simple accretion or partial denudation, while in the bronzes we have statues which are not in origin the direct work of the artist and which, in addition, have suffered a certain metamorphosis which prevents us from claiming the surface that we see as the surface which was seen and approved by the artist.

The bronzes which have survived best are those which have lain at the bottom of the sea. The Artemisium Zeus, the Marathon boy, the Antikythera athlete, and a surpris-

---

[1] Paus. v. 15. 5. They were known as the Φαιδρυνταί. The name of one of Imperial Roman times is preserved at Olympia. See N. Gardiner, *Olympia*, p. 109.

[2] Richter, op. cit., p. xxxi, gives some instances of various patination.

ingly large number of other works have emerged from their resting-place with their bronze but slightly altered and without that great depth of fine malachite patination which is considered by connoisseurs to give an added beauty to a bronze. They serve, however, much more clearly to illustrate the detailed work which was done on them by the original artist. Oxidization is really the great enemy of bronzes, and under the sea only a slight oxidization can take place.

3. *The Model made by the Artist.* How the original from which a bronze statue was cast was made involves many important considerations. It is generally admitted that the first method by which a bronze life-size or large-scale figure was made was that known to the ancients as σφυρήλατον. No example of this survives in Greece, but instances are known from Egypt. In Greece it was applied to figures either of gold[1] or of bronze, and it is likely that the gold-plated figures were the earlier. The colossal gold Zeus dedicated by Periander at Olympia must antedate the work of Klearchos of Rhegium, and it is quite possible that bronze plates or gilt bronze was later adopted as a cheaper way of making metal statues. But what is quite clear is that such metal plates can only have been affixed to a background of wood or some similar material. The main shape of the statue would thus have been achieved not in the metal but in the wood. Metal-work was thus, at its birth, involved with wood-carving. The plates would have been riveted or nailed to the wood, and artists gradually learned how to make a statue so that the wooden core could be removed. But rivets would naturally have been regarded as blemishes and some better method of joining the plates had to be found. Thus by necessity the art of soldering with a hard solder (probably an alloy of copper and lead and tin) came into use, though how and when it was discovered remains unknown. What is quite certain, as Kluge has pointed out,[2] is that the

[1] Cf. *Anth. Pal.* xiv. 2. An Athena of gold.   [2] Kluge, *Jahrb.* 1929, p. 8.

Egyptians had little or nothing that they could teach the Greeks, for they had not themselves learned how to cast bronzes or how to rivet them at a period before the Greeks practised casting and riveting.

The invention of casting bronzes of large scale or even of more than life-size must inevitably be attributed to the Greeks. But the invention was a great one and marked an enormous step forward in technique over the relatively simple methods of the σφυρήλατον process. It seems almost certain that the Samian artists Rhoikos, Telekles, and Theodoros must be credited with the invention. We are indeed told as much by Pausanias,[1] and the fact that both Rhoikos and Theodoros were men of extreme ability and of an inventive turn of mind gives colour to an attribution in which sheer inventiveness and mechanical knowledge played a primary part. The mere fact that Theodoros introduced a system of central-heating into the temple at Ephesus by means of coal fires, marks him out as an inventor in this line who had no worthy successor in Greece until Roman times and is significant in that it shows that he had developed an interest in furnaces.

Whichever of the three made the invention of bronze casting for large bronzes is of no material importance. But that it began in Samos there seems little reason to doubt, and that it began in the middle or soon after the second half of the sixth century is certain. Nor can antecedents for the technique be discovered outside Greece.

It has hitherto been assumed in the text-books that the process so discovered by the Samian artists was that of *cire perdue*. But recently very weighty reasons have been adduced by Kurt Kluge[2] which make it very difficult to believe that this was the case. He has called attention to the fact that the immediate technical predecessors of bronze statues were the plated figures fitted on to wooden cores referred to above. Consequently wood-carving was deeply involved in the

---

[1] viii. 14. 8.   [2] Op. cit. and *Die Antiken Grossbronzen*, i.

early experiments of the metal-workers. Their plated statues
were first conceived as *carved* statues.

From a close examination of all large sixth-century bronzes
Kluge is convinced that they were cast not from any wax
model on the *cire-perdue* process but from *wooden* originals
from which a sand cast was made. Into this sand cast, which
could only be made in two pieces, a rough core was inserted
before the actual casting began. The core would, of course,
be supported by bars against the sides of the hollow moulds,
and it would be made of the usual casting clay. It would not
be easy for the maker of the core to get a very exact fitting,
and the space between the surface of the core and the surface
of the mould would, in consequence, be large. This is, in
fact, the case with sixth-century bronzes where the thickness
of metal is extraordinary. It is true also of some parts of
many early fifth-century bronzes such as the Charioteer of
Delphi. In the *cire-perdue* process the clay core can be
moulded so near to the final surface that is to take the wax
that in nearly every case of a statue made on the *cire-perdue*
method the bronze is extremely thin and rarely over 3 mm.
in thickness. In the earlier bronzes it may be as much as
2 or 2·5 cm. in thickness, a difference which must imply a
different method of fabrication.

Kluge's theory, based on a meticulous examination of examples, seems to be remarkably borne out by the literary
evidence. The famous story [1] of how Telekles and Theodoros
each made half of a statue, the one in Samos and the other in
Ephesus, which were found to fit exactly when joined, seems
but the slightly distorted version, made by one who was not
conversant with the technique, of the ordinary process of
sand-casting from a wooden model. Sand-casting must imply two halves of the model, each represented by a hollow
mould in a box. When the two boxes are joined the whole
statue emerges after the metal has been poured in.

Further, we have the story [2] of the Apollo Philesios of

<hr>

[1] Diod. i. 98.   [2] Paus. ix. 10. 2.

Kanachos, of which a version made of cedar wood by the same artist stood in the Temple of Ismenian Apollo at Thebes. That they were identical figures seems clear from the remark of Pausanias that διαφέρουσι δὲ τοσόνδε· ὁ μὲν γὰρ ἐν Βραγχίδαις χαλκοῦ, ὁ δὲ Ἰσμήνιός ἐστι κέδρου. In other words their only difference was one of material. From this it seems likely that Kanachos disposed of the model for his Apollo to the minor temple at Thebes, while the more expensive bronze was sent to Miletus. Wooden original models would in any case be sought for and so have a market value.

Kluge suggests that Theodoros learned the method of casting from a wooden model in Egypt, where it was possible to see the process used for the casting of doors,[1] which was the nearest the Egyptians got to employing a casting process at all for works of art on a large scale. But the casting of doors was relatively simple and the casting of large-scale statues implied an inventiveness and enterprise far more characteristic of Greeks.

Kluge's theory necessitates a drastic revision of all those aesthetic judgements which are made on the assumption that all bronzes must be from clay originals or from waxen surfaces. The word 'plastic', which is so freely thrown about whenever a bronze is under discussion, must now be abandoned if Kluge's views on sixth-century bronzes are acceptable. For such bronzes are hardly 'plastic' at all. They are reproductions of *carved* originals in which all the qualities of wood-carving are visible. I must confess that it would be impossible to say at a glance whether the surfaces of the Piombino youth or the Acropolis bronze head[2] would preclude them from being cast from wooden models. On the other hand, I cannot accept Kluge's proof for the wooden model of the Acropolis head. He identifies the gouge-cuts on the scalp on the left side of the head as cuts made on the wooden model which have been reproduced in the casting.

---

[1] As in the Rekhmere pictures. See P. E. Newberry, *Life of Rekhmara*, p. 37 and Pl. xviii.   [2] De Ridder, *Bronzes de l'Acropole*, p. 291.

I have examined these cuts closely and am convinced that they are cuttings or parings made in the cold bronze, after casting, by a bronze-worker's gouge in order to reduce the size of the head so that the helmet which was to be added later might fit. In any case this evidence is capable of both interpretations and so cannot strictly rank as proof.

The Charioteer of Delphi, on the other hand, is a much more cogent case. Here Kluge shows that the bell-shaped skirt below the waist as well as the main upper part of the body and drapery are all from a wooden original while the head, arms and feet are separately cast by the *cire-perdue* process. Here the style of the drapery fully bears out his view. It is certainly not 'plastic' drapery, but can be paralleled from very many medieval wood-carvings where drapery tends to fall into similar deep channels and grooves.

Kluge's theory assumes a perfectly logical development from plated wooden statues to bronzes cast on the *cire-perdue* process and has the merit of giving us a logically developed series of inventions which all culminated in the final intricate and elaborate process which, in substance, has remained un-altered and incapable of alteration down to to-day. That the Greeks should have perfected the method is testimony to their untiring and efficient handling of difficulties which even to-day with perfected mechanical aids are universally ad-mitted to be serious and risky. Only a people accustomed to use their hands and wits in perfect combination and ac-customed also to rapid adaptation to changing methods could so early have mastered so complicated a process. It must remain to the credit of Greek artists and craftsmen that they were able to do what no oriental civilization had done before them.

But it must be remembered that no large bronze statue in antiquity either in the Greek or Roman period was ever cast in one whole. It was composed of different pieces soldered together. Heads, arms, and legs were almost always separately made.

But it is not my intention here to describe the *cire-perdue* process in detail. The topic as such is alien to the purposes of this book and in any case full and adequate descriptions are accessible elsewhere.[1] To repeat them would be superfluous. The technical processes of sculpture as such are my main consideration and Greek bronze statues must rank as sculpture if only because they were never allowed to leave the artist's studio before they had been dealt with as intractable material with tools designed to cut, to chisel and to gouge. In this respect bronzes can no longer be considered as 'plastic' even though, when done by the *cire-perdue* process, they are based on an original of soft and plastic material.

The problems here discussed concern rather the final processes on the cast bronze and the ways in which the rough-cast figure was finished.

To-day a bronze can be repeated, almost *ad infinitum*. The original model is made in clay or plaster or wax and a mould is taken from that original model. From that mould the wax version which is to be used in the *cire-perdue* process is made and the original work of the artist never enters the furnace. The process of casting, however, has not changed from the process used in early Greek times. There has been no simplification of the *cire-perdue* process as such, for the simple reason that no simplification is possible. But there is reason for supposing that the Greeks of Hellenistic times did indeed discover the method in use to-day of making a mould from the original work and then making the wax version from that mould. The original work could thus be in clay, if desired.[2]

In this connexion it is not easy to explain the scene shown on the Berlin vase[3] where Athena appears in the guise of a bronzeworker, modelling a horse in clay. She is adding a lump of clay to the muzzle which, like the off hind leg, is unfinished. At her feet is a mass of clay for use. But the horse

[1] Richter, op. cit., p. xix; Pernice, *Jahreshefte*, vii, pp. 154 ff.
[2] Pernice, loc. cit.   [3] F. and R., *Gr. Vasen.*, pl. 162. 3.

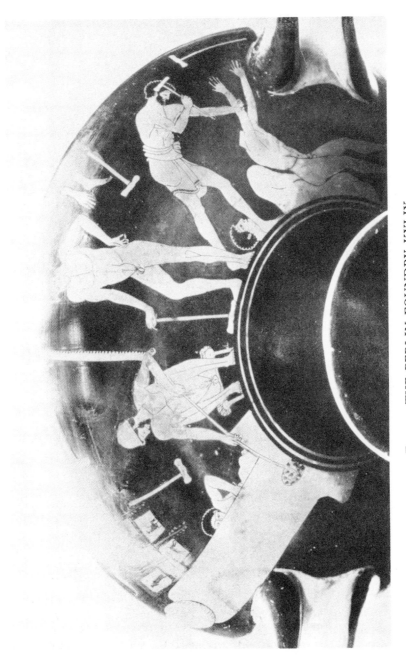

FIG. 52. THE BERLIN FOUNDRY KYLIX

FIG. 53. THE BERLIN FOUNDRY KYLIX

is apparently finished in full detail on the upper part of the head, and even the detail of eye and ear are shown. The Athena is thus finishing a clay statue and not making a rough figure on which the detail can be finished in wax. It is thus difficult to say with assurance [1] that she is modelling for a bronze, according to the early Greek method. Indeed there is some presumptive evidence that we have here proof that at this date the casting of a wax from a clay original was known, and that the invention antedates Hellenistic times.

What we do know from the indisputable evidence of vase-paintings is that large statues made on the *cire-perdue* process were not necessarily cast in one piece, but piecemeal. The head, feet, and perhaps arms, were cast separately and then joined together by ordinary smithing.[2] The famous Berlin kylix which shows a bronze foundry (Fig. 52, 53), shows this process in full detail. We learn further from it that a statue was scraped and smoothed, just as it is to-day, after the process of casting. On the vase is shown a completed statue of a striding warrior, with shield, helmet, and spear. Two workers, one of whom, by the distinctive sign of his Hephaestean hat, may be the artist himself, are scraping the bronze surfaces of the legs with strigil-shaped rasps. The statue itself is about 10 feet high, judging by the proportions it bears to the men.

On the other half of the vase is seen a studio and furnace-room combined. Here the artist himself is watching the furnace while two assistants are near him, one also watching the furnace and holding a hammer while the other is working on a male figure whose arms have just been attached and whose head lies on the floor ready for fixture. Kluge[3] suggests that he is actually about to release the molten metal from the oven into the mould—the most exciting moment of the whole process. The third assistant behind is working the

[1] As does Miss Richter, *Sculpture and Sculptors of the Greeks*, p. 141, n. 37.
[2] Kluge, *Die Antiken Grossbronzen*, pp. 164 ff., where methods of joining parts of statues are discussed.   [3] *Jahrbuch*, 1929, p. 8 ff.

bellows and looking anxiously round the oven to see how the metal flows. The statue in this case is of normal size and is held against a block or support of wood or rough material. The hands of the figure seem to have been attached separately, and on the wall hang a spare pair of feet or models for them, presumably for a statue of this type. It seems possible also that the arms of the statue were attached at the shoulder, for the blow from the hammer which the assistant holds would apparently fall on the shoulder of the statue. There is, however, a more convincing explanation of the actions of this man.[1] On the walls hang various instruments which will be discussed below.

A very similar scene appears on a large fragment from the Acropolis (Fig. 54).[2] Here on the left is a horse, apparently in bronze, very much of the type of the horse on the Berlin vase of the Athena artist. The fragment is here defective, but enough remains to show that on the extreme left an artist is seated on a folding stool with what is probably a hammer in his hand. With the hammer he is giving the finishing touches to the cast bronze. Immediately adjoining on the right is a vase-painter, who does not concern us. Further along is a splendid seated figure of Athena holding her helmet in her hand. This figure is intended to be a statue. It is improbable that a deity would have been interpolated in the middle of a studio without taking an active part in the scene.[3] Taken as a bronze statue the Athena is of great interest. The curious box on which she is seated would thus be of bronze, and the apparently hollow shape of the box is consonant with bronze technique. It is true that no seated bronze is known or recorded at this period, but so few full-scale bronzes of the fifth century have survived that we cannot dogmatize as to what was possible and what was not. Until the discovery of

---

[1] See below, p. 229. [2] Graef, *Vasen von der Akrop.*, II. 1. 6.

[3] Prof. Beazley calls my attention to a vase shown in *Annali*, 1876, Pl. D and Richter, *Craft of Athenian Pottery*, p. 71. But here the Athena and a figure of Nike are crowning potters at work on their pots with gold crowns. There is, therefore, no real comparison between the two Athenas.

Fig. 54. VASE-PAINTING FROM THE ACROPOLIS OF ATHENS, showing bronze-workers, statues, and a painter of pots.

the Artemisium Zeus no figure of full scale in that attitude was known. This Athena at least follows in the tradition founded by Endoios. Her attitude, with one hand outstretched holding a helmet, at least precludes the possibility of her being a stone statue, for such a gesture would be impossible in stone. The serpents of the aegis also are of a type only to be rendered in bronze. A possible interpretation as Athena Ergane is improbable, for, if she were so identified, it would have been certain that she would have been taking some part in the artistic activities, on the lines of the Athena moulding the horse on the Berlin vase.

To her right is apparently the master of the bronze-workers, with his Hephaestean cap hung on the wall behind him, together with his tools.

What we know for certain, even if questions of patina and structure and casting are not settled beyond dispute, is that the surface of a bronze statue or of its parts was never left in the condition in which it came from the foundry. The whole surface, as we have seen, was filed, scraped, smoothed and prepared for subsequent treatment with graving tools by the master himself, or under his direct supervision. The hair was in almost every case carefully worked over with various engraving tools; the eyes were nearly always added after casting, either in the form of inserted stone or glass, or as enamel. The lips and the eyebrows were sometimes given a covering of silver or other metal. The nipples were often fashioned of copper and attached separately. Embroidery to drapery was sometimes added in silver insertion. Eyelashes were on occasions made as small separate plates[1] and inserted along the eyelids between the stone iris and the lid. They can be seen in place, undamaged, in the fine bronze head of a Cyrenean in the British Museum, a Hellenistic work.

But there were no general rules about these adornments. Only in the method of covering defects did Greek bronze-

---

[1] Richter, *Sculpture and Sculptors*, p. 147, fig. 454.

workers follow the same rule from start to finish. Where a bubble of bronze had burst and left an unsightly crater or, without bursting, a large wart or knob, the whole area of bronze involved by the defect was removed, usually to a depth of about a millimetre, and a small plate of bronze was welded in to cover the cavity so made.[1] This can be seen in many cases, the most obvious being the Piombino figure in the Louvre, where there was originally a patch about 2·5 by 1·5 cm. in area added to the flesh surface on the inside of the right leg just above the ankle. The patch has since fallen out. A similar patch is seen on the right side of the back of the neck of the so-called Demetrius, a Hellenistic statue in the Terme Museum at Rome, and another on the neck of the Cyrenean in the British Museum. The Florentine 'archaic' torso is patched at the back.[2]

There was no general rule about silvering the eyebrows or lips. The Zeus of Artemisium has eyebrows inserted in silver but no signs of any kind to show that the lips were ever so covered. The Charioteer of Delphi, on the other hand, had silvered lips but not silvered brows. The band round his forehead has a maeander pattern cut cold into the bronze which was intended to be filled by silver or some metal other than bronze. The Benevento head in the Louvre had silvered lips but plain brows. The Piombino figure had no silver on brows or lips, which were fashioned in the bronze. The head of the Cyrenean above referred to had lips of silver but plain brows.

Nipples were covered with copper in most cases in the fifth century. They are found on the Piombino figure, the boy from Eleusis at Berlin, the Zeus of Artemisium, and the Florence torso. On the other hand, the Idolino at Florence is without them, and they do not seem to occur after the fifth century. Unlike silver lips they can be looked on as realistic. But it is doubtful if the metal used for lips was, as is generally

---

[1] Kluge, *Grossbronzen* I, pp. 116 ff.
[2] Kluge, I. 117 who shows that it is a Roman casting from an archaic original.

believed, always silver. It may equally have been a reddish copper. Eyebrows, as in the case of the Artemisium Zeus, where they are preserved intact, could certainly be in silver, and it can be argued from examples such as this that silver was used for the lips, but the argument is not a sure one. The horse found in the sea near Artemisium has a mouth and tongue, separately cast in copper, to contrast with the colour of the bronze.

The most important process to which a bronze was submitted after coming from the foundry was the detailed engraving of facial hair and of the hair on the head. Quite as much skill was put into the proper working of the hair as the artist put into the original wax. But with the cast bronze the work was of a totally different character. The artist had to work on the cold metal with tools, gravers, and burins, which ploughed grooves and furrows. This required a steady hand and a detailed knowledge of *caelatura*. Whether it was all done by the sculptor of the statue itself is uncertain. Painters were employed for painting statues made by sculptors,[1] and it is equally possible that metal-workers of eminence were called in to work on bronzes. Engravers and sculptors in any case worked together. Often a sculptor was also an engraver.[2] Certainly workers in gold and silver of the eminence of those who made the superb silver-gilt kylix and omphalos cup found at Bashova Mogila [3] or the silver-gilt horns from Trebenishte [4] might have helped in any of the work in which the knowledge of a metal-worker was specifically required. At the same time, the fashioning of the hair of a bronze may be the particular detail in which the statue achieves its attraction. Certainly Polykleitos devoted a major

[1] Richter, *Metropolitan Museum Studies*, I. i. p. 25.

[2] Kalamis had repute as a metal-chaser (Pliny 34. 47), Boethos also worked in silver (ibid. 34. 84), while Skymnos, a silver-engraver, was a pupil of Kritios the sculptor.

[3] Filow and Welkow, *Jahrb.*, 1930, Pls. 8 and 9, and p. 281 ff.

[4] Filow and Shkorpil, *Die archaische Nekropole von Trebenischte am Ochridasee*, 1927.

part of his energy to hair. Consequently it seems probable that the main working of the already moulded outlines of the hair was done by the artist of the whole work.

The treatment of hair after casting seems to have followed the same general lines from the sixth to the fourth centuries. The main structure was produced in the casting, the detail afterwards. The detail in every sixth- and fifth-century bronze to judge both from originals and from marble copies (where hair is recorded with unusual and almost mechanical fidelity) was rendered by means of tools which were either propelled by a series of gentle and continuous hammer strokes, or by steady hand-pressure aided by the great leverage induced by a firm and solid handle. To judge by the methods of workers in cold bronze to-day, grooves can be cut that are either angular or curved in section without any difficulty or risk of accident up to a depth of a little over an eighth of an inch or about o·3 cm. The finer lines, less than this relatively great depth, are done mainly by hand-pressure, the deeper by steady but light tapping of a hammer on the butt of the graver. It must be remembered that gouges or gravers or chisels used in such metal-work are all of solid metal; the gouge of the sculptor is hollow (see Fig. 71). Consequently the metal removed in the process of cutting a groove in a bronze surface, is really *pushed out* of position in one piece rather than removed, as in sculpture, piecemeal, or worn away as with abrasion. A long groove cut with a metal gouge will produce a long strip of metal that curls up in front of the nose of the gouge as it advances. Grooves cut by hand-pressure differ from those cut by hammer strokes in that the former are continuously smooth along the cut faces and need no subsequent clearing, while the latter show at regular intervals in the form of ridges the marks of the hammer strokes, and require to be worked over by hand if their cut faces are to be quite smooth and clean.

The tools used by the Greek bronzeworker must have corresponded almost completely with the tools used to-day by bronzeworkers who chase or cut lettering and formal designs in cold bronze. Very few modern artists chase or chisel bronzes after casting.

The technique of bronzework cannot easily be used as a criterion of date, partly because the number of authentic original large bronzes is so small and partly because the tools employed and the ways in which they were used did not vary much at any period. There is no gradual process of trial and experiment and so of gradual development of technique in the use of these tools that can be analysed. The casting of the Artemisium Zeus marks the highest point to which Greek foundry-work attained as well as the highest point to which it could reasonably hope to attain. That statue is as perfect an example of fine casting as any period in the history of art can show. Once that level of perfection of technique was attained no further perfection in the process was possible. It can safely be said, then, that Greek bronzework was a finished art by the early fifth century B.C.

With stone and marble sculpture, on the other hand, the story is different. Here there was from start to finish enormous scope for invention and experiment. The history of Greek carving, as I have attempted to show, is the history of new inventions, new fashions and new processes, sometimes with continuous advance, sometimes with periods of inactivity or contentment with the conventions of the time. Style and technique interacted the one upon the other and the individual tendencies of particular artists often entirely remoulded both.

Perhaps the early establishment of the technique of bronzework and the realization that no further advances were possible made sculpture in bronze a more alluring activity for the great artists than stonework. The Greek love of perfection led them naturally to a technique that was early perfected. In bronzework, too, there was the added allurement of a wider scope for purely artistic experiments in attitude and composition. Marble naturally limited this.

Greek love of artistic invention would thus naturally lead artists towards bronzework in the periods when ambition was high. And finally the great risks involved in the making of a bronze statue—the risks so graphically described by Benvenuto Cellini—were perhaps an added inducement to an adventurous spirit, on the accepted principle of καλὸν τὸ κινδύνευμα.

PART II

CHRONOLOGY OF STONE-CARVERS' TOOLS

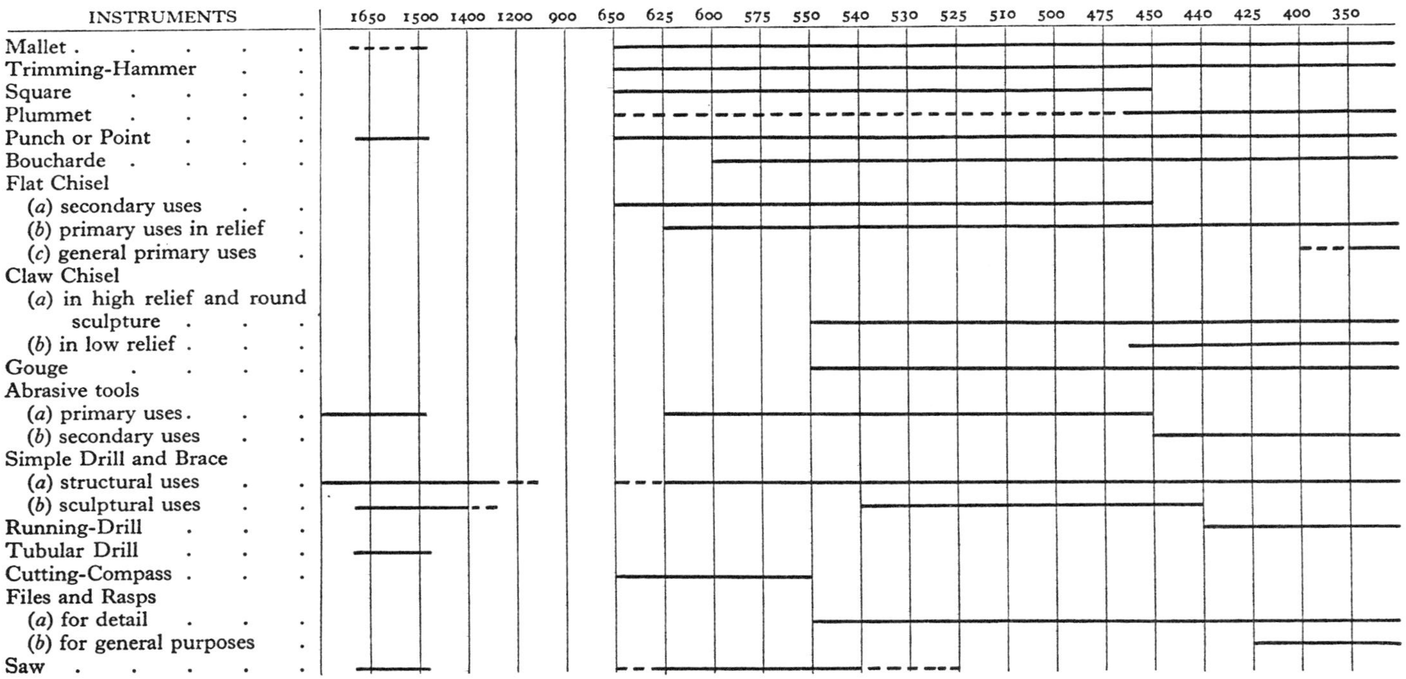

INSTRUMENTS
1650 1500 1400 1200 900 650 625 600 575 550 540 530 525 510 500 475 450 440 425 400 350
Mallet
Trimming-Hammer
Square
Plummet
Punch or Point
Boucharde
Flat Chisel
(a) secondary uses
(b) primary uses in relief
(c) general primary uses
Claw Chisel
(a) in high relief and round sculpture
(b) in low relief
Gouge
Abrasive tools
(a) primary uses
(b) secondary uses
Simple Drill and Brace
(a) structural uses
(b) sculptural uses
Running-Drill
Tubular Drill
Cutting-Compass
Files and Rasps
(a) for detail
(b) for general purposes
Saw

PART II

THE TOOLS AND METHODS USED IN ANTIQUITY

VIII

FOR WORKS IN HARD AND SOFT STONE

PARADOXICALLY enough the processes of bronze-casting are illustrated in ancient documents and works of art with some degree of fullness while those of stone-carving are hardly illustrated at all. The extraordinarily difficult and complicated process of *cire-perdue* attracted attention in ancient times as it does to-day and provided, at any rate for vase-painters, a first-rate subject of interest. No reader of Benvenuto Cellini can fail to be excited by his account of the casting of the 'Perseus', and no amateur of art and science in antiquity could fail to be attracted by the same process. Greek curiosity was stirred by the one but not by the other. In the same way the diverting process of casting attracted more attention than the relatively dull processes of finishing the work after casting. Nevertheless both the Berlin kylix and the Ashmolean kylix tell us something of these. From a technical point of view the hazards involved in the casting of a bronze statue were considerable, those involved in the cutting of a stone or marble statue few. Of the unfinished statues in stone or marble which survive few indeed were abandoned owing to errors of judgement on the part of the artist either in his choice of material or in his treatment of it.[1] Kurt Kluge's monumental work on the ancient processes of bronze statues has already covered much of the ground and left but little to add. But for work in stone there is no complete study. The preceding pages form an attempt to fix the outlines for stonework and work in softer materials that required to be cut as solids in much

[1] The archaic Kriophoros from Thasos is thought by Blümel to have been abandoned owing to faults in the marble (op. cit., p. 52).

the same way. In the pages that follow I shall attempt to summarize all that can at present be discovered about the actual instruments used in the cutting, working, and finishing of statues in marble, in soft stones and in wood. The chronological conclusions about the various tools, that is to say, the attempt in each case to establish the period or periods in which they were individually in use must, as has already been said, be considered as conclusions drawn from available evidence which may in some cases have to be revised in the light of evidence still to be discovered. They must be looked on as provisional conclusions.

1. *The Square.* This, the ordinary carpenter's square, might be assumed to have been one of the preliminary instruments by which the sculptor, especially in the archaic period, made certain that his frontal and lateral planes in a round sculpture were correct. But assumptions form no part of a sound analysis of ancient methods. It is, therefore, satisfactory to find that specific record of its use is found in a curious sculptured relief which is cut in the native rock in the Cave of Vari on Hymettus (referred to above, p. 95). This relief forms part of a series of sculptures and inscriptions which were apparently cut by a certain Archedemos of Thera who resided in the cave in the beginning of the fifth century.[1] Even so his sculptures seem old-fashioned even for this date. The sculpture that concerns us is a low relief in two planes cut in the rock just below the hewn stairs that lead from above down into the cave. It is extremely difficult to photograph, but the illustration here given, though taken from an angle (Fig. 55), is as accurate a version of it as it is possible to get. Here a sculptor, probably Archedemos himself, is seen clumsily rendered. He wears a simple exomis girt at the waist, and falling in folds to his knees. His head, which is badly preserved, faces the right, but the direction of his stance or movement is the opposite way. It is consequently

[1] See *A.J.A.*, 1903, pp. 263 ff.

FIG. 55. RELIEF BY AND OF THE SCULPTOR
ARCHEDEMOS OF THERA, in the cave at Vari on
Hymettus.

difficult to say which is intended for his right arm and which for his left! In the hand seen on the spectator's right is what is, without doubt, a carpenter's square. That it was one of the sculptor's tools is clear from the fact that in his other hand is a trimming-hammer, pointed at one end and flat at the other. In short he is holding the two instruments which were the first to be used by a sculptor. The square helped him to get his planes of side and front correctly laid, the trimming-hammer blocked out the surfaces of those planes. The whole relief together with the shallow steps which serve as a moulding below are cut in the non-crystalline blue limestone of the lower levels of Hymettus and the cutting is entirely done with hammer and pointed punches. Elsewhere in the cave is a seated figure of a kore-type, standing free and in the round except for its back, which remains in the living rock. This kore (whose head is missing) is in the tradition of sixth-century seated korai, so that Archedemos may be considered as an old sculptor who, perhaps through unemployment, had retired to this cave, whose guardian he made himself—to judge by some of his entertaining inscriptions[1]—where he practised his art in the manner of a preceding generation to his heart's content. What other tools he used we do not know, and none were in fact found in the excavations carried out in the cave in 1902. But the tools he shows us were those of the first processes only. He must subsequently have used mallet and punch, but perhaps no other tools at all. Certainly he employed no abrasives for a final surface treatment, probably because he could not get them or afford them, for he must be looked on as a poor hermit, an artistic monk, self-consecrated to the Nymphs and Pan, an alien in Attica and Dorian by race, for he calls himself Archedamos more often than Archedemos, and is a Theran.

2. *The Trimming-Hammer.* This, the first tool to be used in

---

[1] Ἀρχέδαμος ho Θεραῖος κᾶπον νύμφαις ἐφύτευσεν or Ἀρχέδημος ὁ Θηραῖος ὁ νυμφόληπτος φραδαῖσι νυμφῶν τἄντρον ἐξηργάξατο. His dialect varies.

the preparation of a block of stone for sculpture, was a hammer, not unlike the modern geological hammer, with a point at one end and a flat butt at the other. As Blümel points out,[1] such a hammer can only be used to strike blows at right angles to the stone in the earliest stages, for it stuns the stone and destroys its crystallization for a depth of about a quarter of an inch. But the right-angle stroke

FIG. 56. The hammer of Archedemos.

serves the purpose of cracking the marble in the vicinity of the blow so as to make it flake off in large and convenient flakes. It is thus useful in clearing off considerable masses of unwanted matrix. But it has to be used with extreme care or else it will remove too much. As the work progresses the angle of the stroke must become more oblique and the stroke less hard. A gradual slowing-down process is necessary. Traces of pointed hammer work are to be seen on most unfinished statues. In work of the archaic period they are best examined in the Thasian Kriophoros (see Fig. 60) and on the unfinished colossi in the quarries at Naxos.[2] Sometimes the long marks of oblique strokes can easily be seen where the hammer has been used obliquely to strike a furrow. Nevertheless, traces of this tool are not common except in the structural parts of unfinished statues, since few statues survive which have been abandoned in their first stages. But the structural parts, such as the base or supports, may often be left in the first stage of completion when the rest of the figure has reached a more advanced stage. No name has been preserved with certainty for this tool to distinguish it from the ordinary smith's or carpenter's hammer, which has a flat end and strikes to beat rather than to penetrate or pierce. As in English and most modern languages the term hammer included all kinds. The σφῦρα of antiquity applied equally

---

[1] p. 3, and see pl. 1 f. In the illustration on that plate, however, he shows a type of hammer slightly different from that on the relief of Archidemos.

[2] Blümel, pls. 3 and 4 and fig. 14.

to the smith's tool[1] and to the carpenter's[2] and presumably, though there is no specific reference, to the sculptor's hammer. At any rate we know what shape it was in the early fifth century from the humble record of Archedemos (see above, fig. 56). It may be reconstructed from his battered relief as follows:

To judge from the proportions which the hammer in his

FIG. 57. Mallet from the relief in New York.

FIG. 58. Relief of Megistokles, son of Philomousos.

relief bears to the figure, this particular hammer was a heavy one with a handle about 35 cm. in length and a metal head some 20 cm. in length.

3. *The Mallet*. Of the type of mallet used by the Greeks we know all too little. Modern mallets can be either of wood or of metal and are sometimes rectangular in shape with flat heads or ovoid and shaped like a mace-head. Of Greek mallets of archaic times we know nothing, but later records of Graeco-Roman and Roman times show us exclusively rectangular mallets with flat heads. One such is seen on the relief in the Metropolitan Museum at New York,[3] a dedication of a sculptor, and another of the same type is seen on the relief of a certain Megistokles son of Philomousos now in the museum at Chalkis, also a sculptor's dedication.[4] In

[1] Hdt. i. 68.   [2] *Anth. Pal.* vi. 205: αἱ σχεδὸν ἀμφιπλῆγες σφῦραι.
[3] Blümel, p. 48, fig. 12.
[4] Unpublished. The relief is in marble in a panel inset into the stone. The total height of the relief is 66 cm., the width 32 cm. The panel in relief measures 30 by 22 cm.

the former the mallet and a flat chisel appear side by side as votive offerings. In the latter the sculptor is shown hitting the flat chisel with the mallet held in his right hand; he is chiselling the rim of what appears to be an urn.

It would, of course, be unsound to argue as to mallets of the sixth and fifth centuries from these examples of several centuries later; but there is a conservatism in the shapes of sculptors' instruments which may justify us in supposing that throughout the Greek period the mallet was of this rectangular shape. A rectangular shape presupposes wood as a material rather than metal.

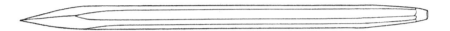

FIG. 59. Point or punch.

4. *The Point or Punch*. This tool, perhaps the most important of all in sculpture, is often called a 'pointed chisel'.[1] This is a misnomer. The punch is used only for the process of *removing* stone in order to reveal the shape conceived in the artist's mind as underlying the stone or inherent in it. It is more rarely used as a means for cutting detail of design or decoration, and only so in the first half of the sixth century: this is one of the functions of the flat chisel. Consequently to call the punch a chisel is to misconceive its proper function.

To Carl Blümel must be given the credit for being the first to point out clearly and unequivocally that the bulk of the work on ancient Greek statues was done with the punch. He also makes it clear that work done with a punch has a totally different quality from work done with a flat chisel. The punch, working always either at right angles to the surface or else at an acute and not a wide angle, keeps in contact all the time with the essential solidity of the material and the matrix. A flat chisel will tend to produce a flat effect, a punch a rounded effect. He contrasts effectively the

[1] So Richter, *Sculpture and Sculptors*, p. 144.

FIG. 60. BUST OF THE KRIOPHOROS AT THASOS

Thasian crystalline marble. The front is unfinished and shows the marks of the
punch and hammer over the face, neck, and breast, and on the ram. There is
no chisel-work.

original heads of the Olympian sculptures with those later restorations to the pediments, done in a period when the flat chisel had replaced the punch for all essential work. But the punch, so used, is the more laborious as well as the more difficult tool. To-day only a very few eminent sculptors use the punch right down to the antepenultimate stages, before the final smoothing and polishing is given. In Greece, on the other hand, the punch was in use for round sculpture until the mid-fifth century and by some sculptors to the beginning of the fourth century. Its precise limits at the lower date are, however, a matter of some dispute.

Traces of the punch are unmistakable and vary from the heavy hard-driven holes made by a heavy instrument to the faint and almost imperceptible holes made by a gentle tapping of a very small tool. The heavier marks can always be seen round the sides of unfinished parts of the basis of a statue or on the main body of a wholly unfinished sculpture. Heavy tooling with a large punch can be observed on most of the unfinished backs of the pedimental sculptures of Olympia, and the very fine almost microscopic tool-marks of the smallest type of punch can be seen on those Olympian heads whose hair is not treated with the flat chisel, and equally on the features of the original Olympian pedimental and metopal heads. Other good examples of heavy punch work can be seen on the unfinished backs of the pedimental figures of Athena and the Giants from the Peisistratid pediments of the Hekatompedon. The marks of a medium-sized punch—the tool which achieved the bulk of the work on a statue in early Greek times from the beginning down to the middle of the fifth century—can be seen most clearly on the back of the torso of Athena from the Temple of Apollo Daphnephoros at Eretria (Fig. 37), where also can be seen the claw-marks made by the next process of the period (see below, p. 185). Numerous other examples of partly finished or unfinished sculpture show clearly these marks.[1] A close

[1] See Blümel, pls. 5, 6, 8, 11, 12.

inspection will show when the punch was used almost at right angles and when it was used more obliquely. The unfinished torso in the National Museum at Athens[1] shows the marks made by both modes of striking.

It might be considered as axiomatic that the sculptor uses the heavy punch rather in the manner of the trimming-hammer with force and at right angles in the earlier stages, then employs it more obliquely, and finally applies the medium and smallest punches almost at right angles to the stone. Many think that right-angle strokes, or strokes nearly at right angles, tend seriously to 'stun' or 'bruise' the stone. Provided the strokes are not hard this is not in fact the result[2] (see below, p. 236). A certain amount of breaking of the crystalline structure of the stone and of 'stunning' inevitably occurs, but if the strokes are light, but steady and continuous, the depth of 'stunning' is so slight that it is all worn away by the subsequent abrading processes and the surface left entirely undamaged.

The chronology of the punch is interesting. It was the earliest tool to be used after the prehistoric period and coincides with the beginnings of sculpture in hard stone. From 650 B.C. it is in use, and it remains as the principal metal tool for nearly two hundred years. After 450 it falls out of fashion and gives way to the flat chisel, which is then used on a more extensive scale and at an earlier stage in the construction of a statue than was the case in archaic times. How much the pedimental sculptures of the Parthenon owe to the flat chisel it is difficult to say, since there are so few unsmoothed or unweathered surfaces to examine. But it is doubtful if the flat chisel was there used to any extent. The change probably came later and the popularity of the flat chisel was probably due to the increased popularity of relief work in the last quarter of that century. The punch was

---

[1] Blümel, pl. 5. The bulk of the marks indicate direct right-angle strokes.
[2] I have experimented on Pentelic marble to establish the truth of this statement.

FIG. 61. THE SO-CALLED 'TÊTE RAMPIN' (Louvre)
The curls of hair are done with a punch.

Fɪɢ. 62. THE HAIR DOWN THE BACK of No. 613 in the
Acropolis Museum.
This is a good example of hair-curls rendered solely by means of a punch,
used at right angles to the marble.
Scale 1/1.

sometimes used for very fine and meticulous work. The 'Tête Rampin' in the Louvre (Fig. 61) is a masterpiece of detailed punch work in so far as the hair and beard are concerned. Every lock of hair is pointed by a punch which, in some cases, must have been as fine as a knitting needle. The hair of the warrior on the Aristion relief is similarly pointed with a fine punch. The kore No. 613 in the Acropolis Museum is unique among the korai in having hair which has been carefully pointed in the same way. The ancestry of this mode of rendering hair goes back, of course, to the Dipylon head and the sculpture of the late seventh century. Small globes of hair held for long a dominating influence in archaic sculpture. The Rampin head shows the last masterpiece of this particular mannerism.

In prehistoric times punches of hard copper or bronze must have been used for minor work on small areas. They were so used in almost all periods of Egyptian sculpture, and that their use continued in Cretan and Mycenaean art down to the fourteenth century B.C. is certain. The spaces between the circles in the 'Pole-end Frieze' from the façade of the Treasury of Atreus and much of the Lion Gate Relief can only have been rendered by a laborious process of punching. Copper tools were probably more popular than tools of bronze, since copper can be hardened by cold-smithing;[1] but, even so, the wastage of metal tools must have been very great. In Egypt and Sumeria[2] the use of metal punches for the removal of surfaces on statues of material as hard as diorite and granite is established beyond question. Here too the wastage must have been enormous, and a process of continuous resharpening must have been essential.

No word is preserved in Greek that may be held to describe the punch as opposed to the flat chisel. Nor is it likely that the word presumably used for flat chisel—σμίλη—can be

[1] T. A. Rickard, *Journal of the Institute of Metals*, xliii (1930), p. 305.
[2] As, for instance, in the case of the spirals on the turban of the Sumerian head No. 55 in the Louvre.

used for punch also, since that word is evidently used to describe a tool which has a cutting edge (see below, p. 184).

5. *The Boucharde.* There is no name in English for this interesting tool. It is largely used by French sculptors and but little known in England. Hence I have here employed its French name. Blümel[1] refers to it as the *Stockhammer.*

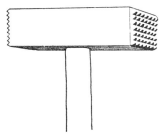

It consists of a double-ended mallet-shaped hammer, with each end flat. The flat surface at each end has been scored across by deep incised V-shaped grooves that divide the area into a series of rectangular squares. Since the dividing lines are V-shaped incisions filed into the surface of the

FIG. 63. Boucharde.

metal, it results that the rectangular squares each come to a sharp head. The flat surface is therefore transformed into a surface which consists of a series of small pyramids each of which ends in a point. The flat surface when struck on the plane surface of stone or marble thus makes a series of sharp indentations corresponding with the points of metal. In effect the *boucharde* is a multiple punch, and must therefore be classed with punches both on account of its structure and on account of the resulting marks made on the stone. But, unlike the simple punch, the multiple points cannot penetrate deep into the stone—hardly more than half their actual depth is the maximum penetration—and, unlike the simple punch also, the points of the *boucharde must* penetrate exactly at right angles to the stone. It is, in effect, the one tool which can only be applied at right angles, and it is the one tool which breaks down the surface of the stone over a controlled area and not at a single point or along a single line. In a sense it is the sculptor's most interesting tool, for it allows him to work with certainty over a restricted area and to know

[1] Op. cit., p. 5.

exactly that at each stroke that area is the equivalent or almost the equivalent of the area of the flat head of the tool.

The marks of this tool can be detected only from very close inspection. Where a series of parallel marks are seen to form a patch composed of *dots*, as opposed to the parallel striations of the claw-chisel which form parallel *lines*, then one can be certain that the *boucharde* was used. In fact its traces are not common, and it was never a popular tool in Greek times. Egyptians, on the other hand, used it extensively for working over and wearing down the surface of granite. It is essentially a tool for use on hard stones only. As such, a coarser version of it is widely used to-day by stonemasons in their treatment of granite surfaces. Sculptors to-day value this tool for the control it gives, especially in the final stages of shaping a surface. If a surface is thought by the sculptor to be in need of reduction he will prefer the *boucharde* to the claw or flat chisel since it enables him to remove, by a process of gentle tapping, the depth that he wishes, giving him great certainty. The tapping process gradually reduces the stone surface to dust, which fills up the interstices of the *boucharde*, making it necessary periodically to clean it. It stuns the surface of marble to an appreciable extent, but far less than a punch. A brief smoothing with stone will remove the stunned area and get down to the natural unstunned matrix. Parian marble is worked with particular success with the *boucharde*, since it is a tough and not brittle marble, compact in its crystallization and not liable to flake. Pentelic, on the other hand, flakes too quickly, and the *boucharde* must be used on it with care.

No chronology for this tool can be fixed. Its traces are seen in the ripe archaic period and as late as the second century B.C. Its marks have been identified on an archaic head in Berlin, on the structural parts of the archaic seated goddess in Berlin, on the Ludovisi Throne, and on the small block under the right foot of the Venus de Milo.[1]

[1] See Blümel, p. 5

It is hardly to be expected that any Greek name will have survived for an instrument that has so poverty-stricken a nomenclature in other languages.

6. *The Flat Chisel.*[1] As has been explained above (p. 36 ff.) the flat chisel was hardly used in hard-stone sculpture at all in the prehistoric period. The reason is, simply enough,

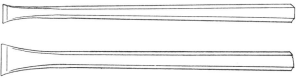

FIG. 64. Flat chisels.

that a cutting-edge of copper or hardened bronze would blunt in a very short time. In the same way the punch, though frequently used, is used very sparingly, as, for instance, in the case of the Atreus façade, where much work that would have been done at a later period by the punch is done with the saw or abrader. In fact there seems to be every reason to think that the flat chisel in prehistoric times was used almost exclusively in woodwork.

With the appearance of iron, however, a cutting-edge could be made to a flat chisel which would last a reasonably long time. Whether, as has been suggested,[2] there was any method of hardening all or part of an iron instrument so that it could have a cutting-edge of the hardness of modern steel is uncertain, at any rate for the early Greek period. But there is exact evidence for the process of case-hardening being known in the ancient world[3] at a later date.

As has been made clear, the flat chisel was used invariably

[1] Students must be warned to use Miss Richter's illustrations of sculptors' tools with discretion (see *Sculpture and Sculptors*, 1st ed., Figs. 440 and 441). The so-called chisel in Fig. 440 is an unusual type of punch; the four tools on the left in Fig. 441 are woodworkers' tools, not sculptors' tools at all.

[2] Richter, *Catalogue of Bronzes in the Metropolitan Museum*, p. xxiii, and Pernice, *Zeit. für bild. Kunst*, xxi, p. 223.

[3] See H. Sandars, *The Weapons of the Iberians*, p. 37. An Iberian *espada falcata* was found, on analysis, to have had its cutting-edge case-hardened. What process was employed to this end remains obscure.

for all work in soft stone as the principal tool. It was used apparently for much, if not most, of the primary work and for all the final stages except the actual smoothing of the stone with pumice or sandstone, which were preliminary to the decoration with thick paint.

It has also been seen how the flat chisel was used in all relief work which can be classed as low relief, with a conscious knowledge that this particular instrument produces more successfully a 'flat' technique. Those who deliberately aimed at this particular aesthetic style favoured the flat chisel.

But the chisel, like all tools that strike an oblique stroke, works more rapidly than an instrument such as a punch. Ten strokes of a flat chisel will remove as much material as a hundred from a small punch. It is only natural therefore to expect that the flat chisel will increase in use as the demand for sculpture increases. The tremendous output of tombstones carved in relief which began in Attica and in many parts of central Greece in the second half of the fifth century was the result of a demand which had originally been stimulated by great public works in relief, such as the frieze of the Parthenon. The domination of *motif* and style as seen in the Parthenon frieze over the compositions of fifth- and fourth-century grave reliefs is most marked.

The great demand for tombstones that increased steadily until the close of the fourth century in some ways commercialized the quality of the output. Reliefs were cut rapidly, and originality of composition fell into a decline. One class of relief in particular, the large urns decorated with a small panel in relief, were cut exclusively with a flat chisel. They form a definite class which continues the older sixth-century tradition of very low relief. Like much sixth-century work, the depth of relief in their designs rarely exceeds one centimetre.

The popularity of the chisel in the latter part of the fifth century was very great. Works like the Nike Balustrade show that, with the drill, it was one of the most important primary tools. The artist called by Rhys Carpenter 'Master E' worked mainly with the chisel and file.[1] The whole technique of relief sculpture had, indeed, changed by this time from what it had been in the earlier part of the century, except in that restricted class of very low relief of a commercial type referred to above. Here only the archaic methods continued unchanged.

Blümel has emphasized the change in technique,[2] but he has failed to isolate that class of low relief in which the chisel was used as the main tool and he has not realized that, in low relief, the same technique was continuous for over two hundred years. His main contention that the flat chisel and the gouge were not extensively used in the fourth century is therefore untenable.

Chisel-work that has not subsequently been smoothed over can be detected at once (see above, p. 140 and Fig. 66). The chisel-edge leaves an indentation at the end of a stroke, since in the course of a stroke it follows a course that is not along a straight but along a slightly curved line. Sometimes also if it is held too steeply against the stone it will cut a similar indentation, or several of the kind, at the beginning of the stroke. In the cutting of drapery-detail also, or in the cutting of any groove over an inch in length, certain unevennesses are perceptible in the lines and in the edges of the grooves: a chisel-cut line never has the certainty of 'run' of a line that has been rubbed with abrasive, nor can it ever achieve any great length (Fig. 65). A comparison of the lines of the drapery on the Athletes Basis with those of the drapery of the best Attic korai or—to take an extreme case—with the lines on the drapery of the Hera of Cheramyes, shows at once how long a line can be made by abrasion and how short and uneven is the span of a chiselled line.

[1] *The Sculpture of the Nike Temple Parapet*, p. 80.
[2] Op. cit., p. 16. Miss Richter reviewing Blümel in *A.J.A.*, 1929, p. 334, also fails to make this distinction between low reliefs cut with the chisel and other works.

FIG. 65. DRAPERY FROM THE ATHLETES BASIS

The surfaces and lines of the drapery are done solely with the flat chisel. The uncertainty of line of the lowest fold on the right is characteristic chisel-work and every plane surface shows chisel marks. No abrasive has been employed at any point.

Scale 1/1. *From a cast.*

FIG. 66. PART OF THE ATHLETES BASIS, showing a surface cut with a flat chisel and not subsequently smoothed over.

The outlining also of the figure is clearly seen. The width of the chisel can be accurately determined from the marks behind the head and shoulders of the athlete.

Scale 1/1. *From a cast.*

It has been stated that the flat chisel can be used for the final smoothing' of a statue and that smooth surfaces are done with a chisel, especially in the fourth century.[1] This is an entire misconception. The flat chisel can prepare for a smooth surface by paring off in small strokes all unevenness. But it can never under any circumstances produce a uniformly smooth surface. Nor has any sculptor ever pretended that it could. Much modern work, like the 'Genesis' of Epstein for instance, has moderately smooth surfaces that have been treated with the chisel and not subsequently smoothed or polished even with a dull polish. But an examination with the naked eye will show at once the distinct marks on every square inch of good chisel-work.

As has already been explained the flat chisel seems at the close of the sixth century to have become more popular than it had been largely owing to the growing influence on stone carving of large-scale bronzework. The various burins used for the cutting of hair-detail on large bronzes produced brilliant effects of cutting which made the stone-cutter try to use the flat chisel on stone for producing similar effects. There is no question of his attempting to copy the effects of the bronzeworker. On the contrary, he had far too much conscious appreciation of the type of technique that suited marble. But the similarity, each according to its own material, between marble statues and bronzes, especially in the hair on late sixth-century and early fifth-century bronzes, is definite. The hair on some of the Olympian heads, notably that of the 'Seer', is cut in close parallel grooves in a way which is as totally distinct from the manner of the hair-cutting of the korai as it is similar to the hair of full-scale bronzes such as the Delphian Charioteer or the Zeus of Artemisium.

[1] Richter, *Sculptors and Sculpture of the Greeks*, p. 144 and n. 60: 'From the fourth century onward the straight chisel was used also on the nude parts for the final smoothing.' 'The smooth surfaces of the bodies of fourth-century finished statues show conclusively that the straight chisel must have been used.' Of course they show nothing of the kind.

The only Egyptian chisel shown on the Rekhmere paintings is a flat, broad-bladed instrument, shaped like an early Bronze Age bronze celt. It is shown in the paintings as being used only for smoothing surfaces of relief carvings. The Greek chisel was long and usually narrow and bears no relation to the Egyptian mason's chisel. The latter may, indeed, be compared with the very broad-edged mason's chisel, known as a 'pitcher', in use to-day for dressing stone. The shape of this is identical with the shape of the Egyptian tools and the cutting-edge may be as much as 3 inches in breadth.

The chisel seems to have been designated in Greek by the word σμίλη. That it meant the flat chisel and not the claw or punch seems certain from the way in which it was used and the context in which it appears.

Aristophanes[1] speaks of the σμίλης ὁλκοί—the chiselled lines or furrows—cut into a wooden surface. In the Palatine Anthology[2] Alcaeus of Mytilene in his epigram on the tomb of the enigmatic Chilias (alias Phidis) commences with the lines:

Δίȝημαι κατὰ θυμὸν ὅτου χάριν ἁ παροδῖτις
δισσάκι φῖ μοῦνον γράμμα λέλογχε πέτρος
λαοτύποις σμίλαις κεκολαμμένον.

An inscription on a tomb-stele could only be cut with a flat chisel, so that we need fear little ambiguity in the sense in which the word was used.

Another word which may also mean 'flat chisel' is the rare word κολαπτήρ. It appears in an inscription[3] in verb-form in the phrase δόγμα κολαφθὲν εἰς στάλαν. Here alone without the addition of σμίλη as above it can be interpreted as σμίλη. A decree could not be cut with a punch, still less with a gouge or a knife. Consequently we are driven to give to κολαπτήρ the meaning of flat chisel and make it an equivalent term with σμίλη.

[1] *Thesmophoriazousae*, 779.
[2] vii. 429. Another form of this word—σμῖλα—means usually a small knife; cf. *Anth. Pal.* vi. 62 and 295.   [3] *C.I.* 5475. 25 and 5491. 22.

FIG. 67. BACK OF THE HEAD OF THE 'SEER' FROM THE
TEMPLE OF ZEUS AT OLYMPIA

The hair is a fine example of the best chisel work. The centres of each curl have
been drilled with a simple drill.

The size of the flat chisel varied, to judge from the surviving marks, from a narrow blade of about 0·5 cm. in width to 1 or 2 cm. Rarely, as in the case of a bearded head in the Louvre,[1] a chisel with an extremely narrow blade of some 2 mm. breadth was used for minute work. In the head in question the oblique strokes are clearly seen over the entire surface. But a tool with so small a blade is hard to differentiate from a punch in its methods and achievements. No doubt tools like this were used in archaic times for details of face and feature.

7. *The claw-chisel.* As has been explained above (p. 127) there is reason to believe that this tool came into use soon after the middle of the sixth century. At present no evidence for its earlier use is available. Nor are its traces found on sculpture in soft stones, although in *hard* lime-stone of the Attic or Anatolian type it is usually employed.

FIG. 68.
Claw-chisel.

This type of instrument allows of considerable variety. Its teeth can vary in size from a fraction of a millimetre to nearly 2 millimetres in width and the number of teeth on the edge of the claw can vary, that is to say, the area affected by the teeth may be as wide as 3 cm. or as narrow as 1. Further, the teeth can be pointed so as to dig well into the marble or they can be blunt so as to pare the surface only. It is in fact a tool of very considerable adaptability.

The claw is very widely used by all sculptors at all periods after the middle of the sixth century. In Greek times its use remained more or less constant for round sculpture and high relief: that is to say, it was not extensively used at one time for primary work and confined at another only to secondary work and detail. Its use became necessary after the statue had achieved its complete outline and was within a centimetre or so of the final surface. It was exactly at this point

---

[1] Langlotz, *Frühgriechische Bildhauerschulen*, Pl. 63.

B b

that the claw served its purpose. In wise hands, indeed, the claw-chisel could express in stone the ultimate surface before actual abrasion of polishing finished it off. But it could express rounded surfaces and mouldings only. The claw can never cut the intricacies of hair or drapery or face. It is essentially the tool that moulds body curves and, in fact, gives the final form to the sculptor's finest conceptions. In this connexion it is of the greatest interest to see how practically every work of Michelangelo that is unfinished or partly finished shows the clearest traces of the claw. Usually two separate claw-chisels were used by him (see above, p. 128). For final smoothing Michelangelo seems to have dispensed altogether with the flat chisel in the last stages. He went on, in the Greek way, direct from the claw to pumice and sandstone, or other abrasives.

The claw was also widely used in the Romanesque and Gothic period in Europe. In many sculptures there is no final smoothing, but the striated surface made by the claw is left. Probably this rough surface was more suitable for the holding of the paint, which in medieval sculpture was often of a thick pasty consistency. But the claw remained throughout the Middle Ages as one of the technical tools employed. Michelangelo unconsciously adopted the technical traditions not of Donatello, Agostino di Duccio, and the earlier Renaissance artists, whose technique was that of the flat chisel, but rather those of the Greek periods which had preceded the earlier Italian sculptors.

The outlines of the Greek claw of the sixth century can be reconstructed with certainty from the surviving toolmarks (Fig. 69). The usual claw had blunted teeth, the separations between the teeth being made by filing a V-shaped incision into a straight edge. If the V-shaped incision was widened the teeth inevitably became pointed. Such a tool was used on some parts of the sepulchral frieze from Xanthos, No. B. 310, though elsewhere on the same sculpture the blunt-toothed claw is used. A claw with very small

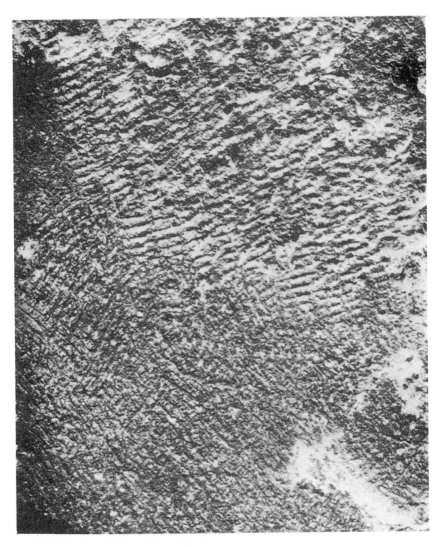

FIG. 69. SURFACE WORKED WITH TWO DIFFERENT
TYPES OF CLAW-CHISEL

The upper part of the photograph shows ordinary claw-work. The lower part
shows finer claw-work done with a spike-toothed claw-chisel. From the Xanthos
Sepulchral Frieze B. 310, in the British Museum.

Scale 1/1.

FIG. 70. CHARACTERISTIC SURFACE WORKED BY A CLAW-
CHISEL IN THE SIXTH CENTURY

The photograph shows part of the 'Cock and Hen' frieze from Xanthos, in the
British Museum, B. 303. The area photographed is from the rectangular space
below the tail of the cock. See B.M. Cat. of Sculpt. Fig. 183.

Scale 1/1.

teeth, a fraction of a millimetre in width, was used on the marble pedimental sculptures of the Hekatompedon (see above, p. 127). The sculptures of Olympia from the Temple of Zeus, on the other hand, show the use of a heavy and coarse type of claw. But there is no distinction of merit between fine claws and the coarse claws. An enormous sculptural project like the Olympian pedimental sculptures involved much sketchy work and much unfinished work, as a glance at the extant sculptures will show. But a mighty undertaking like this could produce as fine results by the aid of heavy tools as could a smaller undertaking with finer tools.[1] There was no room at Olympia for finicky work or for perfection of intricate detail. There is a swift grandeur of creation about these works which precludes any adverse criticism on grounds of technique. Olympia indeed sounded the death-knell of that tendency to over-elaboration which had become apparent in much archaic work of the late sixth century. At the same time the flat chisel was used with exquisite precision for some of the various conventions for hair, and it was used in just that clear incisive way that belongs to the whole manner of the pediments (see Fig. 67).

In relief the claw is, as a general rule, used only for high relief.[2] I have already attempted to make clear this distinction between high and low relief, with the distinction both of technique and of the tools employed that follows as a general rule. But the claw was used early in the sixth century to prepare a surface. But at the close of the fifth century B.C. and in the early fourth the distinction was not so rigid as regards the use of tools. For we find that what is an essentially flat relief such as that of the 'Fourth Frieze' of the Nereid Monument (Fig. 51), has its background prepared by a claw-chisel; and in the same way its outlined figures are done with a punch instead of a flat chisel. This is due not to

---

[1] The use of a moderately fine claw can be seen on the head of the Lapith woman (Olympia).

[2] The rule is not adhered to consistently. The Aristion Stele has a background prepared with a claw, and there are other early exceptions.

a persistence of ancient technique but to a confusion of the two types of relief; for no early fifth or sixth-century relief of such low depth is ever rendered by tools appropriate to sculpture in the round. The fact that it is done in the Nereid Monument is proof either of the provincial quality of those sculptures or of a growing confusion of method.

At the same time it must not be thought that in the fifth century the claw-chisel was totally ignored in low relief. Its advantages as a safer instrument than the flat chisel for preparing a flat ground were obvious. In the sixth century the flat chisel is more often used for a background. But from about 460 onwards the claw becomes more popular in low relief. It is used for the background of parts of the Ludovisi Throne, which, while varying in depth of relief so as to be classed in parts as high, is largely in low relief; it is used throughout on the background of the relief of Philis from Thasos, now in the Louvre. In the third quarter of the fifth century it is more extensively used in low relief, as for instance in the case of the Huntsman of Thespiae, in the National Museum at Athens. But the combination of claw and punch seen on the Nereid frieze referred to above is probably a fourth-century development. The Thespiae Huntsman and the Stele of Philis alike have their relief design cut with a flat chisel and not picked out with a punch.

For those who wish to study the way in which the claw forms the principal outlines of a statue in its closing phases, the unfinished works of Michelangelo afford the clearest illumination.

8. *The Gouge.* This is sometimes called the 'round chisel'[1] or 'curved chisel', a name as unsuitable as it is misleading, since it gives no indication as to the whereabouts of the roundness or of the curve! It also ignores the distinction between the flat 'bull-nosed' chisel, which has a curved edge, and the concave-blade of the gouge. Gouge, on the other hand, is a term which has a reputable ancestry.

[1] Richter, *Sculpture and Sculptors*, p. 144.

At all periods the gouge has been a minor instrument designed for a specific and specialized purpose. Hundreds of statues have been cut without recourse to it, and there is no essential reason why it should be used at all except for certain kinds of incidental work.

From its nature the gouge is a delicate instrument. Having

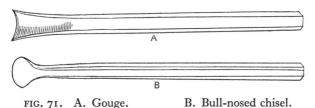

FIG. 71.   A. Gouge.   B. Bull-nosed chisel.

a curved cutting-edge it cannot be used quickly or hit violently with the mallet or its cutting-edge will splinter. It must be used gently for working patiently along furrows already outlined by other means,[1] or it can be used on a smooth surface for cutting shallow grooves into the surface. If used too fast and driven too hard, it will, if it does not break its own edge, splinter the edge of the furrow which it cuts. This helps to explain why in the early sixth century and in the seventh century grooves were usually done by abrasion.

The sculptor's gouge differs from the bronzeworker's gouge in being hollow. The bronzeworker's gouge is a solid instrument of steel or iron which cannot be broken: it removes the bronze by displacing it in a long strip (see p. 164) which curls up as it is displaced. The sculptor's gouge is like one half of a tube that has been bisected lengthways and given a sharp cutting-edge at one end. The back of the sculptor's gouge thus has little displacing power.

The sculptor's gouge differs again from the woodworker's gouge in the shallowness of the arc of its cutting-blade. The woodworker's gouge works on soft material that cannot

---

[1] See p. 132 above. Furrows can be outlined with the flat chisel used from the side.

damage the instrument. Consequently the cutting-blade of his gouge can, if necessary, describe even more than a semicircle and attain the shape of an ogival arch. But a gouge designed to work on stone cannot even describe a wide curve or a semicircle, without endangering the corners of the cutting-edge. It must always have a very open curve and form but a small segment of a circle. All sculptor's gouges designed for hard stones are of this type and Greek gouges were no exception. Every gouge-mark I have examined has been made by a gouge which had a very flat curve.

A variety of the gouge which was perhaps used in antiquity is that which has a V-shaped cutting-edge. This can only be used for the barest surface work and is a most delicate instrument. It cuts, obviously enough, a V-shaped groove in a stone surface. But it is more a woodworker's tool. On the whole I am inclined to think that it was used mainly for soft stone and that the bulk of very narrow V-shaped grooves seen in archaic sculpture, particularly in the lines of hair, are done by the simple flat chisel. The chisel blade would cut down one side of the groove and then down the other. I am the more persuaded to this conclusion since sculptors tell me that for working on marble the V-shaped gouge proves to be almost impracticable. It either splinters the stone or its own corners.

Work done with a moderately wide gouge whose curve is flat, is best seen on the hair that falls down the back of No. 673 in the Acropolis Museum, a kore in the full 'Chiot' style. It is also used on the under-chiton of No. 690, a Nike of the close of the sixth century, and on lines below the waist on the drapery of No. 684, a fine kore associated in style with the Nike; it is also used on the under-chiton of No. 685, a kore of the last quarter of the sixth century.

It is clear that in the finely decorated korai of the sixth century the gouge was used in many cases for drapery. In the main, its use was confined to thin garments like the under-chiton, whose ripples and folds were best suggested by grooves.[1]

Almost every kore of the island type (Dickins's 'Chiot' style) exhibits the use either of the gouge or of the 'bull-nosed chisel' (see p. 192 below) in some part. The most extensive use of a gouge is seen in that remarkable statue No. 683, which wears a chiton without super-imposed garments. The main part of the figure therefore is covered to the thighs with a thin rippling garment which is rendered solely by gouge-work. The ripple lines do not run vertically up and down the figure but rather in serpentine form. The gouge was used for very short cuts, hardly more than half an inch at most at each stroke, and the turns of each serpentine twist were negotiated with care and some difficulty. Examined closely these rippling lines show that very great trouble was taken to cut them and that the surface has been worked over with infinite patience with a gouge and no other instrument: the gouge here used was much smaller than the groove cut.

The gouges used on these drapery folds are various: they vary in size from a very small gouge such as that used on No. 685, thus: ∪
to a large shallow gouge as used on No. 690, thus: ◡

Another use to which gouges were put in the sixth century was for the cutting of locks of hair (see above, p. 110). Sometimes very narrow grooves were cut on the head in parallel lines, wavy or straight. For this purpose a small V-bladed tool may have been used in the case of small lines: this is possibly used on the very fresh surface of the miniature head No. 641 in the Acropolis Museum, where each stroke of the tool has carried it about 0·8 cm. But, as explained above, a very narrow flat chisel may equally have been used. On the front hair of the same head the gouge (or small flat chisel) has been used at right-angles to the stone, producing

[1] These ripples on soft drapery are probably intended to suggest the close folds caused by washing and drying. See Dickins, p. 44.

a series of small V-shaped nicks in the stone that represent the frontal curls, carefully coiffured.

Very heavy gouges are sometimes used to make the transverse hollows of waving locks; these are sometimes ordinary gouges, sometimes V-shaped.

Often the same transverse horizontal hollows are done by abrasion, as in the hair of the figures of kore-type in the Archaic pediments of the temple of Apollo at Delphi, and also in the acroterial figure from the same group.

Although the gouge was a tool that a sculptor could use on almost any occasion for certain types of detailed ornament or accessory, it does not seem to have been in use in the seventh century or in the early sixth. In Attica from 550 onwards its use is common. But since it is an incidental instrument and not one for primary work in any sense, it would be hard to chronologize its use with certainty. The fifth century certainly sees its decline and the flat chisel supersedes it for the cutting of hair.[1] In any case it was not a tool popular in periods when the artist aimed at the broader conceptions and the more general effects. Nor was it ever the kind of tool which could affect style or produce definite aesthetic effects. Its use is largely confined to Attica, and neither the Peloponnese nor east Greek regions, mainland or insular, used it extensively. The Samo-Naxian group dispense with it altogether as, indeed, they dispense with all tools designed for minor effects. The flat chisel also is unpopular in Naxos and Samos, though not absolutely ignored.

To-day the gouge is the least used and the least popular tool of all those employed by sculptors. Its fragility is not compensated by any superior effect that it can produce. It originated as a woodcarver's tool and will always be preferred as a tool for that material.

8a. *The Bull-nosed Chisel.* A brief account of this tool is

---

[1] The hair of the female head, No. 182, in the National Museum at Athens, found near the Asklepieion, is a fine instance of chisel-cut hair in the late fourth century B.C. The use of the chisel is here both bold and simple.

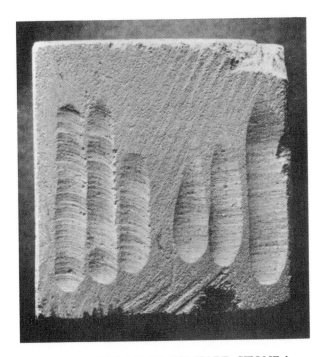

FIG. 72. MARKS MADE ON HARD STONE by:
(1) A 'BULL-NOSED' CHISEL (the three marks on the left).
(2) A GOUGE (the three marks on the right).
Both tools began the cut at the bottom and finished at the top.

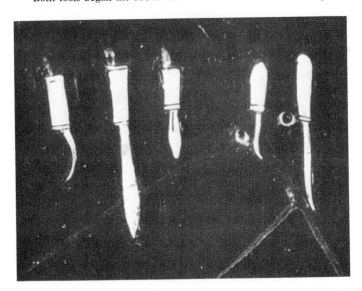

FIG. 73. BRONZE-WORKER'S TOOLS, from a Kylix in the
Ashmolean Museum.
In order from left to right they are: 1. Strigil rasp. 2. Straight long rasp.
3. Small straight rasp. 4. Small strigil rasp. 5. Long straight rasp.

essential, since it is extremely difficult to tell the difference
between its traces and those left by the gouge. The grooves
made by both are hollow concave grooves, while the shape
of the bull-nosed chisel is totally distinct from that of the
gouge. The bull-nosed chisel has a semi-lunar blade that is
quite flat and, as such, it must be classed with the flat chisels.
But the cut it makes is a shallow groove. In many ways it is
the best possible instrument to use when working in hollow
areas of cutting depressions. The only difference between it
and the gouge in working is that it can only make the shallow-
est of grooves and cannot be used continuously to deepen
those grooves, as can the gouge. But a single furrow made
by the bull-nosed chisel is almost indistinguishable from a
single furrow made by the gouge (see Fig. 72). The only
difference is that the bull-nosed chisel seems to require
more strokes of the hammer than the gouge and that the
striations which represent each new hammer-stroke are
more numerous. Further, the striations are, like the edge
of the blade, semi-lunar while the striations made by the
hammer-strokes of the gouge are strictly horizontal. The
difference is perfectly clear from the attached illustration
(Fig. 72) where the two strokes are compared.

One important peculiarity of the gouge-mark that distinguishes it from the abraded groove is that the gouge-cut
groove is, in effect, an elongated oval in outline, with the
head of each end of the oval often prolonged into a narrow
tip, thus:

The abraded groove, on the other hand, 'fades out' at
each end into a surface that blends with the surface which is
cut into, whereas the gouge-cut groove has a perfectly sharp
and well-defined beginning and end. This again is made
clear from the illustration (Fig. 72).

The bull-nosed chisel was in antiquity almost certainly the
tool most usually employed for the cutting of grooves.
Its corners, unlike those of the gouge are not fragile and,

unlike the gouge, it does not require such continuous re-sharpenings.

It is very difficult to distinguish on ancient statues whether a given groove was made by a gouge or a 'bull-nosed chisel' because the surface of the groove is rarely fresh enough to preserve the minute striations referred to above that make the distinction possible. But the one thing that is quite certain is that the 'bull-nosed chisel' was never a wood-worker's tool. It can only cut material that is without grain, material that is frangible. As such it is far more likely to be used by stonecarvers than an instrument whose structure shows that it was designed for wood.

9. *Abrasive tools of stone.* This classification is here made in order to distinguish stone abrasives from the file and rasp of metal; for the principle of use and action is the same in both cases.

Stone abrasives can be used for several separate processes. They can be used to cut, to hollow, to smooth, to polish, and to engrave. Every sculptor to-day employs abrasive in the process of carving stone or marble. Sometimes he uses blocks and pencils of emery-composition, sometimes hard stones other than emery such as 'snake stone', which is used for polishing. For work in softer stones than marble he often used sandstones as abrasives, and for the final surfacing he may even use sand-paper. But abrasives get him only as far as the final *smooth* polish. The high shiny polish so favoured by sculptors of the nineteenth century is obtained by other means which do not here concern us.

Ancient sculptors in Greece seem to have acquired their knowledge of the use of abrasives from two separate sources: from the ancient traditions of the Stone Age, which were most faithfully preserved in the islands, in Crete and on the mainland through the medium of whatever Mycenaean traditions of technique had survived; and secondly direct from Egypt.

Into the Egyptian origins of abrasives and their uses it is not my purpose here to inquire. But it is sufficient to say that almost every process of stone-cutting or working by the aid of stone tools was known to the Egyptians from the earliest Predynastic periods, and that there is no process used by the Minoans, Mycenaeans, and Hellenes which had not previously been known to the Egyptians. It is therefore apposite to mention here the two extremely important paintings from the tomb of Rekhmere which show Egyptian masons and sculptors giving the final polishing and detailed treatment to sculpture in hard stones. A detailed account of what is illustrated is given on pp. 196-7 below the pictures (see Figs. 74 and 75).

What is important to realize is that, except in so far as the Cycladic sculptors of the second millennium worked wholly independently of Egypt and, by the good fortune of having deposits both of emery and of marble, learned early to use the one as a means of cutting the other, the Minoans, Mycenaeans, and Hellenes did not invent any of the methods of using stone against stone. This marks a strong contrast between their knowledge of stone tools and that of metal tools, for the bulk of their iron and steel instruments seem to have been of Hellenic invention.

The most powerful abrasive in existence is emery. It is universally used by sculptors to-day. Emery is the second hardest mineral after the diamond. It can only be smoothed or polished by means of its own dust on the principle of 'diamond cut diamond'. Emery stone is an impure form of corundum. Corundum is a mineral identical with the ruby and the sapphire, which are but two forms which have been stained by intrusive matter. It is naturally rare in its pure crystalline form but it occurs in heavy deposits as emery stone. The Naxian mines, for instance, export no less than 20,000 tons a year of this mineral, which constitutes one of the most important examples of the mineral wealth of modern Greece. Other deposits of emery exist in the island of

Ikaria as well as on the mainland coast of Asia Minor. Emery in its natural state is a sparkling stone, not unlike non-crystalline pyrites in appearance, brown or yellowish in colour. But its hardness and tremendous resisting power

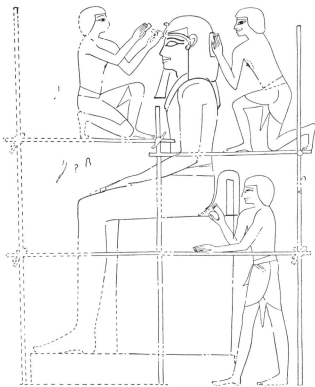

Fig. 74. Sculptors finishing a colossal seated statue: from the frescoes of the tomb of Rekhmere of the 15th century B.C. The man in front of the head is finishing detail with a small chisel and hammer. The man working on the hair is using a rubbing-block. The man working on the throne is using a rubbing-stone of oval shape for polishing.

The smallness of the hammer shows that this chisel work could only have been of the most superficial character.

distinguish it at once from the inferior mineral. A brief search in an emery quarry would provide a sculptor with various fragments of the stone which could be selected to suit his requirements. A large block, broken up with the hammer, could serve equally well. Small splinters with sharp-pointed ends or curved chips with semi-lunar ends or butt-ends would carve lines or grooves of almost any kind. The raw material thus provided the ancient sculptor in Greece with a ready-made tool-case.

Sculpture in marble in the seventh century seems to

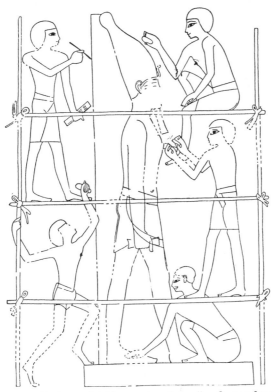

FIG. 75. Sculptors finishing a colossal standing figure: from the frescoes of the tomb of Rekhmere of the 15th century B.C. The workman on the right, in front of the face, is smoothing the headdress with an ovoid rubbing stone. The man below him is working with a small hammer and chisel on the breast. The man on the left at the bottom appears to be holding a rubbing stone. The man above him is painting (probably an inscription) on the back.

employ tools of emery for many purposes. They are used for engraving detail, for rubbing grooves, and for final smoothing. The Dipylon head in the National Museum at Athens is a perfect example of marble sculpture which has been achieved more by abrasive than by metal tools (see above, p. 86). The furrowed ridges over and under the eyes, the jaw curves and hollows at the sides of the nose are all abraded. Details are done with smaller splinters of abrasive. The hair alone seems to have been done with a metal punch, as was the hair of almost all early sixth-century figures.

Before the seventh century there is no certain knowledge that abrasive was known or used in Hellenic times. It rather seems as if increased contact with Egypt had reintroduced Egyptian methods that had been forgotten since Mycenaean times.

Mycenaean stonework and the only Mycenaean sculpture in hard stone, the Lion Gate, owe much to abrasion. The surfaces of the Lions' limbs have been softly moulded by continuous rubbing: the façades of the Atreus tomb have had much of their detail laboriously hollowed by abrasion, and one feature of the Lion Gate (the division between the supports of the Lions; see above p. 27) owes its technique to the Cyclades.

Earlier still, Cretan stonework was worked in the same way.

In the sixth century abrasion did not actually decline as a method, but, on the other hand, much new detail that abrasion could not easily accomplish could be achieved by the flat chisel and the gouge, which increase in popularity after about 550 B.C. That helps to explain why statues like those of the kore series at Athens increase in complexity of detail as the century advances. The earliest of the series are almost wholly devoid of intricate chisel-work and the gouge is scarcely employed at all. They rely (like kore No. 679) for effect mainly upon broad sweeping curves or flowing straight lines, both of which are best rendered by abrasion. How such lines and curves were, in fact, cut can be understood after a close examination. The same type, where broad general effects were aimed at, is illustrated by the Samo-Naxian group of sculptures discussed above (p. 100). Perhaps the best example of drapery which has been almost wholly rendered by abrasive methods is that on the early kore-torso No. 593 in the Acropolis Museum.

FIG. 76. INCISIONS BETWEEN THE FLAPS OF THE
CUIRASS OF THE WARRIOR ON THE STELE OF
ARISTION, National Museum, Athens.

Pentelic marble. The incision on the left is unfinished and shows two grooves.

Scale 1/1.

FIG. 77. FOOT ON PEDESTAL, No. 168, in the Acropolis Museum. Pentelic marble. Incisions made by an abrasive tool worked from above are to be seen continuing the toe-divisions on to the plinth.

Scale 1/1.

For wide grooves in drapery we may presuppose a method of roughing out the hollows by the flat chisel (see above, p. 132) and then widening the groove or deepening it as desired by steady abrasion. A pebble-shaped piece of emery would serve this purpose as well as any. Probably the pebbles held in the hands of the masons in the Rekhmere picture (Figs. 74, 75) are of this type, and in this particular illustration it need not be assumed that the masons are simply *polishing* the surface of the sculpture.

For sharp narrow grooves we can presuppose a disk of emery with a semi-lunar cutting-edge, which is thin like a cutting-blade. Such an instrument is presupposed by the curious grooves on the cuirass flaps of the warrior on the Stele of Aristion.[1] Here the technique in detail can be understood from an examination of the last groove between flaps on the left. This particular groove is left unfinished; the groove is, in fact, double with a projecting core standing between the two cuts. The sculptor should have removed this unnecessary core by further abrasion afterwards with other instruments, but he did not do so, though in the other grooves he has finished his work (Fig. 76).

Very similar marks are seen on two interesting fragments, Nos. 168 and 499 in the Acropolis Museum. These are in each case part of the feet of a figure together with the pedestal on which the feet are carved. No. 168 gives one foot only of a crouching figure, probably male, and 499 feet of a figure certainly male and probably standing. Both seem to belong to figures of the early fifth century. In each case the toes in the process of fashioning the statue have been divided not by chisel-strokes but by the aid of one cutting process done at right angles to the toes vertically from above. This process was one of abrasion, since the tool which cut the divisions between the toes continued the original dividing

[1] Curiously enough in the similar and contemporary warrior relief in the National Museum at Athens (No. 3071) the cuirass grooves are rendered with a flat chisel. Different artists followed different methods and this is a very flat relief.

mark on to the plinth surface. Four cuts are clearly seen continuing the toe divisions on to the edge (Figs. 77, 78). From their nature and position they could not possibly have been made with a file, still less by a saw. They are due to vertical rubbing and presuppose a process which worked from above the toes down on to the marble surface of the plinth. Similar marks are just perceptible in the case of No. 571 (a plinth with horse's hooves and human feet), though here the final polishing has nearly eliminated them. Again in No. 12A in the National Museum at Athens, a pair of feet of the mid-fifth century placed on an oval basis, the same lines are faintly visible. These four examples in any case suffice to illustrate the method which seems to have been widely used for the cutting of toes. And what is important is that it was a method of abrasion and not of chisel-work, except in the later stages. The roughing out of the toes was done with a stone tool, presumably a sharp disk-shaped slice of the best cutting emery.

This minor example of method has been elaborated to show that abrasion was not confined to the paring off of surfaces and the smoothing of planes or curves. Abrasive could clearly be used as a major tool for biting into the surface of marble so as to make grooves narrow and deep or thin incisions that were both accurate and clearly defined. On bronzes similar lines would have been made with a burin, an instrument which works in much the same way as a sharp tool of emery.

Fine surface lines for detailed design could sometimes be ruled with an emery point. A very clear example of this is seen on the belt end of the waistbelt of the torso No. 593 (Fig. 36). Here the chequer pattern of the belt-end, intended no doubt to indicate embroidery, was done by ruling eight lines horizontally and four lines vertically. The four vertical lines were cut after the horizontal lines and were cut a little deeper. The instrument which made these lines was a pointed tool not unlike a blunt-pointed pencil. A file would have given a sharp indented V-shaped line. But these lines

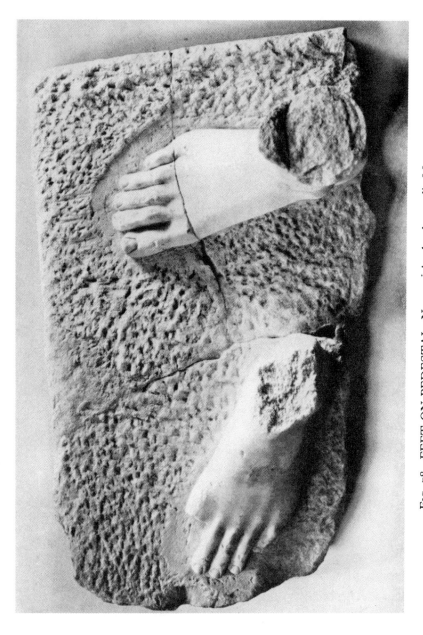

Fig. 78. FEET ON PEDESTAL, No. 499, in the Acropolis Museum.

Similar incisions to those seen on No. 168 are seen continuing the toe-divisions on to the rougher part of the plinth.

Scale 1/2.

FIG. 79. MEETING-POINT OF FOLDS OF DRAPERY BY THE
LEFT HAND OF THE KORE OF ANTENOR

These folds have been rendered by abrasion: perhaps the deeper folds on the
right have been cut with a saw. (The lower part and extreme right of the plate
show some restorations in plaster.)

Scale 1/1.

are made by an instrument with a rounded cutting-point.
The belt-ends of No. 679 in the Acropolis Museum (Fig.
43) are rendered by the reduction on each side of the vertical
belt-ends of the surface of the marble. This reduction is
achieved by abrasion and the horizontal ends of the belt-
ends are left undefined. One of the most impressive instances
of minutely and subtly abraded hollows is to be seen in the
Attic korai of the late sixth century. At the point where the
folds of the chiton are drawn together by the right or left hand
there is a convergence and diminishing of folds towards an apex.
These converging folds are most carefully rendered right up
to the apex mainly by the process of abrasion (Figs. 79 and 80).
One of the best examples is seen on the Antenor kore.

It would be impossible to classify all the various uses to
which stone rubbers could be put. On the whole, abrasion
can be distinguished from file-work or rasp-work by the surface produced. A filed or rasped surface is not smooth. Traces
of the teeth are always left. Abrasion gives a smooth surface.

Abrasives used for the purpose of hollowing grooves,
smoothing ridges, deepening hollows or rounding surfaces
must have lasted a very long time in Greek sculpture. To
work stone with stone was a tradition which did not easily
die. It was ultimately killed by the increased demand for
sculpture, which in turn led to a speedy output. That it
lasted as late as the Parthenon sculptures is perfectly clear.
The bulk of their surface finish, except in the case of the
frieze, is stoneworked. In this context it is interesting to recall
the principal reason which was given by Richard Payne Knight
in evidence before the Royal Commission on the proposed
purchase of the Elgin Marbles in 1816; for his refusal to see
in them masterpieces of the first order, was that their technique
did not seem to him to be the authentic technique of Greek
times; asked his opinion on the so-called 'River God' he replied:[1]

'It is highly finished but it is differently finished from the first-rate
pieces; there are no traces of the chisel upon it; it is finished by

[1] *Minutes of Evidence*, 29. 2. 1816, London, 1816, p. 100.

polishing. In the Laocoon and the things of acknowledged first-rate work, supposed to be originals, the remains of the chisel are always visible. That is my reason for calling these of the second rate.'

From this it is evident that Payne Knight was an observant man, even if the inferences from his observation were wrong. Certainly no other of the witnesses who gave evidence was able to correct him and none of them gave evidence of a technical type to justify their attribution of the works to the first rank and to the fifth century.

Whether the Greeks had a special term with which to designate a stone used as an abrasive is not certain. Conceivably they used the term ξυστήρ which was also applicable to files. Pollux in the Onomasticon, in his list of words used to indicate the working of statues,[1] mentions διαξέσαι. Since it is a general term ranking with κοιλᾶναι λίθον, ἀναγλύψαι and διατυπῶσαι to indicate the main processes, we can reasonably take it to refer to the smoothing of the statue as a whole rather than to the filing of certain parts. The two words διαξέω and διαξύω seem to have had distinct usages and the distinction is not quite clear. The latter is used by Aristotle in reference to facial wrinkles,[2] which suggests that διαξύω is concerned with the cutting of grooves. The former has no such specific meaning. The further occurrence of words like ξυστρωτός as descriptive of the fluting of a column or of διαξύσματα for the flutings themselves (or the alternative ξύστραι) suggests that in some derivative or compound of ξύω lies hidden the word used to describe an abrasive tool.

Certainly there is no suggestion of engraving or cutting either in the word ξέω or in ξύω. Both indicate abrasion in the case of stone, planing or smoothing in the case of wood. τὸ ξυστόν in the *Iliad*[3] is the polished shaft of a spear and παλτὸν ξύσασθαι in Xenophon[4] means to shape a javelin shaft. The word λαοτύπος used adjectively may also have been employed to describe a stone tool.

10. *The Simple Drill, the Auger (or Wimble), and the Running*

[1] i. 1. 15.   [2] *Physiogn*. 3. 10 and 3. 17.   [3] xi. 260.   [4] *Cyr*. vi. 2. 32.

FIG. 80. MEETING-POINT OF FOLDS OF DRAPERY ON THE
FRAGMENTARY FIGURE, No. 147 (1360), in the
Acropolis Museum.

This shows a rather different treatment than in the drapery of the Antenor
Kore. The folds on the right are deep and probably rendered by a saw; the
others are done by abrasion.

Scale 1/1.

FIG. 81. ITALIAN GEM of THE FOURTH CEN-
TURY, showing an artist using the simple bow-drill.

The spherical objects at the lower part of the drill near the
point are weights which served to give the drill momentum.
Exactly similar weights are used to-day.

Scale 3/1.

FIG. 82. HYDRIA in Boston showing the preparation of
the coffer of Danae.

The carpenter is using a bow-drill.

Drill. This is in origin a carpenter's tool. As such it is very clearly illustrated on the Rekhmere paintings[1]. Here the drill itself is held at right angles to the surface to be drilled and the butt of the revolving shaft of the drill is covered with a cap of wood or stone which is held in the hand. The cap can be used to exert pressure on the shaft without hurting the hand.

The simple drill bores always either at right angles or else at a very low angle to the surface to be drilled. The running drill is a name given to the same instrument when it is used at so sharp an angle to the surface that the end of the drill can move in any desired direction. There is no *structural* difference of any kind between the simple and the running drill.

The way in which the drill is revolved is as follows. The string of a bow is looped round the centre of the drill and then fitted on to each end of an ordinary simple bow. If the bow is then pulled backwards and forwards in alternating movements and the drill held firm on one spot, the shaft of the drill will revolve at very high speed. A notch cut round the drill-shaft or a projecting boss at the centre with a groove cut in it, will hold the bowstring firmly in position. The point of the drill, in the case of a sculptor's drill, can be of metal, of stone, or of hard wood, and can be fortified by adding to the spot which is bored emery or other abrasive sand. No drill has survived and we have no precise information as to its nature other than what can be gleaned from ancient representations of the drill, and from inferences drawn from the traces of drill-work seen on statues.

Two early gems are known on which the bow-drill can be seen. But in neither is it shown as being used in sculpture. One, recently acquired for the British Museum from the Warren Collection[2] (Fig. 81), is Italian, and shows an artist or craftsman holding the shaft of the drill with his right hand by the top and working the bow horizontally with his left.

[1] P. E. Newberry, *Life of Rekhmara*, pl. xviii.
[2] *B.M. Quarterly*, iv. 2, p. 34.

His left leg is outstretched to hold down the tripod on which he works. The gem is badly cut and itself suffers from a too deep use of the drill. It is not clear what is the object which is being drilled, for below the visible end of the shaft are two globular objects one above the other. Below them is what appears to be the table of the tripod. The object drilled is possibly a gem, since the artist himself was a gem-cutter. The gem may perhaps have been fixed on the surface of the table-top. The two globular objects are certainly detachable weights, not unlike loom weights, which had been slipped over the drill-shaft. By being placed just above the drill-point such weights would steady the drill in revolution, and give it momentum. Spherical weights of metal are so used in modern hand-drills of this type (Fig. 44).

The other gem, also at London in the British Museum,[1] shows a craftsman in a similar position, but facing the other way. His left leg also is raised and his bow is worked with the right arm. As in the other, the drill is boring vertically into some object which seems to lie on a similar tripod.

I do not think that either of these gems shows a carpenter. Both seem to be gem-cutters and in each case the gem cannot be seen. The drills are small, perhaps too small for use by a sculptor. A carpenter is seen using a drill in the Boston vase (Fig. 82).[2]

It is most probable that the gem-cutter learned the use of the drill from the carpenter and transmitted it to the sculptor. Nor, as we have seen, did the sculptor make use of it before the middle of the sixth century. The priority is certainly with the gem-cutter in the matter of time, for gems were drill-cut in Mycenaean times as well as early in the sixth century.

It has also been made clear how the earliest drill in use in sculpture was the smallest and how towards the close of the

[1] Walters, *Cat. of Gems*, No. 645; Blümel, fig. 2; A. H. Smith, *Cat. of Gems*, No. 305.
[2] Beazley, *Vases in America*, Fig. 31, and *Attische Vasenmalerei*, p. 111.

sixth century the size of the drill increased enormously. The school of Antenor favoured drills almost a centimetre in diameter.

But that large drills were used in the middle of the sixth century for purely structural purposes is clear from the drill-holes in the forearm of No. 679 in the Acropolis Museum. Here a drill larger than those used by Antenor was used to drill two holes transversely so as to allow a marble joint to be made. The holes were later filled with molten lead, so effecting the join. Similar holes for joints are common enough in archaic sculpture.

I have hitherto made the assumption that all drill-holes are made by a bow-drill. This needs some modification, for we cannot know this for certain. The earlier stage, in point of development, of the bow-drill would be, of course, the simple auger or brace. Such a tool is used to-day by most sculptors. It has a flanged boring-point which enables the blades of the flanges to cut rapidly into the marble when the tool is revolved by hand. A large wooden handle or a brace-handle would give great cutting power in the process of revolution. Greater speed and boring power is obtained to-day by revolving the auger by means of a wheel on one side, which is turned with the right hand while the left holds the shaft—rather on the principle of the domestic egg-beater. The ancient equivalent of this had far less power and speed but could well be used to drill simple and shallow holes.

We must therefore allow for the coexistence of this simpler type of drill with the bow-drill. The bow-drill, on the other hand, would give far greater penetrative power. Nor need we assume that the bow-drill was a small drill. An efficient penetrating bow-drill for working on soft objects was fashioned by Odysseus out of a pine trunk, when he destroyed the eye of the Cyclops! The substitute for the bow and its action was provided by his crew hauling on a stout rope and revolving the shaft of the drill in the orthodox way. Given two assistants and a stout cord, a very powerful

bow-drill could be used in architectural or sculptural
work.[1]

The running-drill developed naturally from the bow-drill,
but not from the auger. As already explained, the running-
drill was merely a bow-drill whose cutting-point was used
obliquely in motion. Guided carefully, it could trace long
furrows in any direction.

It has been assumed[2] that there was a transitional stage
from the static to the running-drill which can be detected
in a series of parallel borings made by a simple drill which
were afterwards chiselled over and joined up into a furrow
(see above, p. 134). But this is a difficult assumption. For
we find both in medieval sculpture[3] and in the unfinished
work of Michelangelo[4] that rows of parallel holes bored by
a simple drill are found extensively. Their purpose was to
honeycomb a certain area of the marble so as to make it
easier to clear out later with the chisel. A row of a dozen
holes can make the task of the chiseller much more easy.
If the holes are deep his task is still easier, for the whole
fabric of the marble may be eaten into and so there is far
less resistence to the chisel. Exactly similar series of holes
visible in drapery grooves on the Athena No. 140 in the
Acropolis Museum were no doubt cut for exactly the same
purpose. The same purpose was in the artist's mind when
he cut the row of drill-holes seen on a Nike of the Balustrade
of the Nike Temple,[5] though here the original purpose of the
holes was to break down the marble in the primary stages of
the work, and not merely to cut a local groove in the later
stages. These holes are the technical traces of the very first
work on the block of marble which has been cut down
almost to the level of the end of the holes. It is, indeed,
easy to see how the whole modern process of 'pointing'

---

[1] Blümner, *Technologie*, iii, p. 220.
[2] Ashmole, *J.H.S.*, 1930, p. 102.
[3] No. 6 in the Louvre ('Ange Thurifère'). A twelfth-century sculpture.
[4] The 'Slaves' in the Louvre. Long rows of drill-holes along the outline
of the legs.   [5] Rhys Carpenter, op. cit., pl. xxxiv. 2.

developed from this more primitive use of parallel drill-holes made for the purpose of facilitating heavy work.

The date at which the running-drill first came into operation is dubious and still a matter of some dispute. One authority detects its use on the Boston counterpart of the Ludovisi Throne[1] and, on the assumption that this work is of the first half of the fifth century, dates the running-drill accordingly. Professor Ashmole declares categorically that 'the running-drill was introduced in Athens between the time of the Parthenon Frieze and that of the Balustrade of Athena Nike'.[2] Professor Rhys Carpenter,[3] on the other hand, believes that 'the transition from the stationary to the running-drill' was due to the 'experimentation of the Masters of the Parapet'. Blümel[4] believes that the running-drill superseded the saw in the middle of the fifth century.

I am inclined to agree with Carpenter's view, allowing for the occasional use of a running-drill at earlier periods. For, after all, any sculptor in using a drill could use it obliquely and on rare occasions make it serve as a running-drill. But one cannot say that it was in full use until it was extensively used for many purposes. Such an extensive and fully understood use of the drill is seen in the work of that parapet master whom Professor Carpenter convincingly identifies as Kallimachos. Certainly this distinguished sculptor uses the running-drill with the utmost freedom and ease, and there is no sculpture before his time which shows such swift capacity in the use of the drill. This explains on a reasonable basis the statement of Pausanias,[5] λίθους πρῶτος ἐτρύπησε, which, if taken to refer to the simple drill, is quite meaningless, since the simple drill had been in use for over a hundred years before.

It is, however, not within the scope of this book to investigate the period when the running-drill was in full use. And

[1] Richter, *Sculpture and Sculptors*, 2nd ed., 1930, p. 145.
[2] *J.H.S.*, 1930, p. 102.
[3] *Sculpture of the Nike Temple Parapet*, 1929, p. 78.
[4] Op. cit., p. 9.   [5] i. 26. 6.

in supposed early instances of its use, such as the Boston Throne, the greatest care must be taken to ascertain that the drill used is not the drill of a restorer or toucher-up. In the case of the Humphrey Ward Head in the Louvre furrows made by the running-drill over an inch in length are to be seen under the folds of hair that fall over the temples and forehead. These furrows are of the type seen in work of the Imperial age. The details of the face and hair are largely achieved, rather roughly, by means of a flat chisel. I feel no doubt that the drill-marks are not made by a restorer and the whole technique of the head suggests most definitely that it is a Roman copy and not an original contemporary with the Ludovisi Throne. The marks of the running-drill on the Boston Throne are seen between the fingers of the hands of the seated figure on the left. But these may conceivably be adventitious and later, more especially as the Throne has no archaeological pedigree which can account for the time which elapsed between its finding in the earth and its arrival in a public collection. If, on the other hand, the furrows of the Boston Throne are, as I think certain, contemporary with its manufacture, then they serve as some confirmation of those views which make that work later in date than the Ludovisi Throne, for on the latter there are no traces at all of the marks of the running-drill.

There seems no doubt that the Greek word for a bow-drill was τρύπανον. Homer tells us as much when he makes Odysseus say

Ἐγὼ δ' ἐφύπερθεν ἐρεισθεὶς
δίνεον, ὡς ὅτε τις τρυπῷ δόρυ νήιον ἀνὴρ
τρυπάνῳ.

It is indeed satisfactory to get the name of so complicated an instrument so definitely fixed. It is almost equally certain that an auger was called by a different name although its purpose and processes were the same as those of the simple drill. Τέρετρον has ample documentation to justify us in giving this meaning to it. In the same epigram from the

Anthology[1] we hear of τρύπανα ἐλκεσίχειρα and τέρετρα as two of the tools of a retired carpenter, and we can be sure that at all periods these two tools were common both to sculptor and to carpenter.

In gem-cutting the bow-drill and not the auger would have been used. It must also have been used with emery

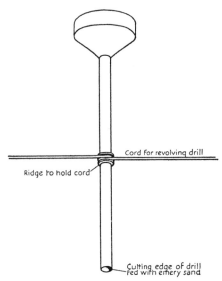

Cord for revolving drill

Ridge to hold cord

Cutting edge of drill
fed with emery sand

FIG. 83. Tubular Drill (conjectural reconstruction).

sand. But there was no fundamental difference between the usage of the gem-cutter and that of the sculptor. The tool worked in the same way and produced the same effects.

11. *The Tubular Drill* (Fig. 83). This instrument was used only in Mycenaean and Minoan times. There is no evidence as yet to show that it was known to or used by the Hellenic Greeks. It has already been shown that it was used extensively at Mycenae and at Knossos in the first Late Minoan period for decorative friezes and façades as well as for the main processes which went to the fashioning of the Lion Gate Relief. Its clear and unmistakable traces are also found in much architectural work and there is some reason to think

[1] vi. 103; cf. also 205, a similar epigram.

E e

that it was also used in quarries for the primary purpose of cutting blocks of stone. Schliemann, with his accurate and observant eye, was the first to note its use in architecture at Tiryns. It is curious to find that no subsequent investigators except Petrie have paid attention to it or observed what an important part it played in Mycenaean stonework. Schliemann's description of the traces left by the tubular drill are so clear and unambiguous that I quote them here as the classic description.

'The appearance of the Tirynthian bore-holes shows us rather that they were made with a simple cylinder, hollow inside, and that thus the auger had the form of a strong reed. With even very rapid twisting one could not bore a hole in a hard stone with such an auger unless, as with the saw, a sharp sand (emery) were strewed into the bore-hole. When the sand was moved about by the auger, it rubbed away small particles of the stone and thus there was gradually formed a cylindrical hole in the middle of which a thin cylinder of stone remained standing. When the hole reached the required depth this cylinder was removed by some instrument, and the dowel-hole was complete. As might be expected, the central stone cylinder was not always by this procedure completely removed at the lower end, but generally a portion of it remained at the bottom of the hole. These upright remains of the little cylinders can be still plainly seen in many dowel-holes and it is from them we have obtained an insight into the method of boring. The diameter of the holes varies from 28 to 45 mm. and the depth from 40 to 60 mm.'[1]

It would be hard to improve on this excellent description. Surprisingly, Schliemann did not detect the use of the same instrument on the Lion Gate and on the Lion Gate Relief, and other sculptures referred to above. In examining the Lion Gate and the Postern Gate at Mycenae in 1932, I found that the same tubular drill had been used in each gate for drilling the large holes in the breccia gate-posts which had held the bars of the gate. The drill was 12·5 cm. in diameter,

---

[1] *Tiryns*, 1886, p. 266. Where Schliemann uses the term 'auger' we should substitute the term 'drill', otherwise there may be some confusion. The auger is a solid drill and here we are dealing with hollow drills.

the largest, I think, yet recorded for Mycenaean Greece. The characteristic ring of the tube and central core are clearly seen at each gate. The thickness of the metal of the tube can be estimated at about 2 mm., to judge from the ring-mark round the core.

Deep holes similarly bored are seen on certain blocks of walls at Tiryns, and they suggest that they were done in the quarry. Doerpfeld illustrates two such stones in his sections on technical matters in Schliemann's book.[1] He suggests that the holes so made were plugged with wood which was then expanded by water, so splitting the stone: for the surviving stones show that they were split exactly along the diameter of the bored holes.

It is clear then that there were two distinct uses to which the tubular drill could be put, one sculptural, the other architectural or masonic. In sculpture the drill was used for making circles that had a decorative value, as the centres of spirals. The depth of these circles was slight and the work involved in the making of them inconsiderable. It was, in fact, secondary work comparable to the work done by the gouge or flat chisel in the later sixth century in Greece. But it was also used for the primary processes, as has been made clear from our examination of its uses on the Lion Gate Relief. Here it cut the main outlines and performed the arduous task of reducing the stone to its principal form, at any rate in the deeper parts. It was used indeed much as the simple drill was used at the close of the sixth century and early fifth century, for the breaking down of the stone. But the performance of this task by the tubular drill would have been a much more arduous process. Why the simple drill was not used by the Mycenaeans and Minoans is not clear. It was known to them as the principal tool of the gem-cutter, but there is no trace of it on stone sculpture.

Schliemann's 'central cylinder' of stone, or 'core' as I prefer to call it, can be clearly seen in each circle cut on a

[1] Ibid., p. 335, fig. 133/4.

decorative frieze or façade and even more clearly on the Lion Gate Relief in the deeper furrows.

The tubular drill and abrasive rubbers were the main tools with which the Lion Gate Relief and most of the other examples quoted were made. As such, it is essentially a tool of the Stone Age which had continued in use for a long period.

Whether the tubular drill was made of metal or of hard wood it is difficult to say. Probably bronze would be the best material, since the cutting-end of the tube, after being used for a short time with emery powder, would soon have its surface full of particles of emery sand which by pressure and revolution would have become embedded in the metal. This leads us to suppose that the cutting-end of the tube was not brought to a sharp edge but remained of the same thickness as the main part of the walls of the tube. This in turn is fully confirmed by the nature of the circles seen on Mycenaean and Minoan sculptures on which it was used. The outline of the ring so cut is a thick one, usually over one millimetre in width and not a sharp line which a knife-edge would have made. It was a blunt-edged tool.

The modern equivalent of the tubular drill, called the 'jumper drill' is, on the other hand, a tube with a sharp edge of hardened steel. Moreover, it is used with a hammer and struck with a succession of short sharp strokes. So used, it soon breaks down very hard stones like granite or basalt.[1] Actually it can be looked on as the lineal descendant of the prehistoric tubular drill, and the way in which it is used corresponds to a modern version of the old methods.

The tubular drill was revolved rapidly in exactly the same way as the simple drill. Probably the metal tube had a notched ring round the middle or a projection to hold the bowstring or wire used for revolving it. The pressure required for the

---

[1] It is an old-fashioned tool for handworkers and in granite work has now been largely superseded by the pneumatic drill, which breaks up the surface by means of a blunt-ended punch driven with great force.

jumper drill is obtained by the hammer and the cutting power comes from percussion and not from revolution.

Note on Egyptian tubular drills. Thanks to Professor Sir Flinders Petrie's brilliant exposition of the types of tubular drills used in Egypt and the manner of their use, we are more fully documented in this matter than for any other detail of the technical methods of stonework in antiquity.[1]

He points out the following facts and illustrates them with examples (Plate VIII of *The Pyramids and Temples of Gizeh*). The Egyptians had perfected tools of bronze in which one or more cutting-points were mounted. These cutting-points were probably of 'tough uncrystallized corundum'. Diamonds were perhaps used, but their extreme rarity and their natural absence from Egypt makes this improbable. Simple burins with a corundum point are inferred from the cutting of inscriptions on diorite bowls. Tubular drills with such points mounted on their cutting-edge, so as to make them, as it were, into tubular saws, were certainly in use, and their dimensions can be established from extant cores and holes in stonework. In the plate above referred to illustrations of several cores and half-finished work by drills are given. The dimensions of the drills varied from a quarter of an inch diameter to one of the astonishing size of 18 inches. This immense instrument was used simply for quarry work. Its traces are to be seen on a limestone pavement at El Berseh.

Tubular drills were invariably used for the hollowing of granite coffers. The process was to make rows of drill holes round the portion to be removed and then to break down the intervening pieces and to break off the cores. The tool was rotated slightly in the case of heavy work, or the object, if a small one, was rotated against the tools. This gives the drill-hole a slightly conical shape. The pressure required on a tubular drill was considerable. He calculates that a

[1] *The Pyramids and Temples of Gizeh*, 1883, chapter vii, and *Anthropological Journal*, 1883, 'Mechanical Methods of the Egyptians'.

load of one or two tons was required upon a drill of a 4-inch diameter cutting granite. Drills with corundum points mounted in the circular cutting-edge made a core which has not a smooth surface but a ribbed one. The ribbing is caused by the corundum point which scratches a spiral line round the core. From the line the rate of penetration can be

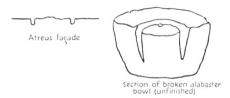

Atreus façade

Section of broken alabaster
bowl (unfinished)

FIG. 84. Contrast of cuts made by a plain tubular drill used
with emery sand and a drill with an inset point of emery.

estimated. In his illustration No. 7 the spiral of the core or hole sinks 0·1 inch in the circumference of 6 inches, or 1 in 60, a very rapid rate of cutting.

No tubular drills have been found, but, he points out, not a dozen of simple mason's chisels are known, and if ordinary tools have survived so ill one can hardly expect the very much rarer and expensive tools, such as jewelled drills, to have survived at all.

Evidently the Egyptians had perfected the tubular drill to a degree far beyond the knowledge of the Minoans and Mycenaeans. The traces of the drill seen at Mycenae, Tiryns, and elsewhere all presuppose the more elementary form with a simple metal blade which was fed with emery sand. The rings on the Lion Gate Relief and on the examples of sculpture from the Treasury of Atreus all show a certain width and not a sharply cut groove. They can be contrasted by comparing them with an example cited by Petrie (Plate VIII, No. 9 a).

The difference is that caused by a drill used with sand on the one hand and a drill whose blade is pointed with corundum on the other. The hole is worn by steady friction by the former and by direct cutting by the latter (Fig. 84).

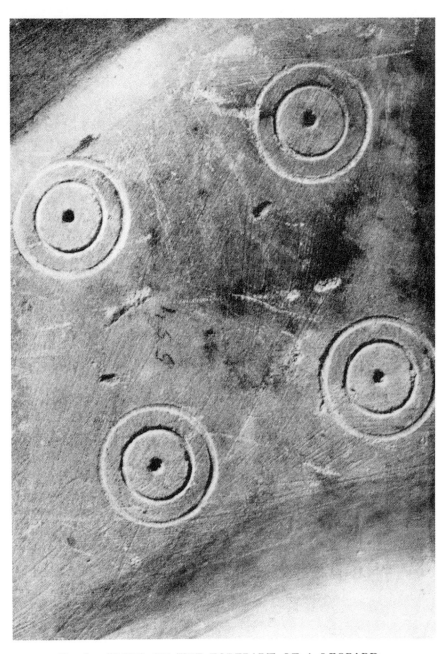

FIG. 85. SPOTS ON THE FOREPART OF A LEOPARD,
No. 554, in the Acropolis Museum, made of Hymettan marble.
These spots are cut with a cutting-compass. The surface of the stone
has been coarsely abraded.

Scale 1/1.

How the weight was fixed on to the drill so as to get the maximum of pressure is not known. Nor is it clear how the drill was revolved, but a central ridge round which the cord ran seems an essential assumption (see Fig. 44 and p. 212 above). For spiral penetration the drill would, of course, have to be revolved only one way and not by an alternate pulling of the cord backwards and forwards. This continuous revolution would involve the use of a long cord and of its resetting every time the pull was completed.

12. *The Cutting-compass*. The evidence for the existence and use of this instrument is inferential. It was used extensively for decorative detail in architecture and on sculpture in the seventh century. Examples of its work have already been discussed in the account of the Prinias sculptures. In the sixth century it was also widely used for cutting the circles of eyes on statues, but it declined in popularity towards the end of the century. It seems to have been popular more in Crete and the Peloponnese and in regions under Peloponnesian influence, and less used elsewhere (Fig. 85).

It was an ordinary two-legged compass of which one leg ended in a cutting knife-edge. There are some grounds for believing that a small version of this type of compass was in use in Minoan times, since small compass-drawn circles are found on certain examples of decorative stonework.[1]

It must have been a development from the compasses used for incising circles on pottery (see p. 82 above), and so may be looked on primarily as a potter's tool. It never played a very important part in the main work done on a statue but it was a useful adjunct. Its extensive use in Crete at Prinias suggests that it belongs to the type of instrument which went with a knowledge of engraving on stone such as is seen in the engraved stelai from Prinias.

13. *Files and rasps*. The file may be distinguished from the

---

[1] Ashmolean Museum, No. Æ. 767, an alabaster vase from the floor of the Throne-room at Knossos.

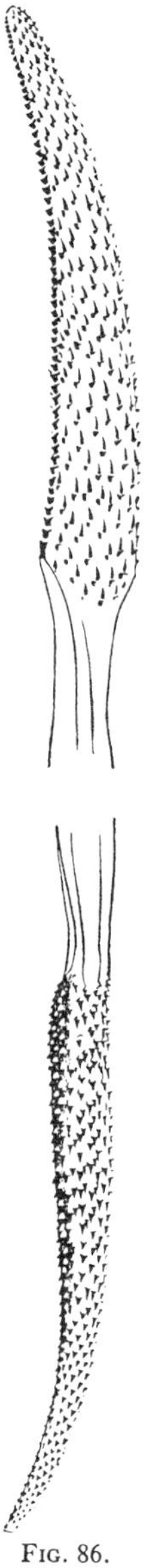

rasp by definition. A file is an instrument that cuts into a surface; a rasp is one which *prepares* a surface. This is a working definition only for the purposes of this book and need not be taken as final. Files cut grooves and lines; rasps wear down surfaces already prepared otherwise, or make hollows or cavities that are not strictly to be classed as grooves (Fig. 86).

Sculptors' files naturally differed from those used by bronzeworkers. There are several excellent representations of files of the latter type but none of sculptor's files. But there is no reason to suppose that they differed essentially from modern files. The same must be said of rasps.

There is no evidence to show that files and rasps were ever used in Minoan and Mycenaean times. None have survived, although bronze chisels, carpenters' tools, are common enough. It is difficult to see that a file or rasp made of bronze or copper could have lasted for any appreciable length of time or for such length of time as to achieve any work of importance.[1] The body of the file or rasp would no doubt have remained intact but the teeth and striated surfaces would have been worn flat after very little use. Nor is there in fact the smallest trace of file-work or rasped surfaces in prehellenic stone carvings.

To what extent the file and rasp were used in the first half of the sixth century it is impossible to say. There is indeed very little to show that they were used at all. The usual process until 550 B.C. seems to have been almost exclusively a preliminary trimming with the hammer, a great deal of punch-work with large and small punches, and then

FIG. 86.
Modern
Double-
Ended
Rasp.

[1] Even a hard steel file or rasp as used to-day is blunted extremely rapidly.

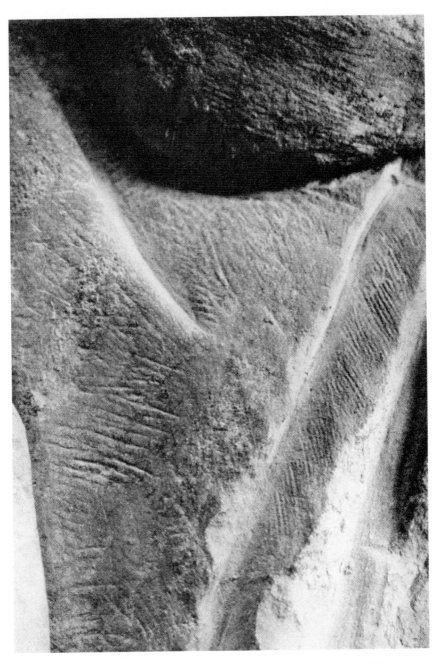

FIG. 87. MARKS OF RASPS ON THE SURFACE OF THE
COLOSSAL FIGURE OF ATHENA, No. 1362, in the
Acropolis Museum.

Two separate rasps have been used. No final polishing has been employed.

Scale 1/1.

a last dressing with a small punch and an extensive rubbing with abrasives. About 550 or perhaps a little earlier, the claw-chisel is used to assist in the last stages before the abrasives are employed. The rasp and file thus do not appear to have been used for primary work. The second half of the century sees the use of new tools for secondary work and detail, but no trace is seen of the use of the rasp and file for primary work. On the other hand, they begin to be used to a certain extent for working on grooves, and rasped surfaces can be detected in a good many cases in the Korai series, mainly on drapery. But they never play a very important part and are never used for primary work.

A filed surface is not so much rough as dull. Actually it is more attractive to the eye than a highly polished surface. This, however, applies only to a surface done with a *fine* file or rasp. Coarse rasped surfaces or a groove whose sides are filed with a heavy file have little attraction. A very characteristic coarsely rasped surface is seen on the male torso in the Berlin Museum figured by Blümel[1] and on a later nude figure.[2] These are surfaces which have been prepared with a rasp for subsequent smoothing and polishing.

There is another kind of rasped surface, such as is found on archaic sculpture, which was left unsmoothed for the reception of paint, so that it might hold the paint firmly. Such also seems to be the explanation of the rasped surfaces of so many of the sculptures of the Temple of Zeus at Olympia.[3] It is also seen in the case of No. 140, the Athena in the Acropolis Museum. One rasp only was used and the surface is uniformly dull. The lovely head No. 699 in the Acropolis Museum, in the early Pheidian manner, is rasped over the top and back of the skull. The lines of the *taenia* are filed. The remaining surfaces are, however, smoothed by abrasion to a dull polish.

---

[1] No. 31, pl. 35 *b*.　　　　　　　　　　　[2] No. 22, pl. 28.
[3] See Blümel, p. 9, for a list of the clearest examples. The fifth century torso of Athena here shown as Fig. 87 is a good instance.

But there is a third type of rasped surface, namely that which is intended to be left unadorned or to be painted very lightly. Such a surface suddenly becomes the fashion in the later part of the fifth century, after the time when the Parthenon sculptures were made and after the time when the Erechtheium frieze was cut. For the pedimental figures of the Parthenon are exquisitely rubbed to a superb smooth surface which does not glisten. Examination of the inner surfaces of the best-preserved examples and of the backs of the figures will explain what I mean more clearly than words. The figures of the Erechtheium frieze are, for the most part, in an appalling condition, badly weathered and hopelessly shattered. But one or two retain their surfaces almost unimpaired. One such, No. 284,[1] shows a smoothed surface similar to surfaces on the Parthenon pedimental sculptures and to much of the frieze surface. But in the Balustrade of the Nike Temple the surface of sculpture is less glowing and rougher, though in no way inferior to look at—merely different. A new fashion had come in and that fashion was popularized by the medium of the rasp. A rasped surface, done with a fine instrument carefully manipulated, was very lovely and suited the bold reliefs of the Nike Balustrade which aimed at catching light and shadow without sharp contrasts. Professor Rhys Carpenter[2] infers a rasp with ridges or teeth spaced 1 mm. apart, and his comments are of great importance.

Rasp cannot be distinguished from file in the traces left on a flat surface. Both alike leave striations clearly defined. A coarse rasp has enormous biting power, sometimes too much, and is with many sculptors to-day a favourite instrument. A few minutes' work with a rasp will abrade a groove half an inch in depth. But treated as a secondary

---

[1] *Acropolis Museum Catalogue*, p. 175, and illustration.
[2] *Sculpture of the Nike Temple Parapet*, p. 8. 'The technical workmanship', he says, 'is for the most part of the highest order; and the tradition of leaving and even exploiting the tool-marks rather than of working all the surface to a monotonously inexpressive lustred finish adds a peculiar charm for an attentive eye.'

tool for the accomplishment of fine surfaces a rasp can, in able hands, make or mar the final surface effects of a statue.

The words for file and rasp in Greek are always distinguished. ξυστήρ is certainly a rasp, the tool that rubs and abrades. The file is called ῥίνη, an obscure word perhaps connected with the name of a fish which had a shagreen-like skin. The qualification χαρακτή[1] indicated that the surfaces of the file were ridged or ribbed. The ῥίνην κνησίχρυσον ὀξυδήκτορα which Demophon the goldsmith dedicates to Hermes[2] can hardly be a rasp, for files and not rasps are the tools of the goldsmith. There do not seem to be any alternative terms for these instruments, and it may be assumed that there were no variants of the ordinary types of file and rasp.

To-day the rasp differs from the file not only in the uses to which it is put but also in the great variety of shapes that it can take. A file is always a straight tool. The rasp, on the other hand, may be curved and can take as many curves as there are concavities to be treated. Its toothed surface can be inserted into the most recondite parts of a statue in order to enlarge a hollow or prolong a groove (Fig. 86).

14. *The Saw.* In Minoan and Mycenaean times the saw was one of the most frequently used instruments in the sculptor's and architect's outfit. Its use at Mycenae on architecture has already been noted by Evans.[3] Schliemann not only detected its traces on architecture at Tiryns but analysed both the methods used for sawing and the nature of the saw used with the greatest accuracy and precision.[4] His account can rank as a standard explanation of this intricate matter. From the sawn stones that he examined he was able to deduce that the process of sawing through a stone block was as follows. The saw attacked the stone from several successive angles until the two parts half-sawn through were joined

[1] *Anth. Pal.* vi. 205.
[3] *Palace of Minos*, II. ii, p. 671.
[2] Ibid. 92.
[4] *Tiryns*, p. 264.

only by a small part in the middle of the mass. This was never finally sawn through, but the two halves or parts were broken apart as soon as the central joint was weak enough. The sawn surfaces thus showed a central rough boss, the remains of the core, and round it were the slightly curved striations made by the sawing, arranged in groups round the central core. He inferred further that the saw had no teeth and was simply a blade of metal. As such, it must have been used with emery sand, which would have hardened its surface and aided the cutting process as a whole. In some cases he was able to estimate the thickness of the blade as being 2 mm. His conclusions are interesting in view of the definite traces of a similar but perhaps smaller saw on certain sculptured decorative fragments from the 'Treasury of Atreus' (see above, p. 31). Here the saw-marks are quite clear and the width of the blade can be exactly gauged.

Petrie's discovery at Tiryns of remains of a saw inside a saw-cut together with small fragments of emery too large to be emery-sand has been noted above (see p. 28). This presupposes a saw which had teeth of emery driven or hammered into the cutting surface. There is no other confirmatory evidence for the existence of this type of saw and it can hardly have been common, but it marks a very important development of the saw as such and would have served as a tool with which to cut the very hardest of stones into slices. At Tiryns it seems to have been a mason's tool, but a smaller version of the same instrument could well serve the lapidary. The use of a graver pointed with emery is attested at least for Egypt (above p. 213) and is presupposed in all Minoan gems. The same principle applied to masons' stonework merely meant the multiplication of the cutting points and so the transformation of a graving tool into a saw.

It is important to make an attempt to ascertain the shape of the prehistoric saws, since the shape probably remained constant even into the Iron Age in classical times. Schliemann suggested that the saw 'had the form of a common knife which a single worker grasped by the handle'. It is certain that the modern stone-saw, that requires two men to work it, was not employed in prehistoric times, for almost all sawn surfaces are slightly curved, showing that they could not possibly have been done with the modern type of saw, which cuts dead straight. It may be as Schliemann suggested, but in the case of sculptures where the saw was used which he did not examine, I am inclined to suggest that the saw there used was a gently curved or semi-lunar blade of metal fastened into a strong wooden back which could be held by one man with one or two hands. As such it could be pressed directly against the stone. Such must have been the saw which cut the rectangular outlines that formed the first stage of the circles on the Atreus fragment discussed earlier (see above, p. 31). Such also must have been the blade which cut the deeper furrows of heavy folds of drapery in the archaic period of Hellenic sculpture. I do not, in fact, know of any indubitable traces of such saw-work in archaic sculpture, but I feel convinced that a small saw of this kind was used on occasions, particularly in very deep and narrow furrows where an abrasive was too thick to penetrate.

The two-handled saw, worked by two men, had certainly come into use in Greece in the earliest period of marble architecture, for not otherwise could marble be cut with the absolute rectangular precision that we see in the earliest temples. This two-handled saw, again, must needs have been a simple untoothed blade, for even the hardest steel blades of a modern saw will not survive the cutting of hard stone and marble for very long. Again, emery sand comes in as the essential medium of cutting, to be used either with oil or with water.

As we have seen, it is probable that some of the more rectangular figures of the earliest archaic period were in the first instance roughly sawn to shape. The Dipylon head has a rectangular quality which certainly suggests that it was outlined in this way.

The Greeks distinguished the toothed from the untoothed saws with perfect clarity. The former was the πρίων ὀδοντωτός[1] and the latter πρίων μαχαιρωτός. This leaves us with no sort or kind of ambiguity.

15. *The Plummet.* Blümel has given a close and reasoned explanation of the use of this accessory in ancient sculpture. He has also added two illuminating illustrations from gems.[2] To the direct evidence he has also added the indirect evidence of the bosses on the heads of some of the figures from Olympia. More than he has told us we do not know. But it would be safe to assume that the plummet, with the square, played an important part in the first stages of the fashioning of a statue in archaic Greek times. The square we know for certain was known as a sculptor's accessory in the early fifth century. The plummet may have been in use as early or even earlier.

[1] The ἰθυδρόμος πρίων of *Anth. Pal.* vi. 103.
[2] Op. cit., figs. 6 and 7.

IX

FOR WORKS IN BRONZE

THE evidence upon which we must rely for our knowledge of the tools used by the bronzeworkers is in the main different from that which illustrates our knowledge of the tools used in marble and stone carving. For the surviving bronzes themselves give us only very limited clues to the tools which were used in their completion. In a life-size bronze the surface has been brought to a uniform smoothness in almost all cases, and no hidden parts are left partly finished. The original cleaning of the bronze immediately after casting largely served to get back to the proper bronze surface itself by the removal of ash, dirt, and accretions and stains fortuitously acquired by the bronze in the furnace. But even the properly moulded surface so revealed was subjected to some kind of smoothing or polishing process of which we are largely ignorant. But a very great deal of modification of the cast surface was in fact carried out in detail, as well as the full completion of detail of hair, face, extremities, and garments which constituted one of the main tasks of the artist of the work.

Our knowledge of the tools employed both in the processes by which the original cast surfaces were modified and those by which the effective detail was added are derived from two quite distinct sources. The first is from the direct evidence of contemporary vase-paintings; the second is from the actual bronzes themselves.

From the vase-paintings we learn a great deal as to the general methods employed in a studio, from the bronzes themselves we learn the detailed methods used by the principal artist. The general processes of welding and smoothing have already been described (p. 159 ff.). But the tools themselves and the relation they bear, if any, to the stone-carver's tools are of primary interest: the following is a list of all the bronzeworkers' tools that can be identified with certainty.

1. *The Saw*.[1] (a) *The long saw.* A very careful representation of this is seen on the Foundry kylix. Here, immediately above the master (who is seated on a low stool in front of his furnace), is seen a long saw with large teeth. One end of it curves slightly to a rounded end which is pierced: at the other it ends abruptly. The teeth are continuous along the whole blade except at the curved and pierced end.

We have no other information of any kind about this saw, and it is difficult to gather the method in which it was used. Sawing as a process in the making of bronzes would only have been needed when the ends of, say, a separately cast limb had to be fitted to a separately cast torso. The rough edge of each would have to be sawn off in order to make a perfect fit. In the process the amount sawn off would hardly exceed an inch. The size of this saw, however, seems too great for so minor a task and something in the nature of actual amputation of a bronze limb seems to be indicated.[2] Such amputations would presumably occur only in the case of castings which had gone wrong. If the limb, as cast, had warped or bent, then it would be essential to saw it off in order that it should be refitted again. The size of this large saw must have been about 4 feet in length, to judge from the proportions it bears to the figures of men. Despite its size it must have been a one-man saw, for it has only one end that is capable of being fitted to a handle. The hole in the curved end is probably the hole by which a handle was screwed on.

(b) *The small saw.* This is only seen on the Berlin oenochoe. It is of a type comparable to a modern carpenter's saw with a bow handle. As such it could be conveniently used for

[1] See Kluge, *Grossbronzen*, p. 142, who does not give much detailed information.

[2] It may be, of course, that this is merely the saw used for sawing logs of wood for furnace fuel.

sawing off small protrusions, or for the minor process of getting a smooth edge to two parts that had to be welded together. It must, however, not be forgotten that its appearance on the Berlin vase does not necessarily mean that it is a bronzeworker's instrument, for, as we have seen (p. 159), there is no certainty that the horse in this scene is ultimately intended to serve as the model for a bronze casting.

2. *The Auger or Drill.* An instrument which may be either of these is seen hanging on the wall in the scene on the Berlin oenochoe, next to the saw. It appears to have a central handle, grooved for the hand-grip, and a loose butt that would revolve with a string. As such this tool is almost identical with the drill of a bow-drill. That drills were needed for piercing holes in large-scale bronzes is evident enough from the bronzes themselves. The eyes, for instance, had to be hollowed for the insertion of their stone or composition irides and holes were needed where two parts of a bronze were riveted together. A drill of this type would have been essential.

If it is thought that the illustration on the vase is inadequate to justify the interpretation as a drill, we can at least assume that it is an auger revolved by hand and not by indirect means; but if this is so, then it is hard to explain the double handle.

3. *The Strigil Rasp.* By this term I mean a rasp in a wooden handle with a blade that curves. Two such are seen on the Ashmolean kylix, two in the Foundry kylix held by bronzeworkers, and one hanging on the wall. The term 'strigil rasp' seems appropriate, since the mode of use is clearly seen. The two workers who are coping with the almost completed warrior statue are using rasps that have sickle-shaped blades and wooden handles, and they are using them with a sideways action that indicates that the process was one of scraping the surface of the bronze just as an athlete's skin is scraped with a strigil. The whole, or at least the greater

part, of the blade is thus in use, not a portion only, as would be the case if the rasp were used as a stone-carver's rasp. The rasps of sculptors and of bronzeworkers seem to be fundamentally distinct in shape and in mode of use.

The purpose of this rasp seems to have been the removal of unevenness and of what modern bronzeworkers, appropriately enough, call the 'fire-skin', and blemishes and accretions on the surface of the bronze acquired in the furnace. It is improbable that it was used or indeed could be used for the modification of the *bronze surface* as such. The way in which it is used by the master and his assistant on the warrior statue seen on the Foundry vase shows that no pressure was possible against the bronze other than the lightest, and that the purpose was, as is here suggested, merely to smooth off excrescences. Where those excrescences were bubbles the resultant holes would, no doubt, later be filled up by patching. All the rasps seen in these various vase paintings are the same. All alike have wooden handles. Those seen on the Ashmolean kylix are smaller and have shorter blades than those on the Foundry vase and the curve of the blades is less pronounced. But no doubt the character of these tools depended upon the individual methods of the artist who employed them.

4. *The Straight Rasp or Burnisher*. Three of these, with various sized blades, are seen on the Ashmolean kylix (Figs. 73, 88, 89). Their handles, like the handles of the strigil rasps, are of wood. That seen second from the left in the row of tools on the Ashmolean vase is clearly a blade for the smoothing or deepening of folds and narrow clefts. It would serve, as such, for working over the inside of vertical drapery folds such as are seen in the Delphian Charioteer, and equally well for the working of the clefts between legs. The very closed Λ formed by the junction of two thighs in a standing figure would be cleared of excrescences by such a tool. The right side of the blade, as seen in the painting, would

be the business end, and its semi-lunar shape would facilitate the work by enabling it to penetrate where a straight blade could not. Traces of rasp work in the form of striated surfaces are sometimes seen in unpatinated or slightly patinated bronzes, but the rarity of unpatinated bronzes is such that only few instances are known. It is difficult to

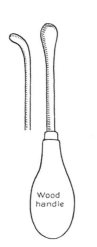

Wood handle

Wood handle

FIG. 88. Modern bronze-worker's burnisher.

FIG. 89. Modern bronze-worker's scraper or burnisher. It should be compared with the similar tool shown on the Ashmolean kylix.

make a clear distinction between rasps and burnishers. The action of both is the same and the burnisher merely has a smooth face. The tool seen third from the left in the Ashmolean kylix corresponds exactly with a common type of modern burnisher (see Fig. 89).

5. *The Hammer* (Fig. 90). Bronzeworkers' hammers differ radically and, one might say, in every respect from the hammers used by stonecarvers. In the Foundry vase no less than six hammers are shown. All alike have long slender handles and light heads which are not pointed. Whether either or both ends of the hammers are edged ends or not cannot be made out, though the fact that in three cases there

is a sensible difference in the profile of one end as contrasted with the other suggests strongly that one end was blade- or wedge-shaped. The hammer used by the assistant who is hammering the headless statue seems to have different ends, and the end actually in use seems certainly to be the blunt end or butt-end of the hammer. This suggestion is strengthened

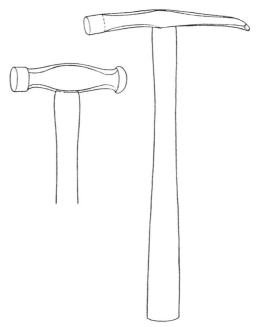

FIG. 90. Modern bronze-worker's hammers.

by the appearance of two hammers which hang, together with a Hephaestean helmet, above the worker who sits to the right of the Athena figure on the Acropolis fragment. They differ from the hammers of the Foundry vase only in the fact that they have their hafts inserted not at the middle but at one side of the central part of the metal head. The butt-end is clearly on the shorter side of the hammer and the longer side holds the wedge-shaped end. The hammer held by the artist is not preserved in its entirety, but the butt-end, with its slightly splayed butt is very clear.

The purpose of the wedge-shaped end would be to make

a furrow or indent a line, while the butt-end would be to beat in a surface and make a hollow or to flatten out a protruding edge. The assistant who, on the Foundry vase, is beating a statue seems to be flattening with the butt-end some area below the neck or shoulder. He is certainly not striking the arm or hand. But his action is difficult to explain, for his grip of the hammer is not that of a man who is using it to strike with. It has been suggested to me by the sculptor Mr. Pilkington Jackson of Edinburgh that this bronzeworker is not using the head but the haft of the hammer and that he is using it to break up the clay core by driving it into the aperture of the neck. This explains why he holds the hammer high up the haft and not in the normal way.

The long slender hafts of the hammers show plainly enough that the hammers were used lightly. Hard hitting would soon break so slender a haft. The hafts of the hammers on the Acropolis fragment are even more slender, and obviously intended for only the very lightest tapping. For the whole process of bronzeworking admits only of light work with the hammer or rasp or gouge. Heavy blows would soon crack cast bronze or bring out latent weaknesses and flaws. Steady and continuous tapping would produce good results. The artist who appears to be striking the horse in the Acropolis fragment (Fig. 54) with a hammer is clearly giving light taps, for he holds the instrument very close. The artist of the Foundry vase, on the other hand, is hitting harder and, in order to safeguard his hammer-haft, is holding it near the head, or at least half-way. Two distinct and intentionally different sizes of hammer are shown in the Foundry vase, one about 2 feet long and the other about 18 inches. The workman standing behind the master at the furnace holds the larger and the workman who is hammering the headless statue the smaller. Two of the large and one of the small hammers hang on the wall in this scene. In the opposite scene is one of the small hammers only, hanging on the wall. The two hammers of the Acropolis fragment, on the wall, are of the small size. The heads of all these hammers seen in vase-paintings correspond exactly with modern types of hammer used by bronzeworkers (see Fig. 90).

6. *Pincers*. These were used presumably for the moving of metal too hot to manhandle. Only one example is known— on the Acropolis fragment, hanging on the wall, and that shows large and heavy pincers.

7. *Callipers* (?). A mysterious instrument hangs on the wall in the scene of Athena moulding the horse on the Berlin oenochoe. It appears to be a very small pair of callipers fixed at the end of a long tapering shaft, presumably of metal. The shaft runs to a point instead of to a handle and must indicate that we have here some kind of a composite instrument which served two or more purposes.

8. *Gouge* (Fig. 91). As has been already explained (p. 189), the gouge used by bronzeworkers was, like the burins, solid. It pushed the metal out rather than cut it out. Clear proof

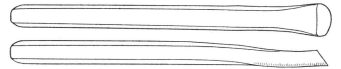

FIG. 91. Modern bronze-worker's gouge (and side view).

of the use of this instrument on full-scale bronzes is provided by the life-size head from the Acropolis.[1] One side of the head proved too large for the helmet, which was to be fixed separately, and the artist planed it down by means of a broad gouge, removing quite a considerable amount from the surface. The gouge to-day plays an important part in bronze-craft, and one can assume that in antiquity it played a part in every way as important. But no representations of it exist on vases.

[1] De Ridder, *Bronzes de l'Acropole*, p. 290, No. 768; *J.H.S.* 1930, p. 318; Kluge, *Jahrbuch*, 1929. Fig. 10. But see above, p. 157.

9. *The Multiple Burin* (Fig. 92). In appearance this instrument must have resembled the stone-carver's claw-chisel, though in structure and use it was very different. In effect it was a row of small graving tools combined in one blade. If a blade of hard steel is fashioned into a heavy chisel-edge and that edge divided up into three or four clear burin-points, the resulting blade would serve to plough a series of parallel

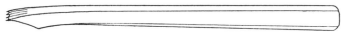

FIG. 92. Modern bronze-worker's multiple burin.

striations in a bronze surface. A superb example of the use of this tool on the hair of a small bronze is seen in the bronze from the Acropolis.[1] The finest possible multiple burin has been used for the lines of the hair and the surface is almost as fresh as when cut. With such a tool the Greek bronze-workers cut the fine hair-lines on locks of hair. A skilful artist would have great opportunities with it, and that he made the fullest advantage of it is clear from such an example as the head in the Polykleitan manner which is in the Ashmolean Museum at Oxford. Here the hair, where it survives, has a very finely preserved surface with a light patination. The grooves are as clear as when they were first cut. A multiple graver or burin has been used here with prodigious success. How the artist could control it in its sinuous turns and twists without letting the continuous hammer-strokes make themselves evident in halting lines or jerky grooves is astonishing. It is added testimony to our accumulating knowledge of the Greek artist's perfect control of his tools. It is of course possible that the artist used hand-pressure alone for his burins, but this, if anything, makes the feat of long-drawn lines of hair even more remarkable. Gentle curves only were possible with this burin or indeed with any burin. Sharp turns of hair-lines are never found on the hair of bronze statues.

[1] De Ridder, *Bronzes de l'Acropole*, p. 268, No. 740 (6445 in the National Museum.)

10. *The Simple Burin* (Fig. 93). This was the bronze-engraver's principal tool. It was a blade of steel, mounted in a wooden handle, with a cutting-point. The cutting face of the blade was either rectangular or triangular, the actual cutting being done with one of the pointed angles. The groove so made was, as a result, a V-shaped groove. Where the groove is semicircular in section the instrument that made it is called a gouge. That is in effect the only difference between the two tools, gouge and burin. The process by which the bronze is removed and the tool employed is the same in both cases, though the gouge, having a less fluent blade, because of the wide area of resistance which it meets, is usually driven by a hammer and the burin by hand-pressure.

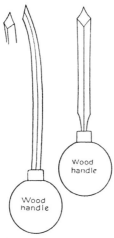

FIG. 93. Modern bronze-worker's simple hand-burins or 'scorpers'.

Burins can vary enormously. They can be of minute size, like copper-plate engravers' burins, or they can be large and heavy, strong enough to remove quite thick strips of bronze from a smooth surface. Heavy and light burins alike are best driven by hand. Tremendous pressure and great control can be obtained if the burin has a broad handle shaped rather like a flattish door-handle. The ball of the thumb and much of the palm of the hand can be used to control its direction and give it pressure, by leverage.

Actual representations of burins are lacking, but the evidence for their variety in antiquity is enormous. All surviving bronze statues, with a very few exceptions, testify to their continuous use from the earliest times down to the latest. Artists in the early times never left the hair untouched after casting. The practice developed only at a later date when impressionistic influences were aimed at, or carelessness had set in. There is no actual proof that wooden

FIG. 94. GOLDSMITH'S PUNCHES AND CHISELS
FROM GALJÛB

In order from left to right: 1, 2, punches; 3, 4, chisels.
Scale 1/1.

handles were employed, but since we have already seen that wooden handles were used for all rasps, and since only the heavy burin can be used without a handle of some kind,

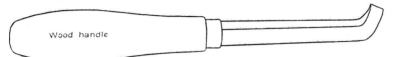

Wood handle

FIG. 95. Modern bronze-worker's burin for cutting grooves by a process of downward pulling instead of hammer-driving.

FIG. 96. Modern bronze-worker's simple burin or 'scorper', for use with a hammer.

it seems reasonable to assume that most burins in antiquity usually had handles similar to those of modern burins. The heavy burin shown in Fig. 96 needs no handle, and is hammer-driven.

11. *Punches and Chisels.* We know very little indeed of the punches used by bronzeworkers. Indeed, we are not sure that they were in use to any extent. But one is driven to infer the use of the punch from the appearance of various small hollow depressions in some bronze surfaces, and it is certainly known that punches were part of the stock-in-trade of Greek jewellers and metal-workers. The complete stock-in-trade of an Hellenistic bronzeworker, found in a jar at Galjûb near Cairo, has provided information of the highest value.[1] Not only were partly finished figures found but also a series of no less than twenty-seven complete or broken tools and several bunches of similar tools oxidized into a solid mass. It is true that the bronzeworker in question was an artist of small bronzes only and that he cast solid from wax models. But the surviving tools may perhaps be taken

[1] A. Ippel, *Der Bronzefund von Galjûb*, Berlin, 1922.

as throwing some light on the methods of larger bronzes, although as a general rule I have assumed that the processes were different in large bronzes from those used in the case of small works.

Among these tools were punches on the one hand and chisels on the other. In Fig. 94 we see two perfectly preserved examples of each. The punches look as if they had never been used, and this may well be the case. For there is no sign that one end or the other has been blunted by percussion. But either end would well serve the purpose of beating out design into repoussée, and as such they correspond exactly with modern metal-workers' punches.

The chisels also look fresh and unused and have thickened middles to give them strength in use: they also have flattened butt-ends which show little or no signs of use.

Such tools for work on a smaller scale in gold, silver, and bronze may well be miniature versions of tools used in the larger bronzework.

APPENDIXES

I. EMERY

I AM indebted to Messrs. Harrison Brothers, Ltd., of Middlesbrough, for the following information about emery and artificial abrasive.

Emery is an impure form of corundum. It is to-day obtained from Naxos, from the basins of the Sarabat and Mender rivers in Asia Minor and from the region of Chester, Mass. and Peekskill in the United States of America. Emery is a unique mineral, as it is a mixture of alumina oxide and iron as magnetite and haematite.

Corundum theoretically contains but two elements, alumina and oxygen, its chemical formula being Al_2O_3. Commercial corundum generally contains a trace of silica, ferric oxide, and combined water. As found in a mine it is not in a pure state and is mixed with other minerals such as felspar, hornblende, margaritite, muscovite, &c. It is largely found in the United States and in Ontario, Canada as block corundum, crystal corundum, and sand corundum. It occurs usually in igneous rocks, principally syenites and in several gneisses and schists. Canadian corundum occurs in nepheline syenite associated with Laurentian gneiss.

Artificial corundum is produced by the fusion of lead oxide and alumina in a fire-clay crucible, so forming lead aluminate. Silica enters into the composition of fire clay and, under the influence of high temperature, the silica of the crucible gradually decomposes the lead aluminate, forming lead silicate which remains in a liquid state while the alumina crystallizes as white sapphire. By mixing a small amount of chromium, rubies have been formed.

A German scientist changed natural emery into iron-and-water-free corundum by the mixture and fusion with charcoal or coke.

Carborundum is the trade name for carbide of silicon, which is a chemical combination of the two elements carbon and silicon. The material was first made by Edward G. Acheson in 1891 when he discovered a few bright crystals surrounding the carbon electrode in an iron bowl in which he had fused by means of an electric current a mixture containing carbon and silicon. Coke and silica sand, which supply carbon and silicon, are the raw materials which enter into the manufacture of this remarkable abrasive.

Aloxite is an abrasive, artificially made, used for grinding steel tools. It is a pure form of crystalline aluminum oxide and is made from a clay called bauxite which is fused in an electric furnace.

I am also indebted to Mr. A. Lucas for the following information: It has been said that the sand at Aswan contains 15 per cent. of emery, but there is otherwise no evidence of its occurrence in Egypt. What Pliny's 'Coptic' or Ethiopian sand was is not known. For imparting the final polish to stone the Romans used an Egyptian commodity called 'Thebaic stone'. Objects of emery have been found at Naqada and Ballas, Hierokonpolis, and a piece of the raw material at El Amrah and Abydos.

II. THE FITZWILLIAM STATUETTE

To make quite certain that my inferences were based on sound evidence, I obtained a piece of red breccia as nearly like that of which the goddess is made as possible, and carved on its surface a series of grooves by means of an ordinary sculptor's steel gouge measuring 0·6 cm. across the arc. With this gouge I was able to cut a series of grooves exactly similar in dimensions and outline to those on the apron of the statuette. I found that one stroke was usually not sufficient to make a groove of the requisite depth and that a series of sharp single strokes were required for each groove. The second and subsequent strokes, achieved by one sharp tap of the mallet, did not, naturally, leave the series of horizontal lines which are left by a large gouge across the groove in large-scale sculpture, since each of such lines (which can be seen on Fig. 72 above) are the result of a separate blow with the mallet for each line. Instead, the inside surface of the groove showed vertical striations, only detectable with a good glass, which were caused by the various unevennesses of the blade of the gouge, which had, in each stroke, not stopped at any point. I found that on the Fitzwilliam statuette there were precisely the same minute vertical striations. This made it plain that I had employed the gouge in exactly the same way as had the sculptor of the statuette and that we had both probably employed the same type of gouge. Such gouges can be bought at any tool-maker's for about a shilling. The type used in each case seems to have been a standard type and size and is almost the smallest sculptor's gouge obtainable.

III

MR. ERIC GILL originally expressed to me his disbelief in the method of using the point in marble sculpture which Blümel attributes to the

Greeks and which I accept as strictly accurate. This method, in brief, is that the point was held as much at right angles to the plane surface of the marble as was possible. Mr. Gill maintained that to strike the stone at such an angle would hopelessly stun it, and not remove it in adequate quantities. I pointed out to him that the stone would no doubt be stunned by such a procedure but that, provided that the blows were not too hard and that the punch did not penetrate too deeply into the stone, the stunned surface so produced could easily be removed by abrasive or chisel. I maintained that such was indeed the practice of the Greeks.

Mr. Gill now tells me, and gives me permission to repeat what he says, that he now himself uses the method in question—as in his recent sculpture in Hopton Wood stone which stands in the entrance hall of the building of the British Broadcasting Company in London —and that the effect of this way of using the punch is certainly to stun the stone. But he finds that the forms so produced by this method are more solid and sculptural than those produced by oblique use of the punch. The stunned surface is removed by the chisel or abrasive down to the unaffected surface of the stone a few millimetres deeper and the result is definitely more satisfactory from an aesthetic point of view.

Mr. Gill adds the following notes on the above (with a diagram).

'I have always (ever since I began carving, long before our discussion) used the "vertical stroke" for parts of a carving when it was impossible to do otherwise, e.g. in deep places where you couldn't use the chisel or point at any other angle. But after our discussion I started using the "vertical stroke" for the whole job.

'Nevertheless the *realization* of sculptural mass (i.e. as a thing contrasted with surface or contour) is the important thing, and this is attainable even though the "vertical stroke" be not used. The mere use of a certain method may help, but it won't *ensure* the sense of mass. The use of another method may hinder, but will not necessarily destroy the sense of mass, if the sculptor *has* such a sense. It is what you are thinking about while you do it that matters.

'It must also be remembered that the "vertical stroke" is not the only alternative to the "carving stroke". The stroke called the "mason's stroke" is again quite different and has much of the advantage of the "vertical stroke". I have always used the "mason's stroke", and for the same reason (though without knowing much about it and without trying to put it into words) as that on account of which you advocate vertical use of a point, i.e. it gives or helps solidity of form and puts off any seduction which *surface* might have: it helps to keep mass-form (not contour or surface) the thing uppermost in the mind.'

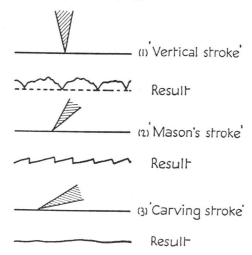

(1) 'Vertical stroke'

Result

(2) 'Mason's stroke'

Result

(3) 'Carving stroke'

Result

INDEX OF MUSEUMS

INDEX

Ypsilanti Area Public Library

Ypsilanti, Michigan